The Tao of Potter:

Growth and Healing in the Magical Universe

By

Brian Donohue

The Tao of Potter: Growth and Healing in the Magical Universe, by Brian Donohue

Copyright © 2010 by Brian Donohue
All rights reserved. No part of this book may be reproduced by any means without written permission from the author.

Note: This is a work of literary criticism, and as such, claims no affiliation with or endorsement from J.K. Rowling, Warner Bros., or any other holders of copyrights or trademarks associated with the Harry Potter names, brands, and products. All citations in this work are made in the conventional form of literary citation.

Published in the United States by Brian Donohue and Lulu.com.

ISBN: 978-0-557-67178-6

Table of Contents

Introduction: Entering the Way of Natural Magic 6

Exercise: Hagrid's Answer 7

Inner Matriculation: The Feeling-Sense of Natural Magic 10

"The Burrow" and The Magic of Lived Experience 11

Asking for Help: Freedom Through Natural Magic 15

Chapter 1: Principal Characters in The Way of Natural Magic 20

Professor Albus Percival Wulfuric Brian Dumbledore 20

Hermione Granger 23

Tom Marvolo Riddle, a/k/a Lord Voldemort 26

What's "Evil" About Religion? 29

Ronald Weasley 35

Draco Malfoy 38

Harry Potter 42

Environment as Character: The Aura of Hogwarts 49

Chapter 2: The Room of Requirement: Getting Help Where You Need It 53

Chapter 3: Memory and the Way Forward: Entering the Pensieve 59

Siphoning the Excess: Entering the Pensieve of Meditative Practice 66

Another Exercise in Unburdening 70

Chapter 4: The Boggart in the Wardrobe: Defeating Fear Through Humor 73

Dispersing the Boggart: Practical Steps in Separating from the Realm of Ego 80

Chapter 5: The Cloak and the Mirror: Self-Images of the Individual Ego 84

Meeting Lord Voldemort.. *92*

An Insight Meditation: Experiencing Invisibility.. *93*

Looking into the Mirror of Erised.. *97*

Chapter 6: Priori Incantatem: Engaging Cosmic Protection.................... **100**

Meditation: Engaging the Personal Energy of Protection........................ *111*

Chapter 7: No. 12, Grimmauld Place and The Voices of Neurosis............ **114**

The Noise of Neurosis: Kreacher the House-Elf.. *120*

Silencing the Demons: An Approach to Healing *122*

Chapter 8: The Black Door, the Circular Room, and Dreams of the Present **124**

Unlocking the Black Door: Nurturing Communication on the Inner Plane of Being *141*

Chapter 9: The Ministry of Magic: Bureaucracy and Other Ideologies of Fear **146**

Attributes of the Ministry of Magic (and other fear-based institutions) *149*

Weapons in the War on the True Self: Guilt, Blame, and Dread *156*

Separating from Guilt: Banishing the High Inquisitor *160*

Chapter 10: Inside the Department of Mysteries: Time, Death, and the Search for Truth **164**

Katabasis: Journeying Beneath the Surface of Death................................ *174*

The Unnamed Force in the Locked Room: The Unconscious Potential Buried by Ego *178*

Penetrating the Mysteries of Time and Death: Reaching Past the Appearance *180*

The Use of Oracles: Drawing on Cosmic Resources.................................. *184*

Chapter 11: Moaning Myrtle and Self-Distortions of the Human Psyche 187

The Egg in the Bath: The Birth of Insight *193*

Exercise: Transformation Through a Word *199*

Dumbledore's Response: Returning to the Room of Requirement *200*

Appendix: References and Further Reading **205**

References *208*

Notes: **212**

In the very earliest time,
When both people and animals lived on earth,
A person could become an animal if he wanted to
And an animal could become a human being.
Sometimes they were people
And sometimes animals
And there was no difference.
All spoke the same language.
That was the time when words were like magic.
The human mind had mysterious powers.
A word spoken by chance
Might have strange consequences.
It would suddenly come alive
And what people wanted to happen could happen–
All you had to do was say it.
Nobody can explain this:
That's the way it was.

—traditional Eskimo[1]

Introduction: Entering the Way of Natural Magic

> Harry had never even imagined such a strange and splendid place. It was lit by thousands and thousands of candles that were floating in midair over four long tables, where the rest of the students were sitting. These tables were laid with glittering golden plates and goblets. At the top of the hall was another long table where the teachers were sitting....Mainly to avoid the staring eyes, Harry looked upward and saw a velvety black ceiling dotted with stars....It was hard to believe there was a ceiling there at all, and that the Great Hall didn't simply open on to the heavens. —J.K. Rowling, from Chapter 7 of *Harry Potter and the Sorcerer's Stone*

Imagine, for a moment, that you are walking into the Great Hall of Hogwarts School of Witchcraft and Wizardry; that, with the open heart and silver-dollar eyes of a child, you are entering a place that is thought only to live in the realms of fiction and fantasy. See if you can feel the glow of candlelight hovering above your head; see if you can sense the seemingly universal vastness of this immense hall and its boundless firmament of ceiling, as you shuffle forward in a clot of classmates, nearly overcome with a mixture of humility, gratitude, awe, a little dread, and above all, open wonder at the *reality* of it all. Now hold your awareness there, in that moment, and remain. Continue walking through this spacious, starry hall for a minute or so, and then turn slowly, to look back through the door that had stood, a little time before, between this reality and that dream, and ask yourself the question that an old Chinese philosopher once asked:

> Once upon a time, I, Chuang Tsu, dreamed I was a butterfly flying happily here and there, enjoying life without knowing who I was. Suddenly I woke up and I was indeed Chuang Tsu. Did Chuang Tsu dream he was a butterfly, or did the butterfly dream he was Chuang Tsu? There must be some distinction between Chuang Tsu and the butterfly. This is a case of transformation.[2]

Transformation *is* the way of natural magic. As Chuang Tsu suggests, transformation is a kind of change; but not merely a changing of outer circumstances—a reordering of the furniture of life. No: transformative movement involves the total being, and starts from within, where the universal is realized through the liberation of individuality. This book, this journey through the world of Hogwarts and its transformative symbols, is a simple guide to applying the magical stories of Harry Potter's quest to the everyday experience of our own lives, here in the Muggle world. We all have the inborn ability to move freely between the manifest and the unconscious; from matter to energy; between distinction and union, until the divisions dissolve amid a cleansing mist of expansive awareness.

"One thought fills immensity," said the poet of eternal childhood.[3] This is the spirit in which we will here explore the grounds, people, objects, and events of the world of Harry Potter. For the journey of Harry Potter is an inner voyage of return—to one's personal truth; to one's entire being in all its diversity of feeling, thought, and vision; and finally to one's inimitable yet universal connection to the Origin of life and form. This is a connection made between the open luminosity of individuality and the sable glow of the universal Source. For the purpose of this exploration of the world of Harry Potter I call this journey "the way of natural magic."

Exercise: Hagrid's Answer

> "Hagrid, I think you must have made a mistake. I don't think I can be a wizard."
> To his surprise, Hagrid chuckled.
> "Not a wizard, eh?" Never made things happen when you was scared or angry?"
> (*Sorcerer's Stone*, p. 58)

Hagrid, I'm wondering if you could re-phrase that last question for the benefit of our Muggle audience here? I mean, for folks who question whether there can even *be* such a thing as magic in living?

"Okay...well, sure...right. Firs' thing yeh need ter ask yerself is, has there ever been somethin' unus'l or even strange happen in yer life—somethin' that couldn't be explained in the nermal way?...Well, yeah, that's the magic, on'y it's not serposed ter be strange or mysterious or...whaddya call it...S-O-teeric. That's what's nermal abo' yeh; that's the way yer life is meant ter be lived all the time.

Now you Muggles on'y miss the magic in yer lives because yeh dinna seem able ter take a step outside yer doors without worryin' over yer logic and science. Always goin' on abo' yer Laws of Nature, are yeh, as if Nature were goin' ter obey a great Muggle like yerself if yeh told Her what the Laws were. They're all right, mind yeh—yer logic and science—but there's more tuh yer life than can be fit inside a book or a brain...and that's yer magic. It's right there, inside yeh—yeh'd have ter be blind ter miss it."

Well said, Hagrid. Perhaps what you're telling us is exactly what Shakespeare told us through the voice of Hamlet:

> There are more things in heaven and earth, Horatio,
> than are dreamt of in your philosophy.

This is not about denying science and intellect their natural place in life and knowledge. To me, it all boils down to a simple anatomy lesson: you can only push intellect out of your life by cutting away your forebrain, and that would leave you dead. And you can only push feeling and inner sensing out of your life by cutting out your heart, which would leave you just as dead.

So why do we in our culture attempt to do exactly that with our heart-lives, through the institutions, rules, and commandments of our various insular social groups? Can we not trust feeling and thought, heart and brain, to work together as one? A man named Albert Einstein did exactly that—he made it the foundation of his life's work; and many would argue compellingly that he thereby got more out of his brain than any scientist before him ever had.

When Einstein talked or wrote about the universe, he was speaking as a scientist, a man involved with the exploration of lived experience. When he talked or wrote about God, he was referring not to a powerful and distant cult figure that rewarded obedience and punished outsiders, but to the universe. In other words, when he spoke of God, he was on the same level of awareness as when he scribbled those equations of a relativistic universe across a blackboard.

It seems like a very practical and successful way to conduct one's life, this idea of letting the heart and brain work as one. I have a meditation that you can try and then adapt to your personal needs. I call it, "Heart, Brain, Infinity":

> Look within yourself, and feel: there is an active, working relationship among the parts of the self that we abnormally imagine as disjointed or even opposing organs and functions. The heart sits at the top of the thoracic cavity, sounding the rhythm of Nature, sending nourishment throughout the body, and sharing information along electrochemical pathways with the brain and the rest of the central nervous system.
>
> The heart is the primary feeling organ of the self: like a woman breathing into her lover's ear, it feeds inspiration to the brain, which then transforms that inspiration into the expression of insight and invention. When you let this happen, it is bliss beyond comparison—something like sex on warm, moonlit sand, moistened by an evening ebb tide.
>
> So visualize, if you will, a continuous current of energy that begins in the heart, rises and flows upward, emanating like light from a windblown candle along the upper spinal column and into the brainstem. From there it glows onward, diffusing across the seemingly infinite neural pathways of the midbrain and forebrain, awakening and inspiring everything in its luminous path. It curls, like jasmine smoke, over the forebrain, along the face downward, through the mouth and the throat, back toward the origin and destination of this infinite loop of perception and expression, the heart.
>
> Now consider the shape made by this pathway: it is the symbol for infinity. That is who you are; it is the simple essence, the core of your uniqueness. Discover it.

Inner Matriculation: The Feeling-Sense of Natural Magic

Harry is invited to attend Hogwarts and enter the way of natural magic because he possesses some inborn ability or potential that distinguishes him from the children of the "Muggle," or non-magical world; yet there is no clear-cut definition ever given of *what* exactly it is about him and other wizard kids that makes them eligible for admission into Hogwarts. There are certainly no national, financial, racial, or class restrictions.

Mrs. Rowling's ambiguity on this point is, I think, intentional: the experiences of Harry and his friends in their response to the call of magic are meant to speak freely and without restriction to *all children*. What people call "magic" (whether in awe or derision) is really the *ordinary human way of feeling and action in the world*. It's just that we've somehow forgotten that simple fact. Otherwise, as actually happens during Harry's journey through Hogwarts, the division between Muggle and Wizard tends to dissolve. We're all familiar with the "Muggle-mind" of the Dursleys—a cultural program of repression, accumulation, and artifice; but as Rowling later shows us, there is plenty of "Muggle-mind" to be found amid the magical world as well.

So there is no fixed ideological qualification for an introduction to magic: it appears that the children simply need to have grown enough to be ready. They do not have to perform heroic actions, pay tribute, pass a test or suffer through an initiation ritual; walk through fire, receive ablutions, enter apprenticeship, go on retreat, or perform penance—*they only have to grow to be eleven years old*.

When they're ready, they go—not by flying broom or magic carpet, but via a slow, daylong journey on that transformative means of modern transportation, the train. Childhood, and especially adolescence, cannot be rushed—to force it to a conclusion in a supersonic moment of linear development is an invitation to disaster and regret.

To force conclusions aborts solutions; development that is driven to a fixed point of culturally-defined maturity only sets the stage for a lifetime of regression. Therefore, the students of Hogwarts both arrive and return via a long journey, pulled by an old steam locomotive, during which they will have time to adjust inwardly, form relationships, contemplate, and literally *feel* the time and energy that is needed for growth.

"Grow up" is a message of forced urgency; often the phrase itself is spoken in a kind of harried impatience, usually to a person who we think is acting immaturely ("can't you *grow up?*"). In the linear, upward model, development is pictured as a rapid succession of stages, which can be compressed and foreshortened through the technologies of progress, until childhood comes to resemble the boot-sequence of a computer.

Rowling's Harry Potter novels are marked throughout by this tension between the natural, omni-directional movement of growth, and the culturally-defined "upward and onward" obsession, familiar to nearly all of us. This again reveals that tension between the magical reality and the Muggle delusion—the forced separation of heart and brain. But early on, as she introduces her characters and settings, Rowling is careful to remind us that true magic is found not in the flick of a wand, but during a slow train ride, or through long nights of solitary gazing into a mirror that reveals the images of an unknown and idealized past.

"The Burrow" and The Magic of Lived Experience

> The clock on the wall opposite him had only one hand and no numbers at all. Written around the edge were things like Time to make tea, Time to feed the chickens, and You're late. Books were stacked three deep on the mantelpiece, books with titles like Charm Your Own Cheese, Enchantment in Baking, and One Minute Feasts—It's Magic! And unless Harry's ears were deceiving him, the old radio next to the sink had just announced that coming up was "Witching Hour, with the popular singing sorceress, Celestina Warbeck." (*Chamber of Secrets*, p. 34).

Another way that Rowling invokes the way of natural magic in her fiction is through the earthy settings and domestic movements that are the pulse of these stories. We are taken out of the fantastic realm of Merlin-esque fiction, and drawn instead into a world where magic is the way of daily living.

This is what happens at "The Burrow," the home of Harry's friend Ron Weasley. There, Harry discovers that magic is about washing the dishes, doing the knitting, clearing pests out of the garden, and, of course, getting the mail. One is reminded of the well-known haiku from a Zen poet:

> I draw water, I cut wood—
> How miraculous, how mysterious![4]

This is how a life of natural magic *feels*. It also appears that this sense is best nurtured within a simple practical setting, where empty excess does not distance us from lived experience. But it's not about pursuing some stupid ideal of poverty, as you see in many religions. The Weasleys are a large, middle class family, living on the single income of a civil servant-level employee of the government (Ron's father, Arthur Weasley). They get by not through fantastic feats of powerful magic, but by the thrift and natural wisdom of Ron's mother, Molly Weasley, who gets her children through school in hand-me-down clothing and second-hand books and supplies. Ron is painfully self-conscious of his family's simple circumstances, yet Harry only sees the richness of natural magic at The Burrow, and so he warmly tells Ron that "this is the best house I've ever been in."

This practical and domestic vein of the magical runs through every one of the stories, and probably accounts for their immense popularity more than any of the more heroic or dramatic moments in the series. The principle female among the child characters is Hermione Granger, who introduces herself to Harry by magically repairing his broken eyeglasses. She is the intellectual leader among the children in the story, yet she is repeatedly seen magically knitting, conjuring portable heaters on wintry days, preparing healing potions for cuts and sore skin, and performing other feats of practical legerdemain without the mildest sense of awe or self-consciousness. This is a practical guide to a way that we can all live our lives: through the leadership of the inner life, which both includes and surpasses mere intellect. This kind of living engages invisible forces that lead us to success in every phase of our outer lives. It is a principle that will course through this entire book and its meditations, exercises, and practical examples of ordinary magical living.

It seems to be a message that needs to be more clearly heard in our culture today, because most of us are so deeply trained to compartmentalize our lives, with work here, in a box labeled "office, Monday through Friday, 9 to 5"; with family there, in another compartment marked "home, after work and weekends"; and with spiritual life perhaps shunted off into another corner of time and space. There are other, smaller boxes and labels ("nightlife," "shopping," "girlfriend," "gym," "TV," "Internet"), which each receives its place in the order of living, or else is given over to the random compartment of "spare time."

The compartments are neatly divided and arranged according to the dictates of a *perception*, based on appearances, which is too easily mistaken for reality. Thus we may continue in seeming abundance and contentment until an event, an illness, or an act of fate scatters the neat but brittle compartments into rubble; or until the boxes seem to merge into a mountain of mid-life anxiety. These are the times when we turn within and seek help from some realm of being that surpasses and underlies the superficial. It could happen amid a divorce, a death in the family, job loss, mental illness, bodily injury, or conflict in any of life's major arenas. Or we may find ourselves crushed by a mid-life, "existential" crisis, which appears to result from the spirit's final collapse beneath the weight of a lifelong plod amid routine and the oppression of sacrifice.

Nature didn't create us to live on a treadmill, yet somehow many of us do. Thoreau also saw the effects of sacrifice-by-conditioning, when he wrote his famous line: "the mass of men lead lives of quiet desperation."[5] So the natural question that arises in contemplating such events of fate or existential crisis is, "why do we have to wait until adversity, illness, malaise, or disaster strike, or until a moment of belated emptiness overcomes us?

There is a long tradition underlying this treadmill mindset. It is a tradition that has appeared in the societal doctrines of both the East and West, and it is summarized in the belief in the *necessity of suffering*—that every life is lived on a wheel of fortune (and its opposite), with the further assumption being that the only way beyond this realm of suffering is in a bodiless paradise that one may arrive at after death. It may be called Heaven, Nirvana, or any of a number of synonymous names, but it is usually described the same way—as a distant, separate, and perfect place, whose entrance requirements are stringent indeed, in terms of sacrifice, ascetic restriction, and moralistic behavior. In short, it is the fervent dream of desperation, the reluctant consolation of the oppressed.

The students at Hogwarts are presented with a different view. As we mentioned, they are not subjected to any moral or behavioral requirements to earn their entry into the academy of natural magic, and once there, they are simply asked to show up on time, follow some other common-sense rules of social conduct, and put forward some effort in their learning. The rest is implied to come from each student's unique talents, abilities, personality, and disposition. The crises and challenges come to the children at Hogwarts through the metaphorical embodiments of the same corrupt beliefs and assumptions present in our own institutional ideologies. As Harry and his friends gradually discover throughout the series, the key to successfully navigating the psychological challenges and physical dangers presented by the likes of Lord Voldemort and his followers, or by Dolores Umbridge and the Ministry of Magic functionaries, lies in separating from the attachment that these forces falsely claim on the inner truth and natural personalities of the children.

We will be following a similar process throughout the rest of this book. For now, the lesson of "The Burrow" is that inner life is not meant to be a walled-off place of experience, separate and distant from work, family, play, and love: it is meant to inform and enrich all these aspects of one's life—indeed, to unite them.

Asking for Help: Freedom Through Natural Magic

But how we are to approach the path to freedom from the cubicles of belief and conditioning? One essential aspect to it is suggested during Harry's second year at Hogwarts: it comes at a moment where the very foundation of Hogwarts appears to be under an overwhelming attack from Lord Voldemort's henchmen and their government stooges. It is when Professor Dumbledore speaks his last words before accepting his suspension as headmaster of the school:

> "If the governors want my removal...I shall of course step aside...However," said Dumbledore, speaking very slowly and clearly so that none of them could miss a word, "you will find that I will only truly have left this school when none here are loyal to me. You will also find that help will always be given at Hogwarts to those who ask for it." (*Chamber of Secrets*, pp. 263-264)

This is a message that Harry recalls time and again throughout his Hogwarts journey – first, at a time when he is facing down the dragon of Lord Voldemort's corrupt ideology (symbolized by the basilisk, which is summoned and directed by the voice of a memory-demon from an old book bound in black leather).

The old Taoist Chinese oracle, the *I Ching*, offers the same advice as Professor Dumbledore. In a chapter titled "Difficulty at the Beginning", it reminds us that when there is difficulty, it is "time to gather helpers."[6] It is a simple reference to universal energies that respond to our conscious call for help; that unlock our self-healing potential and support us through painful times. This should come as no surprise, and certainly not as a mystery, to anyone: for helpers are quietly acknowledged even in the language of Western medicine. "Helper T-cells" are immunosupportive components of the blood, which are most notable when they are absent or weakened: this is what happens in those afflicted with HIV. There is also a form of cancer therapy known as "adjuvant therapy", from the Latin word *adjuvare*, meaning "to help."

Every tradition of genuine spirituality has begun from this call for help, and it persists today in the form of propitiatory prayer. Unfortunately, the simplicity of the call for help has been encrusted with the devious commerce, difficulty, and formulaic complexity that are the hallmarks of religious ideologies and their institutional monuments. You don't have to look very far to find remnants of the old Medieval practice of selling "indulgences."

Yet, when he is faced with the basilisk, Harry has no time or inclination to call for help from the god, angel, or spiritual favorite of any insular group—he can only ask from his heart, at a time when there is no rational or objective support for his making the call. "Help me, help me...someone—anyone—" he says repeatedly—"*please help me.*" Immediately, the help arrives—as though from "an invisible hand"—in the form of a protective sword that drops right onto his head from inside the old school sorting hat. An impersonal, directionless—albeit desperate—request is made, and instantly answered in exactly the proper form and measure. This is how the way of natural magic is meant to work, though for us, there is no necessity to wait until a dragon-snake (or a life-crisis) is about to eat us alive before we make that call for help.

Asking for help from the invisible world—Cosmic energies, elemental forces, Nature, or a "god-presence" that is not bound up in the tangled cords of doctrine—is perhaps the most fundamental and natural inner movement of the heart. As Harry himself says in reviewing his exploits of four years, "I got through it all because help came at the right time." Indeed it did, *but only because he asked*. In the text box below is a story from my own experience, which I hope will serve to arouse your own memories of "help coming at the right time," so that we may inspire one another to continue calling for help—preferably before a cataclysm or crisis forces the issue.

It is well known that about half of all marriages in this country end in divorce, so the pain and bitterness of this experience will resonate with many who read what follows. I became involved in the destructive emotional cycle of divorce—the charges and counter-charges flung in a cesspool of malignancy, leading inevitably to the legal profession and its absurdly mechanistic language and procedures (to say nothing of the expense). However, one thing was different in my experience—different, at least, from the stereotypical divorce encounter. I learned, fairly early on in the process, and even amid the swamp of my own negativity, that a call for help from invisible resources would, at the very least, prevent me from making more mistakes than I had already made. I made that call, first as a propitiatory kind of begging (to Saint Jude, to Jesus, to the Buddha, to any known cultural spiritual figure who I imagined could help) that my marriage be repaired, that reconciliation be accomplished, and that love somehow be restored. This, of course, only led to further estrangement and bitterness, until at last my call for help became the kind that Harry makes in facing the basilisk: all the religious deities and symbols were removed from my inner space, and in that seeming emptiness, a direct connection formed spontaneously between myself and the Source of my being. Only the *I Ching*—a plain-speaking, nonsectarian, impersonal source of guidance—remained for me. I consulted it every night, often spending hours with its calm voice and inscrutable ability to capture a broader perspective of events and emotions that seemed to have closed around me like a trap. From this point where I ceased with the desperate demand of prayer and focused instead on the work of simple understanding—free of expectation, claim, or the hunger for influence—help arrived. I found myself able to turn off the noise of resentment and bitterness, able to endure the terrors of isolation, and capable of putting down the inner sword with the poisoned tip, whose use had only brought me defeat, despair, and soul-suffocating guilt. Once I had become clear within (mainly through simply asking), the outer plane responded spontaneously, and channels of communication opened between myself, my former wife (how we use the language matters, and the prefix "ex" before anything tends to demean it), and the child that unites us in principle and purpose. This gift came to, or I should say through, me, because at a time where all conventionally spiritual means had been exhausted in failure, I asked for help without sticking any terms or conditions onto the request. Almost instantly, the basilisk of ego was silenced enough to allow the helping presences of the universe to flow with Nature's deep abundance. This is an example of what I mean when I speak of "the way of natural magic."

Throughout our journey amid the metaphorical landscape of Hogwarts School, we will consider the seemingly infinite range of practical cosmic resources that are able to bring us what we need to live our lives and fulfill our destinies. When these functional presences, these helpers, are free to move through us, they bring fulfillment in a form and degree that far exceed anything that ego, with its expectations and restricted, artificial desires, can possibly concoct or provide. Harry learns this distinction in his encounter with the Mirror of Erised, in which he finds self-images drawn from the past, that only bring him pain and frustration (see Chapter 5). He repeatedly finds that help comes in unexpected and completely unpredictable shapes, and that this is the help that truly furthers life and growth. Harry winds up learning more from his journeys within the magical basin known as the Pensieve than he does in any of his "real" classes (Chapter 3). He discovers a world of invisible helpers in the in the wonderful "Room of Requirement" (Chapter 2); and the helping light of Cosmic protection in the beautiful web which rescues him from Lord Voldemort in the graveyard (Chapter 6).

As he moves along his path of inner learning, Harry finds that there is no textbook prescription for growth. The most effective teaching is gentle and unforced (this is also true of the most effective political leadership or corporate management), and allows room for each student's personal assimilation. I have made an effort here to abide by this approach, in part because it accords with the way that Mrs. Rowling has told her stories. There is not an ounce of pedantry in her work—like Professor Dumbledore, she teaches without projection or ideology. She understands that while books and lectures may help in pointing the way toward learning, it is ultimately experience that brings each lesson into the heart of the student. This is the understanding that is reflected in the poetry of Lao Tzu, where he sings of the teaching aspect of the Cosmic Consciousness, which he refers to as "The Sage":

> Thus the eternal Sage
> Acts with abiding care for all.
> Because of this, it abandons no one:

Its regenerative Presence flows
Through every particle of being.

This is called the penetrating awareness.
Thus the Sage approaches those who lack fulfillment:
For those who lack fulfillment sustain learning;
The Teacher and the student unite in what is learned.

Accept this fully, for if you fail
Success will forever elude you,
However great your erudition.

This is why I call this
The heart of my teaching.
(from Chapter 27, *Tao Te Ching*)

    Harry comes to this same realization amid his adventures at Hogwarts: the teaching presences (both human and otherwise) that enter his life are not to be perceived as "superior beings" who must be feared or worshiped in order that one may receive their wisdom. No: they are familiar, friendly, and supportive helping presences that stand beside us as we learn. As Lao Tzu says, "the Teacher and student unite in what is learned." For when true learning happens, both, after all—the formed and the Formless—are enriched.

    Therefore, the exercises and instructions contained in the individual chapters of this book are offered as catalysts for each reader's unique experience, not as practical applications of doctrine. How you use these portions of the book will be utterly original, and you may well find that an exercise as presented will change within you, and become something entirely different and more personal than the actual text may suggest. This is completely natural, and represents the joyful activity of free will. Growth, after all, is really the process of choosing, from the core of our being, those experiences that most accord with our individual nature and its connection with the Source. As Professor Dumbledore reminds Harry after the encounter with the basilisk, "It is our choices, Harry, that show what we truly are, far more than our abilities."

Chapter 1: Principal Characters in The Way of Natural Magic

Professor Albus Percival Wulfuric Brian Dumbledore

Professor D—I have to ask you about that expression of yours that we just quoted: "It is our choices, Harry, that show what we truly are, far more than our abilities." Surely, you're one pretty talented and powerful wizard—the greatest of your age, most people say—how can you say that choice is more important than ability?

"I have been a teacher and headmaster at Hogwarts for longer than I would care to admit—longer, let's say, than many of my colleagues have been alive. I have seen as many students and wizards pass through the gates to this school as would be sufficient to populate one of your mid-sized Muggle cities; and I can tell you confidently that every one of them has been utterly unique in his and her ability.

"Too often, we equate talent with power—you just did so yourself, if I am not mistaken—until we're claiming that this fellow here is greater in his ability than that one over there. The problem is that such judgments tend to become fixed, particularly when they find their way into the Daily Prophet. *Especially* when they're repeated in the press, such labels turn into pure concrete—many an undeserved reputation and an ill-gotten fame has been perpetuated on the foundation of these fabrications, which are themselves blown up out of an airy obsession with appearances.

"This sort of image-making based on the perception of ability is a spell that has nearly as destructive an effect as any of the unforgivable curses, because it confers power on a person. And power not only places those without it into a position of being oppressed; it also puts an intolerable burden upon those who wield it. Some of the most renowned wizards I have known in my life have been driven to madness by the power that was projected onto them. Perhaps you have had some experience of this in your Muggle world.

"Now I am hoping that you will be more eloquent and efficient at instructing your readers about the consequences of power, but allow me to mention here that all power is an illusion. Indeed, a destructive and horrible illusion (as most are); but fundamentally, a fraud. There is no such thing as the *proper* use of power—there is only the abuse of power, for to use it is to abuse it.

"So to avoid confusion and prevent myself from making more errors than I already do, I tend to focus the children's efforts on choice rather than ability. It is not so difficult to find out what your abilities are—just find out what you love. But choosing what to do with your ability, that can be a challenge. Every wizard gets a wand, one that is utterly unique to his or her personality and ability; but many, I am afraid to say, never learn what to do with it."

In a youth-obsessed culture where middle age is deemed the onset of senescence, and particularly in this country, where the attitude of trust and respect toward the elders of a society breathed its last in the slaughter at Wounded Knee, the appearance on the world's literary stage of Professor Dumbledore is a welcomed blessing. Here is a man of indeterminate age (somewhere over a hundred, we are led to believe), still possessed of the strength and ability that have earned him the designation of "greatest wizard of his time." In *Order of the Phoenix*, he overcomes the attack of three younger opponents in one scene, and then personally tips the balance of the climactic battle scene. Yet he is the farthest thing from an "action hero" imaginable: he is gentle, yielding, soft-spoken, often unabashedly silly, meditative, and modest. He is, of course, the headmaster of Hogwarts School, and apparently has refused the position of Minister of Magic (the highest office of the wizard government) in order to remain with the school and its students. Indeed, he appears to be entirely lacking in ambition, violence, contempt, impulsiveness, acquisitiveness, and the hunger for fame—in short, he is the human embodiment of *Te*, the cosmic principle of Modesty that Lao Tzu speaks of throughout the *Tao Te Ching*. This poem, from Chapter 56 of that work, appears to fit Professor Dumbledore very well:

> Understanding doesn't talk a lot;
> A lot of talk lacks understanding.
>
> Can you be guided by silence?
> Can you shut down your outer senses?
>
> This is called "harmonizing light and dark."
> In this, you possess no one,
> But are loved by many.
> You are equally immune
> To attraction and revulsion.
> You are equally receptive
> To profit and to loss.
>
> You are unmoved by fame,
> Yet you attract honor.
> Because you make no claim,
> You can be free of disgrace.
>
> Thus are you lovingly received
> Into the Heart of Nature,
> Forever.

As a leader, Professor Dumbledore is everything that our current major world leaders are not. He retreats from display; is non-violent, even amid combat; his vision reaches beyond appearances; he embodies archetypally feminine traits; is simple in his needs; modest in both the amount and volume of his speech; and he promotes loyalty from his students and staff by nurturing their independence. His dignity and splendor are gifts of Nature; he makes no outer demand of others' respect, but his inner aura seems always to evoke it anyway.

As will be further discussed in Chapters 8 and 10, Professor Dumbledore is indeed human, meaning that he is subject to error. But he again distinguishes himself from the current crop of political leaders in our society *by displaying the capacity to admit his errors.* He goes further than this even, in his ability to share the blame for the miscommunication that leads to some of the tragic events of the stories. In doing so, he reveals the defining nature of true leadership, which is the ability to open new paths to understanding and correct action for others, through the example of inner truth, expressed in speech, thought, and action. In acknowledging his error and accepting his share of the blame, Dumbledore engages the Cosmic energies that transform the ideological stain of guilt into the cleansing water of remorse.

Hermione Granger

> "Harry—you're a great wizard, you know."
> "I'm not as good as you," said Harry, very embarrassed, as she let go of him.
> "Me!" said Hermione. "Books! And cleverness! There are more important things—friendship and bravery and—oh Harry—be *careful*!"
> (*Sorcerer's Stone*, p. 287)

Hermione, how could you, of all the people at Hogwarts, have come to believe that there are more important things than books?

"Well, that's perhaps the greatest lesson I've learned here. I've learned not to trust what I read in books as much as I thought I had to when I first came to Hogwarts. I mean, I still love to read...always will, I expect. But I've found that books are just the beginning of learning. To read a book is to stick a toe into an ocean of knowledge. And simply reading more isn't likely to take you in any further, any deeper. The best books give you an orienting point for your personal experience—do you know what I mean? Like the one you've perhaps heard me talk about a lot—*Hogwarts, A History*. That book was a nice guide (and I still wish someone around here besides me would bother to read it)—but the real thing, the real Hogwarts, is so different.

"I think the big turning point for me was the end of the

third year, after that exhausting and terrifying year with the time turner. When I looked back on how we had rescued Harry's godfather, and the way it all happened, I finally felt as if I had done real magic. But the reading and the studying, though I had done ever so much of it that year, had so little to do with it.

"So during my time here I've gone from thinking of books as the goal of learning to just the opening to it. Books open the door to experience, but they can't replace it."

Hermione Granger is the brainy girl who develops over the course of her journey through Hogwarts into a burgeoning woman. Her path of inner growth parallels Harry's, with the difference between them being the fact that Hermione rarely requires repetition in her learning—she tends to integrate her lessons, not through mere intellectual mastery, but through the activity of an organic intuition that is perhaps unique (at least in our culture) to the feminine.

While it is Harry's character that provides the focus of the dramatic thread of the stories, Hermione's path is drawn to show us a more purely natural way of inner development. Like many of us who have sought to discover ourselves through spiritual practice, Hermione's circle of growth begins with her lively intellect. This is one reason why there is such an enormous published literature of transformative practice: most of us happen to begin our journeys in this vein through the doorway of an intellectual encounter with a book, or an entire collection of them, before we begin to do the necessary inner work of giving intellect its appropriate (and often rather subordinate) place within the dynamic family of the personality. As Lao Tzu says of the Tao, sometimes it follows, sometimes it leads; but intellect is never meant to be alone.

> Pursue, and it eludes you;
> Follow, and it vanishes.
> Thought cannot hold it,
> But you can't think without it.
> (from *Tao Te Ching*, Chapter 14)

This is what Lao Tzu means when he speaks of

"rediscovering the Mother," or a return to the inner feminine. Thousands of years later, the psychologist C.G. Jung would again call us to this traditionally feminine aspect of human nature in his concept of the *anima*—the element of personality that helps us reach beyond the limitations of thought and toward a more holistic experience of the personality. This is the path that Harry falteringly takes, and which Hermione moves along with far more assurance.

Yet the gender-metaphor here can mislead us, if we're not careful: it is not meant to reflect an inherent *advantage* in being female, but rather to adapt (and at the same time expose) one of those basic assumptions of our culture—that such things as feeling and intuition are the exclusive or dominant province of the female. Like Lao Tzu and Jung, Rowling has chosen to swim amid this cultural current so that she might help us to rediscover the stream. Harry's character develops depth and substance as he learns to discover and accept the various manifestations of his feeling nature, his "inner feminine"—even to the point where Hermione's "voice" arises from within him at certain moments of decision, often to draw him back from an impulsive (or stereotypically "male") action.[7]

Hermione begins her life at Hogwarts under an obsession with books and rules, but her progress from that point is quick and purposeful, which is appropriate, given that her name is derived from that of the speedy "messenger god" of Greek mythology, Hermes. One turning point seems to come in the experience with the troll in the bathroom, from which Hermione learns the value of natural loyalty over conformity. Here, she opts for a temporary disgrace before authority, so that her friends are credited for the valor they showed in coming to her aid. Immediately following this experience, her nurturing and supportive qualities become manifest:

> Hermione had become a bit more relaxed about breaking rules since Harry and Ron had saved her from the mountain troll, and she was much nicer for it. The day before Harry's first Quidditch match, the three of them were out in the freezing courtyard during break, and she had conjured them up a bright blue fire that could be carried around in a jam jar. (*Sorcerer's Stone*, p. 181)

This inner trend grows throughout the remainder of the stories, until Hermione appears as a kind of empathic presence throughout the fifth and sixth books. She is able to sense and courageously expose Harry's more destructive and self-centered moods; she correctly intuits the danger from the death-veil within the Department of Mysteries; and she alone reveals an insight into Harry's ego-obsession with the heroic act, in his repetitive impulse to act before he is clear within.

Hermione, therefore, reveals to us the practical, reality-based orientation of inner truth: her perception increasingly reaches past appearance and ideology, toward the heart of every situation, where the supple, organic quality of truth stands out in contrast to the rigidly forced contrivance of doctrine. It is no random coincidence, then, that she is given the ability to move through time itself (in *The Prisoner of Azkaban*). For, while she never abandons her books and her devotion to study and preparation, she joins her scholarship with the values and abilities of the hearth, the earth, and the insight of the feminine.[8]

Tom Marvolo Riddle, a/k/a Lord Voldemort

> "I decided to leave behind a diary, preserving my sixteen-year old self in its pages, so that one day, with luck, I would be able to lead another in my footsteps, and finish Salazar Slytherin's noble work...Voldemort is my past, present, and future, Harry Potter..." (*Chamber of Secrets*, pp. 312-313)

Tom, many who have heard your story have wondered, how is it that a mere boy could have become—in a beautiful, magical place like Hogwarts—a force of such amazing...*darkness*?

"Well, first I should remind you that Hogwarts is not the idyllic little paradise that you Muggles seem to imagine. To a wizard of true power and ability, it is just another school, filled with snot-nosed runts and teachers who aren't smart or talented enough to make it in the *real* world.

"As for the fluff that Dumbledore and his little circle call teaching, I had learned all the lessons of the magical life long before I got to Hogwarts. I had already learned that there is power and there is weakness; and if you're going to really live and understand the secrets of life, then you'd better have as much power as possible. The more I grew, the more I realized that you can't have too much power—there is *no such thing* as too much power.

"This is what you quickly learn when you grow up as I did—abandoned, alone, rejected by your own parents. When you are forced to live apart, you learn to use that separation to create both mystery and dread.

"It all goes back to power, and power goes back to fear. If you can't make people fear you, then you can't get anything out of them, and that's just when they are most liable to take advantage of you. You can talk all you want about love and friendship, but nothing rules like fear.

"What people call loyalty is just terror with a candy coating or a gilded edge. People were always loyal to me at Hogwarts because I could show them the power I had to control them. In life, you have either followers or enemies. There is no such thing as friendship. I knew, even before I got here, that even so-called friends can turn on you at any moment. So I worked hard at learning those three little...uh...*charms* that you may have heard about, to help me in dealing with both my followers and my enemies. If you want to stay safe in this life, you have to keep people in line; and the way to do that is to treat your friends as if they were potential enemies.

"There's a lot of power in this place; but to use it you have to take it, and take it by force. It's not going to jump into your hands or up the core of your wand, and certainly no one is going to give it to you. No: you have to claim the power, grasp it, master it, and *own* it. Love is a nice fairy tale illusion for Muggles and Mudbloods, but power gets things done—power makes everything possible."

Why is it that the Potter books have so inflamed the

followers of certain fundamentalist sects of Christianity? It's probably a question that can't truly be answered, because to fully explore it only raises deeper questions. But it is clear that some violent passions have been aroused by the Harry Potter stories: the infamous book burnings and the repeated legal challenges against Ms. Rowling's books evoke the inquisitions of medieval Europe and the Salem witch hunts in America. Now, to have one's books burned by a sick fragment of the religious right is harmful only to those who are poisoned by the consciousness that lights such a petty conflagration—especially the children among them. Otherwise, as many a wag has observed, it is simply good publicity.

But could these violent attitudes toward a set of children's books be telling us something more—about both the stories themselves and the emotions they seem to arouse? This is where I think the character of Lord Voldemort comes in, for he is, indeed, the very embodiment of fundamentalism. Could it be that these fearful, paranoid right-wing ideologues that burn Mrs. Rowling's books are simply reacting to the terrible reflection of *themselves* that appears in the characters of Lord Voldemort and his followers, the Death Eaters?

I think that when we look closely at Lord Voldemort, we find a very accurate symbol of the icy and commanding voice of the group-centered ideological prejudice known as institutional religion. The very presence of that word, "Lord" in his title, suggests the exposure of the patriarchal and hierarchical face of institutional religion, with its exclusionary voice and racist overtones. Voldemort lives on the blood and energy of others, through the perpetuation of an image of power. His power is enforced (as all power must be) by the means of Laws and Commandments, torture, and slaughter (respectively symbolized by Voldemort's three favorite curses: "Imperio" representing Law and Commandment; "Crucio," torture, including the inner torture of guilt and blame; and "Avada Kedavra," murder.)

What's "Evil" About Religion?

The question has to arise in many readers' minds, "how can one possibly equate such a stereotypically evil character as Lord Voldemort with religion? What right does this author have to thus globally demonize religion and those who practice it in humility, goodwill, and faith?"

After I had written the main text of this book, it occurred to me that this is a fair question, and one that deserves a fair answer. My primary response to the question "what's wrong with religion?" is, "Intrinsically, absolutely nothing." It has been my experience, personally and through interactions with clients, students, colleagues, and friends, that there are "religious moments" in most people's lives. There may be a time when Christianity is nourishing to a person's inner being, there are moments where Buddhism is a correct path to follow; the same principle may apply for Judaism, Islam, Wiccan belief, Hinduism, Shintoism, or indeed any structured religious belief. In my own life, as in those of many people I've known, even a period of atheism (or a studied ignorance of religious matters entirely) has served a constructive purpose of growth and inner development. So once again, the answer to the specific question of what's wrong with religion is, "nothing's wrong." The problem arises in the ***forced attachment to the ideology***.

This is the danger of religion, and indeed, of any orthodoxy—of spiritual belief, scientific theory, nationalistic affiliation, or the adherence to a corporate, governmental, or other insular system of group-belief. Wherever, through the feudal power of attachment, a religion or other orthodoxy becomes institutionalized, then each individual's growth potential is instantly oppressed, to the extent that each member of the group *finds his identity through the ideology* (see the quotations from Eric Hoffer later in this chapter, in the section "Non-human Creatures of Hogwarts"). We have seen this corruptive influence at work within every one of the world's major religions, in many schools of scientific thought (such as Freudianism, for example), and in fixed structures of government—even in so-called democracies or republics, such as our own here in America. This is what I mean when I speak of "Voldemort-consciousness" in the orthodoxies of our lives, religious and otherwise.

What, then, is the religious person to do? What is he to make of such a perspective? Before you reject it as a slander against whatever faith you may practice, consider this suggestion: remain with your religion and its practices for as long as they serve your inner growth, but remain open in your awareness to the fact that spiritual life is no different from intellectual or psychological life in its natural need for growth, transformation, and movement. Just as your

> body needs room to breathe, and your mind the freedom to learn, your soul needs the space for growth and transformation. I have not met with the ideological system that can successfully accommodate the inner space required for the dance of transformative movement and broadening awareness that occurs in a life fully and deeply lived through to completion. Therefore, I ask my clients, students, and now my readers, to simply be open to the possibility that a time may come where their religion or belief of the moment is no longer appropriate to their inner space—that, like an old garment, it simply "no longer fits." Paradoxically, such a moment can be detected wherever you hear within yourself the phrase, "This is the Truth, the Truth for all and for all Time." Whenever you feel such a belief hardening within you, that's the time to firmly and fully rid yourself of it and move on. That sensitivity to the monumental voice of ego is your protection. In the presence of such an open awareness, any religion can be safely, uniquely, and constructively practiced, free of the Voldemort-consciousness of institutional ideology. We may leave the question there for now, with the hope that the reader may arrive at his own understanding on the matter, after having tried some of the exercises and meditations described in this volume. For the moment, it may be helpful to recall an expression I once saw on someone's T-shirt: "Religion is for people afraid of going to Hell/Spirituality is for those who have already been there."

As we will soon see, there is a lot of room for personal interpretation when it comes to Lord Voldemort. But I think it would be a terrible mistake to simply dismiss him as a stereotypical "bad guy;" and he is certainly not to be forced into the allegorical pigeonhole of the Satanic. For Lord Voldemort, given the scope of the stories themselves and the monumental dimension of his own presence within them, is more than the leader of a cult of devil-worshipers. Rowling is far too modern and urbane a writer to work amid such shallows; to identify Voldemort with Satan merely because of the snake metaphor would be just as careless a reading as would a parallel interpretation of Goethe's Faust.[9] Voldemort, like Mephistopheles, is only "demonic" to the extent that he represents a strain of consciousness that is fixed, derived, artificial, and obsessed with appearances. For me, the connection to the inflexible and power-driven delusions of institutional religion appears intuitively compelling, especially when it is seen to walk in lockstep beside the other significant embodiment of evil in the Potter stories, the Ministry of Magic.[10]

There is, throughout the Potter stories, a recurrent and insidious interdependence between these symbols of religion and state. Rowling holds a mirror of metaphor up to the history of humankind, while also delivering a crucial message to modern society: **there is truly no such thing as the separation of church and state.** Throughout history, these two forces have operated on behalf of one another, disguising their respective depredations with the smoke of their interlocking ideologies, and enforcing their hardened beliefs in human weakness with the oppressive cudgel of Law. This is why Lao Tzu advises us, in Chapter 19 of the *Tao Te Ching*, to inwardly separate from both of them:

> Separate from spirituality;
> Extinguish wisdom,
> And there will be benefit for all.
>
> Discard all pretence
> To piety and benevolence,
> And the people will help one another.
>
> Close the academies;
> Extirpate the feudal rites,
> And sorrow will be annihilated.
>
> Banish investment vehicles,
> Impoverish the profit-takers,
> And there will be neither thieves nor frauds.
>
> These are the ornaments of my teaching,
> But hardly the essence, which is this:
>
> Rely upon your inner discernment;
> Return to your original purity;
> Wear down your ego;
> Break out of the circle of desire.

What Lao Tzu is telling us here is a message that he repeats in other poems of the *Tao Te Ching*: institutionalized religion, with its forced and legally-mandated spirituality, cannot be separated from the oppressive mechanisms of state, *because they are both founded on the same illusion—they are not real.* That is, they don't come from what is real within us. As soon as each individual cleanses himself from within of the false concoctions of belief that support the perpetuation of church and state, then he discovers that the solution to conflict is not the forced separation *of* church and state, but a personal separation *from them both,* and from the claims that they make on our personal freedom. From this separation, "the original purity" arises, along with a more natural social order and the unforced, liberated spirituality of self-discovery.

In several of the chapters to follow, you will find certain exercises described, which are meant to help you begin the work of this process of nurturing your inner freedom. For the moment, it is worth noting the lesson that I think both Mrs. Rowling and Lao Tzu are offering us—that we *already know* how to relate harmoniously to one another; *we already know* the natural principles of inner governance, which can easily be translated into the social realm. All we have to do is "wear down ego; break out of the circle of desire." The transformation of society begins within the heart of each individual.

This message seems especially penetrating in the character of Lord Voldemort. For he, too, is fundamentally an illusion, an abstraction: he spends most of the stories as a vaporous, shadowy, insubstantial parasite. Even after his return to bodily form in the fourth book, he is like a ghoul—a wasted, skeletal form with the head of a snake. It is only fitting, then, that Lord Voldemort and his followers infiltrate the government, whose minions are represented by characters at the other extreme of physical form. Fudge and Umbridge are squat, smug, little tyrants—fat bureaucrats covered in labyrinthine layers of legislative gristle. Between Voldemort and the Ministry officials lies a third element, the unctuous corporate robots of annihilation, known as the "Death Eaters". These are the armies of oppression and destruction, which every institutional ideology of church or state has had occasion to employ—either as physical or economic force (usually a combination of both). The "corps" of armed force is cut from the same ideological fabric as the "corporate" weaponry of greed. This element is personified in the character of Lucius Malfoy, whose oily wealth is the forward advance of Voldemort's infiltration, his army of inner occupation.

As we will see in Chapter 3, which discusses Harry's journey within the Pensieve, the evil represented by Voldemort-consciousness is spread amid the noise and violence of conflict. The rant of litigation at home is merely the echo of the clamor of war abroad; the same distortions of ego perpetuate domestic violence and the destruction of our planet's atmosphere. Evil cannot hear the voice of inner truth because it is deafened by the noise of its manufactured conflicts. This inner deafness of evil[11] is a function of its fundamental lack of reality—it is a distortion of nature, a parallel, artificial construction with no inherent substance. Even as he is tortured by Voldemort, something within Harry perceives that he is dealing with a mere illusion—a power that has no further substance than did the memories he had encountered in the Pensieve. Guided by this insight, Harry is able to deal with Voldemort by drawing upon the pure and vibrant energies of light and help.

Still, there is no need to attach ourselves to a view of Lord Voldemort as a specific reference to religious ideology alone. For example: to a teacher, Lord Voldemort and the Ministry of Magic may represent the monumental ideals and bureaucratic regimes of academia; to a scientist, they may take on the inner meaning of received truth (the god of empiricism) and textbook knowledge; to a businessman, they may evoke images of the hypocritical ethics and oppressive organizational structures of the corporate world.

For me, Voldemort is symbolic of that ideological force in whose name the most horrible acts of genocide, slavery, occupation, dehumanization, destruction of Nature, and global oppression have been committed, enforced perpetually through the agencies of delusory belief and the insidious forces of guilt and fear. Jiddu Krishnamurti was once asked "is not the worship of God true religion?" His response addresses both the Voldemort-consciousness of institutional religion and our other question, posed above, about "what's wrong with religion":

> We have seen that ceremonies are not religion, that going to a temple is not religion, and that belief is not

religion. Belief divides people. The Christians have beliefs and so are divided both from those of other beliefs and among themselves; the Hindus are everlastingly full of enmity because they believe themselves to be brahmans or non-brahmans, or this or that. So belief brings enmity, division, destruction, and that is obviously not religion....When the mind is swept clean of image, of ritual, of belief, of symbol, of all words, mantrams and repetitions, and of all fear, then what you see will be real, the timeless, the everlasting, which may be called God....It is only when the mind is in revolt against all so-called religion that it finds the real.[12]

Ronald Weasley

> "I'm the sixth in our family to go to Hogwarts. You could say I've got a lot to live up to. Bill and Charlie have already left—Bill was head boy and Charlie was captain of Quidditch. Now Percy's a prefect. Fred and George mess around a lot, but they still get really good marks and everyone thinks they're really funny. Everyone expects me to do as well as the others, but if I do, it's no big deal, because they did it first. You never get anything new, either, with five brothers. I've got Bill's old robes, Charlie's old wand, and Percy's old rat." (*Sorcerer's Stone*, pp. 99-100).

Ron Weasley is the ugly duckling figure of the Potter stories—the Everyman through whom the most amazing wonders are accomplished as he plods along in artless insensibility. Throughout the stories, Ron is heard bemoaning his lot in life as the male incarnation of Cinderella—he is constantly self-conscious of his family's financial troubles and his personal fate of always being found at the back of the line in life. He must walk in the shadow of his brothers' past and their accomplishments, and again as the sidekick figure to Harry's fame and daring, while always having to content himself with the residue or leftovers of glory, notoriety, material possession, or love itself. As he makes his way through his distracted and sometimes timorous journey, however, insight is delivered through him, natural virtues are glowingly reflected, and the blessings of friendship are revealed.

As a comic figure, Ron seems to have been influenced by Shakespeare's Falstaff from the Henry IV plays. Happiness consists in a good feast, a full belly, games and other simple diversions, freedom from toil and study, and coarse conviviality.[13] Like Falstaff, Ron's self-preservative instinct is prominent, sometimes revealing a slightly phobic streak. He is afraid of spiders and the intimidating carnivores that Hagrid brings to their Care of Magical Creatures classes. Yet overall, Ron's sensitivity to danger reflects a natural sense of caution, which most parents would not mind seeing more of in their teenagers. He is always available to Harry as an influence of restraint, and his advice is very often appropriate, as when he warns Harry of the dangers of the Mirror of Erised. Ron's voice frequently serves to at least slow the momentum of Harry's more heroic impulses. Indeed, he would agree with Falstaff that "honour is a mere scutcheon" that "comes unlooked for, and there's an end."

To be sure, Ron is no coward: he is always there when danger must be faced, when "the choice between what is right and what is easy" (in Professor Dumbledore's words) must occasionally be made.[14] Yet his magic is not of the dramatic or heroic sort; Ron's preferred magic is about making work less toilsome and play more entertaining. He is too earthbound a child to become lost amid the past, or in fantasy. Although he momentarily indulges a rather provincial fantasy before the Mirror of Erised, of achieving recognition beyond that of his accomplished brothers, he very quickly returns to his center once the inner peril represented by the Mirror becomes clear to him. The self-imagery of sacrifice does not seem to stick to him, as it often does to Harry in his moments of self-conscious heroism—probably because Ron has not been culturally subjected to that form of projection. As we will see in Chapter 5, there is a lesson in this for both parents and children.

Yet something odd does happen to Ron in the climactic battle scene of *Order of the Phoenix*, which is perhaps a reflection of the osmotic power of ego-infection, especially among the young. After a brief separation amid their initial escape from the Death Eaters, Ron rejoins Harry and the others. But Ron is apparently drunk or otherwise intoxicated; he totters comically about, like a clown in a graveyard, and then attempts to "catch" a disembodied but living brain from a holding tank in which a number of such brains are magically preserved. He is instantly trapped within its "tentacles of thought," which do him some severe, though not irreparable, damage.

This is an example of how even the more playful of Mrs. Rowling's metaphors carry a deep vein of meaning. Amid all this warfare, a teenager is seen getting high, and is then trapped within snares of abstract, disembodied Mind. For those of us who grew up in the '60's and '70's, this scene evokes the Vietnam War-era experience of children experimenting with peyote buttons, mescaline, or LSD—trapped in the attempt to escape the seeming prison of the body, to retreat into a realm of pure Mind. Ron's injuries from this encounter are a metaphorical reminder that the madness known as ego arrives in many forms, all derived, however, from the same false belief in the relative insignificance of the physical body. For the psychedelic seeker, as for the grim, self-referential hero, spirituality and salvation are the goals of a bizarre asceticism, which is continually demonizes the body in its fantasy of a higher or more ethereal, "bodiless" realm. The body thus becomes a tool, or worse still, a servant of some superior purpose or ideal. Ron, like many of us who grew up possessed to some extent by this delusion, is able to recover, and the experience will no doubt become a turning point in his own path of growth. As the healer who treats him later declares, "thoughts could leave deeper scarring than almost anything else." (p. 847). It is no wonder, then, that the room in the Department of Mysteries, in which these disembodied brains live, is adjacent to the room of death and its ancient archway and veil. Whenever we are misled, even through naiveté, into beliefs and practices that espouse an escape from, or abasement of, our bodily nature, we are indeed flirting with death.

Draco Malfoy

> Malfoy looked angrier than Harry had ever seen him; he felt a kind of detached satisfaction at the sight of his pale, pointed face contorted with rage.
> 'You're going to pay,' said Malfoy, in a voice barely louder than a whisper. '*I'm* going to make you pay for what you've done to my father...' (*Order of the Phoenix*, p. 750).

Draco, perhaps you could tell us something about what you experienced that summer after the fifth year...you know, after your father was exposed as a Death Eater and put in Azkaban. What was the homecoming like, and how did you spend that summer?

"You saw how Potter and his friends attacked me on the train—the cowards had to gang up and blindside me, of course. But that's how these people are—Mudbloods, half-breeds, and Muggle-lovers. Takes ten of them to match up to the power of one *real* wizard. But like I said, they'll pay, all of them. Most of all, Potter. Dumbledore's lapdog, and his smarmy overgrown house elf with the red head and empty brain.

"These pea-brains, they actually believe that everything in the world is just like it is at Hogwarts...that defeating the Dark Lord is just like winning another Quidditch game. Ha! Wait till you see what Vol—what the Dark Lord does with them, what he has in store for them. He's a kind of a prophet, that man, and he chooses only the elect, only the best, to follow him. There's no force on earth can stop him, least of all Potter and his slimy friends.

"You want to know what happened that summer? Well I can't tell you...there were plans made, plans that would bring Dumbledore and his pasty-faced circle down for good. There won't be any mercy—not for anyone. Not after what I went through this summer, my mother screaming mad every night, with no one to hear her but me. Not with my father in Azkaban...no, no mercy.

"You see, it's different now...everyone is with us—the dementors, the giants, the werewolves—and those who aren't with us will be treated as enemies. Mark my words: there will be such vengeance as has never been seen in the history of wizardkind.

"Do you?" said the boy, with a slight sneer. "Why is he with you? Where are your parents?"

"They're dead," said Harry shortly. He didn't feel much like going into the matter with this boy.

"Oh, sorry," said the other, not sounding sorry at all. "But they were our kind, weren't they?"

"They were a witch and wizard, if that's what you mean."

"I really don't think they should let the other sort in, do you? They're just not the same, they've never been brought up to know our ways. Some of them have never even heard of Hogwarts until they get the letter, imagine. I think they should keep it in the old wizarding families. What's your surname, anyway?"

(Sorcerer's Stone, p. 78)

There can be no doubt that these are the words of a "bad faith dragon." Draco Malfoy[15], however, is the product of the cultural forces that molded him, and thus is but a symptom of an illness that has been recrudescing for thousands of years. Already, at the age of 11, the racism, intolerance, contempt, and insularity of a vicious group ideology can be seen in Draco, as actually happens in real life among children even younger than he. The nearest source of this corruption is indicated in the first book, and specifically identified in the second (Draco's father, Lucius Malfoy); but from a broader perspective, the source is the same cultural distortion that the iconoclastic psychotherapist Alice Miller describes in her books on the depravities of group assimilation among Western children. As she writes in *Banished Knowledge*[16], it all goes back to the inner death whose grip first forms within a home where there is no honor given to a child's uniqueness—in other words, where there is no love:

> It is only from adults that an unloved child learns to

> hate or torment and to disguise these feelings with lies and hypocrisy...The young child knows no lies, is prepared to take at their face value such words as truth, love, and mercy as heard in religious instruction in school. Only on finding out that his naiveté is cause for ridicule does the child learn to dissemble. The child's upbringing teaches him the patterns of the destructive behavior that will later be interpreted by experts as the result of an innate destructive drive. Anyone daring to question this assertion will be smiled at as being naïve, as if that person had never come in contact with children and didn't know "how they can get on your nerves." (p.47)

Draco, like many children who are thus indoctrinated, is a victim of what may be called "learned deceit." The rationale for this corruption is captured in the phrase "for your own good"—as classic a case of projection as can be found in our society. In their commentary to Hexagram 51 ("Shock") from the *I Ching*, Carol Anthony and Hanna Moog discuss the workings of this process of conditioning:

> This hexagram also addresses the shocks employed by the collective ego during childhood, in both physical and psychological forms, to condition the child to have reverence and respect for authority. This use of shock has the effect of deeply impressing the psyche with fears. The conditioning ultimately has the purpose of transferring the child's inner senses from serving his true nature to serving outer authorities. This transfer is made first to the parents, then to other institutions that represent the collective ego. The parents are made to believe, through their own conditioning, that their failure in this duty will create shame for them in the eyes of the collective ego. The child, for his part, is always told that the shocks are being administered for his own good. (*I Ching: The Oracle of the Cosmic Way*, pp. 551-552).

Thus, hypocrisy is encrusted onto the child's heart in the guise of prudence or outright opportunism; while prejudice and racism come decked in the alluring glitter of tribal religiosity ("we are the chosen people") or nationalism ("my country, right or wrong"). Even the more flattering versions of these distortions must be reinforced through the inner weaponry of threat, violence, and guilt. The sneering contempt of Draco's father, Lucius Malfoy, comes from the same attitude; it is the ideological fuel powering the twisted consciousness that smugly bears the "white man's burden." Slowly and inexorably, it blackens the heart, turning an innocent child into a sneering, raging bully. It is the inner force that turns people into walking corpses, families into corporate entities, nations into states; it is the power that causes parents to allow their children to be sent off to kill and die in deserts half a world away—"for your own good." For whose good is never truly made clear, nor will it ever be, as long as this decadence is permitted to rule us.

Therefore, under the painful yoke of this ignorance, a child like Draco is sent out into society to endure one disgrace after another, each of which further hardens his enmity against all who are separate from his ideological inheritance. Finally, the poison becomes his blood, and he will eventually degrade into a Lord Voldemort—a grasping and oppressive monster of self-righteousness; a monument made of shadows. At Hogwarts, Draco must submit to recurrent defeat, humiliation, and increasing isolation, because he has never been free to form relationships beyond the narrow boundaries of his group ideology. His isolation continues to spiral in a cycle of implosive density, until at the end of the fifth book he and his goonish friends are left stuffed in a luggage rack aboard the school train, as shapeless, oozing slugs. By this point, his father has been exposed as a follower of Lord Voldemort, and is now a prisoner of the same government that he had recently held between his purse-strings. On his return home, Draco will find, as do many children of excess and influence, that the manor is empty; perhaps he will also find the lies of his lifetime finally exposed for the vapid delusions that they are, and that his youth has so far been consumed by, in Lao Tzu's words, "an obsessive attachment to life's mere appearance."[17]

We will wish for Draco what we wish for all the children of lovelessness—that from the pit of their isolation they may find their way out of the prison of prejudice and insularity, and back to the innocence with which they began their lives. For Draco has suffered a more acute and malignant devastation than perhaps any of the other children of Hogwarts, since its grip of inner death is so frequently relentless. Its cycle of loneliness and enmity perpetually tends to further separate the prisoner from his only means of freedom—the very nourishment that he has lacked from the beginning: love. As Alice Miller writes, "an injured child lacks everything because he lacks love."[18]

Harry Potter

> If there is one thing Voldemort cannot understand, it is love...to have been loved so deeply, even though the person who loved us is gone, will give us some protection forever. It is in your very skin. (*Sorcerer's Stone*, p. 299).

Harry, you're about to enter your final year at Hogwarts. Is it even possible to capture the lessons learned over these six years in a few words?

"In fact, it's possible to do it in one, but it's a word that needs some explanation. It's love. You heard what Dumbledore said, right at the end of the first year—it's about love. That's what saved me as a baby; that's what brought me the help I needed in facing the basilisk; it's what made Prongs ride again when the dementors attacked; what made those things happen in the graveyard; and what rescued me from Voldemort's possession at the Ministry.

"But let's be clear about this: I'm not talking about some weepy, sentimental kind of love—you know, the kind you see on TV or in Muggle greeting cards. The love I'm talking about is different, and I think, more real. It's a kind of force...of attraction. Maybe it's some sort of power or principle that I don't fully understand yet. Hermione once told me about something she had read in a book she was assigned for Muggle Studies. She said that Muggle scientists talk about something called "quantum gravity;" that it's a force that attracts bodies in space as if they were bundles of light—like the light-stream from a wand. Seems crazy, but that sounds like the sort of thing I learned from

Dumbledore.

"There's something else that might have a lot to do with what happens next. I remember something Dumbledore told me in that long talk we had after Sirius died—you know, when I nearly trashed his office. He said there's a room in the Department of Mysteries that is always locked, and contains something that is stronger and greater than anything else down there—even the death veil and the time jar. Dumbledore told me that I have this...something...inside me, and that it had saved me from Voldemort's possession.

"I have a feeling that I might have to go there, and see what this thing is; how it's stored there and what it does. I think I might need it to find all these Horcruxes, you know. I think it's probably some other force, like Fate—maybe it's the river that opens into that ocean of Love that Dumbledore talked about, that has saved me so often before. I also wonder whether it might save me from having to kill, because that's something that really scares me—the idea of having to kill.

"I don't want to have to kill Voldemort, or anyone else, for that matter. I want to find those horcruxes, and I want to see Voldemort's power finally destroyed, of course. But I don't want to have to kill him—no more than Dumbledore wanted to kill him. I think that the last force in the Department of Mysteries might help me there—that it will help me finish what I have to do without having to kill. If Voldemort has to die in order for our world to continue, then I hope he is forced to kill himself."

Before he'd had time to think, Harry had taken his eyes off the Snitch and looked down. At least a hundred dementors, their hidden faces pointing up at him, were standing beneath him. It was as though freezing water were rising in his chest, cutting at his insides. And then he heard it again...Someone was screaming, screaming inside his head....a woman... Numbing, swirling white mist was filling Harry's brain...What was he doing? Why was he flying? He needed to help her...She was going to die...She was going to be murdered... He was falling, falling through the icy mist. "Not Harry! Please...have mercy...have mercy." A shrill voice was laughing, the woman was screaming, and Harry knew no more. (*Harry Potter and the Prisoner of Azkaban*, pp. 178-179)	A long time ago my father told me what his father told him, that there was once a Lakota holy man, called Drinks Water, who dreamed what was to be; and this was long before the coming of the Wasichus. He dreamed that the four-leggeds were going back into the earth and that a strange race had woven a spider's web all around the Lakotas. And he said: 'when this happens, you shall live in square gray houses, in a barren land, and beside those square gray houses you shall starve.' They say he went back to Mother Earth soon after he saw this vision, and it was sorrow that killed him. You can look about you now and see that he meant: these dirt-roofed houses we are living in, and that all the rest was true. Sometimes dreams are wiser than waking. (from *Black Elk Speaks*, p. 8)[19]

The coming chapters will follow Harry Potter's allegorical journey through the school of inner life, so there is no need to anticipate here what will be covered later. So, as an introduction to the approach that will be taken throughout this book to the character and story of Harry Potter, it seemed that a comparison between two magical visionaries—the one fictional, and the other historical—would be appropriate.

The quotes above—from *Prisoner of Azkaban* and Black Elk's memoirs—reflect two separate instances of remote seeing. Harry's experience comes to him during a Quidditch match, while he is flying on a broomstick, playing a game of skill and speed. In the midst of the outer action, Harry sees the "dementors"—the black, soul-sucking demi-ghosts of the stories—and instantly has a vision of the murder of his mother by Lord Voldemort. In the books that follow *Prisoner of Azkaban*, Harry has dreams and visions of events that are happening in the present—glimpses of the consciousness of a moment. They always involve a threat or destructive action being planned or completed by Lord Voldemort. As these visions become public knowledge, Harry is labeled, by turns, a charlatan and a lunatic—even by people within the magical world. Many of the accusations against him are scripted and spread by Lord Voldemort and his followers, through the machinery of the Ministry of Magic; even the press is manipulated to defame him. Harry's path of inner growth is thus pitted with obstructions, and he is forced, again and again, to learn the same lessons over, until each is fully and maturely worked into his psyche. For he is drawn recurrently into a field of opposition—against Voldemort, the Ministry, sometimes even against his fellow students and closest friends.

Harry makes the additional error of pursuing various heroic and idealized self-images, usually bound up with the notion of sacrificing himself amid rescue missions of near-messianic proportions. These always lead him into confusion, senseless risk to self and others, and finally, to outright disaster. In the first book, it would appear that the Sorcerer's Stone had already been adequately protected and did not need "saving;" the pursuit of the spiders in the second story turned out to have been little more than a nearly-fatal misdirection; and in the fifth book, Harry's literal interpretation of a dream image leads to the death of his godfather.[20]

Harry's journey is thus an amazingly apt metaphor on the psycho-spiritual search of our era, with its tortuous paths spotted with error, false belief, and ambivalence. Harry's very name suggests this image of inner conflict that can only be clarified amid the heat of the cauldron of lived experience. His first name is, of course, a word meaning "to harass, worry, annoy, or make small, repeated attacks;" while his last name is evocative of the earth as the substance from which clay is made into objects of utility and beauty for humans. It may be said that the "Harry" in him is ego's worrisome, annoying, sniping, and meddlesome voice, which recurrently distorts and undermines the earthy, natural intuition of the "Potter" in him. This seems to be a broader perspective on his difficulties in learning the way of natural magic than to dismiss his recurrent error as merely the folly of youth or the turmoil of adolescence. Indeed, the lessons of natural magic lead us to the understanding that youth does not have to be foolish, nor adolescence a period of ceaseless inner conflict. Nature does not dictate that its creatures must grimly endure "stages," "phases," "crises," or "life changes" of physical suffering, emotional turmoil, and misunderstanding; only human institutions and their collective ideologies (religion, science, and cultural belief) project such delusions onto Nature.

The Oglala Sioux healer and philosopher, Black Elk, came out of a very different cultural environment than the Muggle world in which Harry Potter was raised. Yet Black Elk's extraordinary autobiographical narrative contains references to many of the same kinds of struggles, self-doubts, and errors that Rowling writes of in Harry's story. There are also some parallels between their visions of natural magic, beginning with their onset in early childhood; the presence of natural metaphors such as lightning; and concern over being judged as "crazy" or misguided because of the seer's connection with the invisible realm of consciousness. Harry's dreams of the horrible events that occurred while he was an infant seem to go back as far as he can remember, and the strange things that happened around him whenever he was afraid or angry also seem to reach deep into his childhood. For Black Elk, the visions began when he was about five years old, at a time when peace appeared assured between the white man and the Indian:

> The soldiers did go away and their towns were torn down; and they made a treaty that said our country would be ours as long as grass should grow and water flow. You can see that it is not the grass and the water that have forgotten.
> Maybe it was not this summer when I first heard the voices, but I think it was, because I know it was before I played with bows and arrows or rode a horse....It was like somebody calling me, and I thought it was my mother, but there was nobody there. This happened more than once, and always made me afraid, so that I ran home. (p. 14).

Then one day, a bird speaks with him—not unlike the arrival of an owl bearing an invitation to a school of magic. This bird tells Black Elk to direct his attention to the sky; and from out of the sky come two men, singing:

> Behold, a sacred voice is calling you;
> All over the sky a sacred voice is calling. (p. 15)

Then, when he is about nine years old, "the great vision" occurs, in which he is drawn into the sky and taught the way of life by birds, animals, and humans together.[21] Similarly, Harry's experience of magic shows him that learning happens when we allow *all* of Nature to become our teacher; his most enduring lessons come from objects, animals, plants, rocks, spirits, and part-humans. Black Elk feels pain and illness along with his vision, and his first impressions on entering the spirit-realm are of the "thunder beings," represented by the lightning that arises from the shaking of the spirit-horses' manes and the thunder from their breath. In the same vein, Harry's lightning-bolt scar on his forehead, the physical remnant of Lord Voldemort's attack, becomes his entry into the most potent and personal of his magical abilities. In both stories, the wound left by the conflict between ego, with its fearful, predatory beliefs, and the teaching drawn from the encounter with Nature, become the gateway to all understanding and growth.

This is the understanding expressed by Lao Tzu throughout the *Tao Te Ching*; it is also transmitted through many spiritual insights across many traditions, from that of ancient Egypt to Buddhism to the stories of the American Indian. In his classic guide to inner life for men, *Iron John*, Robert Bly has a chapter called "The Wound by the King's Men" which discusses stories of injury and wounding as the way of entry into the more mature depths of psycho-spiritual life. He mentions the boar-wound to Odysseus from Homer's story and the Fisher King's thigh wound, from Arthurian legend.[22] Significantly, Black Elk's pain comes to his thighs as he is embarking on the journey of his "great vision." There is a temptation to look upon this wounding as a symbol of the sacrifice as represented in the stigmata of the crucified Jesus; yet I think it would be an error to look upon either Harry's scar or Black Elk's wound as a symbol of death and resurrection—except as of the death of ego and the recovery of the true, individual self that is progressively liberated from the institutional prejudices of church and state.

Harry, after all, is not by nature a sacrificial being; in fact, it is his self-sacrificing or heroic impulses that lead him into the most egregious errors as he makes his way through the school of natural magic. It is similar with Black Elk: he, like Odysseus, lived a long, active, and fruitful life in which he taught, healed, fought when necessary to protect his people, and finally transmitted the story of his people. For Black Elk, this last act involved a calling to future generations to remember that the earth is our mother, that the way of true magic is the recognition of the human place within the cosmic whole, which is not Lordship or dominion over the earth and its creatures (for that would be the way of Lord Voldemort and the Judeo-Christian institutional religions), but of cooperation, service, and grateful participation with all the things and beings with whom we share our planet. At the end of the "Heyoka Ceremony," Black Elk directs us to the same deep understanding of the human place within Nature that Harry discovers in his own encounters with hippogriffs, centaurs, elves, and healing plants. Note also the specific mention of "fun" in Black Elk's description of the effect that natural magic has on those who allow themselves to be guided by its healing energy:

> When the ceremony was over, everybody felt a great deal better, for it had been a day of fun. They were better able now to see the greenness of the world, the wideness of the sacred day, the colors of the earth, and to set these in their minds.
> The Six Grandfathers have placed in this world many things, all of which should be happy. Every little thing is sent for something, and in that thing there should be happiness....Like the grasses showing tender faces to each other, thus we should do, for this was the wish of the Grandfathers of the World. (p. 149).

Environment as Character: The Aura of Hogwarts

> There were a hundred and forty-two staircases at Hogwarts: wide, sweeping ones; narrow, rickety ones; some that led somewhere different on a Friday; some with a vanishing step halfway up that you had to remember to jump. Then there were doors that wouldn't open unless you asked politely, or tickled them in exactly the right place, and doors that weren't really doors at all, but solid walls just pretending. It was also very hard to remember where anything was, because it all seemed to move around a lot. The people in the portraits kept going to visit each other, and Harry was sure the coats of armor could walk. (*Sorcerer's Stone*, pp. 131-132)

There is a lot of unpredictable movement in the magical world of Hogwarts: objects that seem to possess not only consciousness but a mischievous sense of humor. Indeed, by comparison, the children themselves seem rather staid and mature—they are continually portrayed in attitudes of annoyance or alarm as they react to the petty, playful assaults of magical objects and ghosts.

This kind of environment, with its trick doors, moving staircases, and paintings that invent unfathomable passwords for permission to enter a room, is highly suggestive of the trickster figures of old mythologies and Zen Buddhism. The stairway to heaven may contain a trick step, or lead in the wrong direction tomorrow morning, just when you assume that you've figured it out, that enlightenment is attained. The doors of perception that seem to be portals to the right hand of God or the end-point of realization will, once you have reached for their handles, turn out to be blank, laughing stretches of wall. It is at a time like this that Peeves the Poltergeist (who is introduced in the very next paragraph following the one quoted above) will appear, to drop a water balloon on your head, thus completing the lesson in the folly of spiritual self-aggrandizement.

It is no mistake that the one person at Hogwarts who is

most tormented by Peeves is the caretaker, Argus Filch, who is a person that we all encounter in our lives every day. Filch is a "squib"—a person born of magical parents but having no magical ability; his petty self-absorption in the most superficial aspects of propriety and routine has thoroughly clotted his true nature. He has not an ounce of humor or human feeling in him, it seems—he is the tattletale at school, the procedure freak at the office, or still more ominously, the grownup that beats a child for playing in the mud on Sunday. Peeves is one antidote to Filch-consciousness: without the cackling irritation of Peeves' mindless sport in our lives, we would be far more prone to falling prey to the dark and petty meanness of Filch.

The role of humor in the way of natural magic will be more fully discussed in Chapter 4; it will be worthwhile here to briefly emphasize the playful aspects of the environmental metaphor at Hogwarts and its connection to the pre-institutional stories of ancient cultures. These latter have been delightfully recorded by Joseph Campbell, in his focus on the trickster spirits of myth:

> This ambiguous, curiously fascinating figure of the trickster appears to have been the chief mythological character of the paleolithic world of story. A fool, and a cruel, lecherous cheat, an epitome of the principle of disorder, he is nevertheless the culture-bringer also. And he appeared under many guises, both animal and human. Among the North American Plains Indians his usual form was Coyote. Among the woodland tribes of the north and east, he was the Great Hare, the Master Rabbit, some of whose deeds were assimilated by the Negroes of America to an African rabbit-trickster whom we know in the folktales of Br'er Rabbit. The tribes of the Northwest Coast knew him as Raven. Blue Jay is another of his forms.[23]

Shakespeare, of course, gave the trickster an eternal life in literature, from Puck of *A Midsummer Night's Dream* to the Fool of *King Lear*. Peeves, often helped by the trickster twins Fred and George Weasley, is the modern literary incarnation of the trickster spirit, who noisily enforces attention, humility, and laughter upon those who would otherwise take themselves and their lives too seriously. For when we become too serious, we become self-absorbed; and before you know it, the passing truths of our lives are made into the concrete monuments of insular religion, science, and law. The presence of Peeves reveals another of Dumbledore's qualities as a leader: the poltergeist is tacitly accepted (and even encouraged) by the headmaster, who also has a taste for tipping sobriety onto its ear now and then. At the Opening Feast of the first book, Dumbledore solemnly announces that he has words of wisdom for the students, and then barks out, "Nitwit! Blubber! Oddment! Tweak!" (*Sorcerer's Stone*, p. 123).

Indeed, there can be no inner growth without humor and the ability to embrace life's seeming capriciousness. It is a teaching that has required repetition throughout history: Socrates was a Peeves figure, blowing raspberries within the most holy church of Athenian Democracy; literary figures from Aristophanes to Rabelais to Cervantes to Thoreau to Gogol have made the same blessed sounds, each in his own way. Throughout the Hogwarts journey, the same lesson is heard over and again: wherever there is pomp and self-consciousness, it is knocked flat onto its ass by a false door, a trick step, a violent willow tree, a "blast-ended skrewt," a three-headed dog, or a ghost who can flip his head back like the cover to an ice bucket.

Modesty is the golden thread of the tapestry of magic; humor is the breath that allows Modesty to glow amid the morbid decadence of pomposity. One final trickster story from the American Indian mythology will be appropriate here—imagine as you read it that the "coyote's arms" are the different departments within a modern corporation or a government bureaucracy:

> One day the trickster, in the form of a coyote, killed a buffalo and while his right arm was skinning it with a knife his left suddenly grabbed the animal. "Give that back to me," the right arm shouted. "This is mine!" The left arm grabbed again, and the right drove it off with the knife. The left grabbed again and the quarrel became a vicious fight. And when the left arm was all cut up and bleeding, Trickster cried, "Oh, why did I do this? Why did I let this

happen? How I suffer!"

(from Joseph Campbell's *Primitive Mythology*, p. 269)

Movement is the metaphorical blood that both animates and nourishes the environment of Hogwarts: motion is the medium of spontaneity, of humor, of the magical dance of Nature. Movement is life, and movement across structural boundaries is evolution. So it is at Hogwarts, and in the world that its metaphors describe. In his book *The Hidden Connections*,[24] scientist Fritjof Capra (still best known for his groundbreaking work of the '70's, *The Tao of Physics*) answers the question "what is life?" in the context of a "living systems" view of cellular biology:

> ...the cellular network is materially and energetically open, using a constant flow of matter and energy to produce, repair, and perpetuate itself; where new structures and new forms of order may spontaneously emerge, thus leading to development and evolution. (p. 31)

The more we learn of life—whether from a scientific, psychological, social, or cosmic perspective—the more we see its boundaries expanded. The limitations imposed on life by the science, law, and religion of the feudal past tend to crumble into cosmic dust before an open and receptive effort of understanding. The recognition of the organic nature of truth, its unceasing unfolding, may be considered a beginning step in opening to the way of natural magic. The truths discovered through this book will be expanded upon by every reader who encounters it in a spirit of sincerity and receptivity; there is no end to understanding, because there is no end to consciousness.

Chapter 2: The Room of Requirement: Getting Help Where You Need It

> "Dobby knows the perfect place, sir! It is known as the Come and Go Room, sir, or else as the Room of Requirement! It is a room that a person can only enter when they have real need of it. Sometimes it is there, and sometimes it is not, but when it appears, it is always equipped for the seeker's needs. It is a most amazing room, sir." —*Harry Potter and the Order of the Phoenix*, from Chapter 18

Dobby is a house-elf: a dwarfish creature whose kind have been made into slaves by the humans who rule the wizarding world. Since he has been enslaved by his society, Dobby has nurtured many of the abilities of the servant. He knows things of which his human masters are entirely ignorant; he possesses powers of knowledge, insight, and action that often exceed those of his rulers; and he exhibits many "human" virtues—such as loyalty, humor, resourcefulness, and altruism—which are frequently found to be so violently repressed among his masters that they might as well be absent. Thus, Harry Potter finds himself turning to Dobby during a point in the fifth story where he has a certain specific and crucial need. Harry must find a place within the Hogwarts grounds where he can safely lead a practice-oriented work-study group in "Defense Against the Dark Arts," because the instruction he and his fellow students are getting in that area from Professor Umbridge is so superficial as to be utterly useless.

Yet even though he is well aware, through prior experience, of Dobby's practical abilities, Harry is pessimistic about what Dobby could offer him. He makes the error of casting a negative expectation onto his call for help—this, of course, is a common mistake which we have probably all made at one time or another (the operative phrase that one usually forms or hears in this respect goes something like, "I'll just expect the worst, and anything good that comes will be a pleasant surprise"). Indeed, such negative expectations can be just as impractical as the other extreme, the grasping expectation of inner demand. Both these poles along the narrow linear shaft of expectation are usually set into our minds during the training and acculturation of childhood. We may have learned a false notion of humility (as self-abasement and self-denial), or we might have been taught a horribly restricted vision of how (and what) the universe creates and provides for us. Indeed, traditional societal and religious formulations of what "Providence" does for us leave very little in the way of Provision! Providence, it turns out, is not much of a provider.

The problem, as we will see, is not that we expect *too much* (of the universe, Nature, or God), but *that we expect at all*. For expectation (and its opposite, self-denial) is a closed hand, a clenched fist that is stretched out along a narrow line of division and demand.

The teaching poems of the Chinese oracle, the *I Ching*, offer us an alternative to the extremes of pessimism and greed; this alternative is like an open-armed embrace that encompasses the realms of both giving and receiving, in an arc of natural abundance. The *I Ching's* discussion of this topic can be found in Hexagram 25, appropriately titled "No Expectations":

> No expectations.
> To have no expectations is supremely blessed.
> It is favorable to remain as one is.
> Improper conduct brings misfortune.
> It is not favorable to advance.
> (from Greg Whincup's translation, *Rediscovering the I Ching*)

The "supreme blessing" of discarding the habits of expectation is that we are thereby taken completely out of the arenas of demand and self-denial. The resulting point of balance is "to remain as one is." This expression is succinctly interpreted in Anthony and Moog's book on the *I Ching*, which we will have cause to cite several times throughout our Harry Potter journey:

> Not expecting is a person's natural state of mind. It

means residing in one's center, where discernment springs spontaneously from the feeling of what is harmonious and what is discordant...Not expecting means approaching something free of prejudice, preconceived images, fixed beliefs, inner demands, fears, or doubts.
(from *I Ching: The Oracle of the Cosmic Way*, pp. 299-300)

Thus, "to remain as one is" means simply to *be as one was*, before the forces of cultural conditioning took hold of us, with their artificial notions of demand, sacrifice, negativity, grasping, and longing. It is no more our natural state to renounce desire than it is to define it. Throwing walls around our natural bodily and psychological needs always leads us to failure and instability, as it did for Saint Augustine in his famous prayer of ambivalence: "Lord, make me chaste...but not yet."[25] Unfortunately for himself and countless others who followed his subsequent teachings, Augustine was led to make the wrong choice, based purely on his obsessive attachment to a group-defined belief as to what is good, pure, and true. In doing so, he built one of the most unnatural monuments of doctrine in the history of human ideology. When the door to his own Room of Requirement stood wide open before him, he chose instead to construct a corridor of madness, built from the mud of self-denial.

We can therefore be grateful that Rowling's work has come to be at least as equally influential in our time as Augustine's writing was in the century after his. She has the insight to bring Harry to a far healthier decision than the august saint. What brings Harry this "Room of Requirement" is, first, his trust and goodwill toward a creature that is despised and enslaved by the cultural forces of Harry's world, and second, the fact that he has not rigidly defined what will or won't work for him. Therefore, and his passing moment of negativity notwithstanding, Harry receives much more than he could ever have concocted in his imagination through narrow expectation. The perfect solution to a problem is not meant to be miraculously rare, any more than it is meant to be foreseen.

When we expel the presence of ego, along with its

desultory expectations, from the classrooms of our inner lives, then "magic," or—to be precise—the natural energy of cosmic help, is free to flow through us, bringing us exactly what we need in each situation. The solutions that thus arrive do more than simply suit the need of a passing moment—they endure and flow throughout our lives, in a trickle-down fashion that (in contrast to certain political economic theories going by the same name) really works.

It all begins on their first visit: they find that the hallway where this magical room may be found is guarded by a very silly, though violent, image: a tapestry that depicts "Barnabus the Barmy" (which may be a playful slap on Rowling's part at institutional Christianity, through the name of one of its iconic founding figures). This Barnabus had apparently once attempted to teach trolls the ballet, and the tapestry is a record of the result: a troll (whether or not dressed in a tutu is not specified) is seen perpetually clubbing poor Barnabas to death for his efforts. Well, it would appear that the Room of Requirement is not a place for the idle or the curious. But Harry and his friends only have to practice a brief walking meditation in this corridor, and the door to the Room appears in a wall that had hitherto been bare and solid. Once inside, they discover everything they need to do their work.

But it doesn't end there: Harry finds that, in this environment, he can teach others—that he actually has knowledge from which they can benefit. His friends also discover abilities which they would never have thought themselves to possess. Even the timorous Neville Longbottom is able to reveal his "internal warrior," to use Robert Bly's expression[26]. Together, the children learn that they have the natural capacity to express their true nature, and thus protect themselves from harm—all that is needed is the right environment and the synergy that occurs when people are united by a modest attitude, sincere motivation, and a willingness to allow the teaching energy of natural magic to flow among them. Incidentally, Harry also discovers romance in this room, for it is here that his courtship of the lovely Cho Chang achieves "consummation" (in a holiday kiss under a sprig of mistletoe placed in the Room of Requirement by Dobby). The nourishing inner effect of this Room is so complete and deeply satisfying that Harry feels as if "he were carrying some kind of talisman inside his chest" over the weeks after the children begin using the Room together in their common mission of self-discovery.

The Room of Requirement is, after all, a metaphor for an *inner space*, available to us all. It is the place where the true self makes a connection with its cosmic origin, which is the source of all inner and outer prosperity. Receiving the gifts of life, health, and the maintenance of one's needs in every moment, is about nurturing non-expectation. When we abandon expectation, we are free to experience our natural desires, needs, and preferences as a unique individual. When he puts his wish before Dobby, Harry doesn't say "I need a place where I can discover my ability as a teacher, see others realize their hidden talents, and somewhere along the way get a chance to kiss Cho Chang." No, he simply says, "I need a place to practice Defense Against the Dark Arts with my friends." Yet all these other gifts do indeed come to him and his fellow students. Harry knows he has a specific need, and he is also aware that it is correct for him to want to see that need fulfilled; but he places no projection of limitation, form, or extent onto his desire. Thus, he gets more than he can possibly have dreamt of receiving.

Throughout Harry's journey within the magical world, he is brought the help and blessings he needs—often at the very moment when he has relinquished hope and expectation. For hope is to outer life what faith is to the inner: a grasping projection of belief and demand, which tries to reach beyond the arc of experience. This may fool us for a while; it may even offer us temporary or passing comfort; yet it does not bring us all of what we truly *need* from life. But to let go of hope is not to pass over into despair: it is instead to return to our center. This return to the center of being has the effect of removing the force of power and inner manipulation from the expression of need; instead, we simply acknowledge our desire and allow the cosmos to respond.

In his classic novel, *Siddhartha*, Hermann Hesse has his principal character offer his own perspective on this principle. Siddhartha appears before the beautiful courtesan, Kamala, and almost instantly attains goals that most people might strive mightily to reach through years of forced effort and struggle. He explains the principal that guides him to this seemingly magical kind and pace of achievement:

> "Listen, Kamala, when you throw a stone into the water, it finds the quickest way to the bottom of the water. It is the same when Siddhartha has an aim, a goal. Siddhartha does nothing; he waits, he thinks, he fasts, but he goes through the affairs of the world like the stone through the water, without doing anything, without bestirring himself; he is drawn and lets himself fall. He is drawn by his goal, for he does not allow anything to enter his mind which opposes his goal. That is what Siddhartha learned from the Samanas. It is what fools call magic and what they think is caused by demons. Everyone can perform magic, everyone can reach his goal, if he can think, wait, and fast."[27]

Whenever we are in tune with Nature, with our deepest inner nature, then everyplace you go is Hogwarts; every moment you are living is a magical one.

Chapter 3: Memory and the Way Forward: Entering the Pensieve

> A shallow stone basin lay there, with odd carvings around the edge: runes and symbols that Harry did not recognize. The silvery light was coming from the basin's contents, which were like nothing Harry had ever seen before. He could not tell whether the substance was liquid or gas. It was a bright, whitish silver, and it was moving ceaselessly; the surface of it became ruffled like water beneath wind, and then, like clouds, separated and swirled smoothly. It looked like light made liquid—or like wind made solid—Harry couldn't make up his mind.
>
> —from Chapter 30, "The Pensieve" of *Harry Potter and the Goblet of Fire*

In one of Rowling's more finely placed and crafted scenes within the Harry Potter series, Harry finds himself at another turning point in his young life: he is soon to face the third and final task of an elite wizard's triathlon, which had been designed exclusively for the participation of students much more advanced than he, but to which he has nevertheless been magically called. There is a deepening mystery surrounding him, which began with a troubling dream, followed by a foreboding display of group violence at a major professional sporting event, and continuing with Harry's selection for the "triwizard tournament."

At the moment of the story where we now join Harry, he has come to the headmaster's office to see Professor Dumbledore, for help and advice with another violent and ominous dream that had awakened him from a nap during Divination class. But Dumbledore is preoccupied with an inspection of the site of the aforementioned attack, so Harry waits for him, pondering this odd container with its "light made liquid."

Sitting alone in the headmaster's office, Harry feels his inner strength and poise return. All the elements of his inner truth are symbolized by the aura of Dumbledore's space, and the objects it contains. There is the phoenix, and there the sword and the sorting hat, which had come to his aid in overcoming the dragon-snake known as the basilisk just two years before[28]. He is entering a realm of hidden resources and deep strength, where inner truth connects with cosmic energies; within this realm, Harry will find protection as well as insight. In every story of the spiritual quest, these two functions coalesce and support one another, furthering the seeker's growth in an expansive dance of light and dark, yin and yang, retreat and advance. We all have the ability to draw on such resources: their presence is accessed through such means as meditation, the awareness of dreams, the use of oracles, and transformative practices such as can be discovered in the hut of the shaman or the office of the psychotherapist. All such practices relate fundamentally back to the same simple trust in, and attention to, the invisible realm of being, where feeling-consciousness transforms difficulty and transcends suffering.

But, as we all know, inner life is not a pool of perfect stillness: it is often a journey through choppy seas and hidden depths, especially for those who are new to the seeker's voyage. By the time we encounter him in the Pensieve scene, Harry has had many experiences of the quest; yet he is still but fourteen years old, and there is much learning yet to be experienced. Indeed, the journey is never over, and is continually reaching new depths of discovery and regeneration. Frequently, these depths are encountered in memory, where the path of inner growth is entered upon through the doorway of the past.

Therefore, Harry is brought to the Pensieve, where he goes beyond the comfort of prior achievement and into more mature depths of inner experience. We often approach a path of inner growth with a conditioned position of distrust, suspicion, or outright malice; or we may find the prospect of inner learning to be filled with mystery and a kind of esoteric holiness. Either perspective is, of course, erroneous, and must be discarded before any seeker on the psycho-spiritual path can make true progress. Harry initially approaches the Pensieve, this magical basin and its glistening contents whose diaphanous light draws his attention, with a cautious combination of attraction, suspicion and awe:

> He wanted to touch it, to find out what it felt like, but nearly four years' experience of the magical world told him that sticking his hand into a bowl full of some unknown substance was a very stupid thing to do. (*Goblet of Fire*, p. 583).

Then Harry decides to test the silvery substance with his wand, and things begin to happen. Once he initiates contact with the mist within the bowl, the silvery substance clarifies and takes on a crystalline transparence. This is the symbolic opening of inner clarity, the point at which understanding is synergized with commitment, in which an encounter with the past can point us forward. It is a breakthrough point in the quest, where the silvery cloud of Mystery clears within us, and transformative practice then becomes as natural and effortless a process as eating or going to the toilet—and no less rewarding. In the Zen tradition, it is that moment where "the mountain is again just a mountain," where wonder merges with acceptance to give birth to "ordinary mind," and the quest becomes a natural part of daily life. This is the point at which we, like Harry, are drawn in—"pitched headfirst", as Rowling puts it, into the Pensieve of inner growth.

Harry enters the Pensieve when his nose—the organ of the most primordial and feeling-oriented of our senses—touches the silvery mist within the bowl. We, too, are meant to approach our inner life with our feeling-senses heightened; the seeker's journey is led and nurtured by the senses that are the most commonly repressed or neglected by our culture—even by our religious beliefs (see text box, "God's Nose").[29] When we approach the invisible realm of being, we must discard, or at least suspend, that conditioned obsession with rationality which has been programmed into us by our culture: in turning within, we can no longer "be reasonable"—we must "follow our nose." Healing and growth—the twin goals of all transformative practices—occur when we are able to engage ourselves and our past with all the intuitive and noumenal capacities of our total being.

God's Nose

In the Judeo-Christian tradition, God knows all (mind, intellect); sees all (the omni-eye); and hears all (the cosmic NSA wiretapper). But He doesn't *smell* a thing; and this, I submit, is a problem, a failing of God.

The Greeks and other ancient cultures knew better. They understood that man was not created in God's image, but that it was really quite the other way around. Therefore, they gave God a very sharp sense of smell. This sense is a part of the many stories (usually of the big guy, Zeus), that involve attraction, deception, and even seduction. Read the tales of Homer, Ovid, or Pindar: if you wanted to get a god's attention in those days, you laid out a feast that would usually feature a juicy, burning, smoking sacrificial barbecue. The fumes from the roast would waft toward Olympus and next thing you know you'd have a god at the picnic table.

The only remnant of such stories in the Judeo-Christian Bible that I could find is Gen. 8:21, where Noah, having survived the famous flood, has smoked some sacrificial animals in the BBQ pit and the smell attracts God, who as a result swears never to destroy the Earth again. Otherwise, in both the Old and New Testaments, God's nose has been removed.

Maybe the authors of these texts wanted us to believe that God couldn't possibly be an animal like us, so they made a point of taking away or at least minimizing the most primordially animal sense—smell—from the attributes of God. Once again, in these texts God knows, sees, hears, and certainly acts a lot; but he rarely smells (though he often stinks).

The problem with a God who can't smell is that this deficiency severely weakens the teaching potential of the myth; it saps the metaphor of a crucial strain of pragmatism, since God is suddenly so fundamentally unlike us that His experience is no guide for our lived experience.

And if you think the sense of smell is overrated, check out the animal kingdom: what do two dogs do when they first meet? How do animals in the wild detect enemies or food? Then consider your own experience, and think of how often you've relied on your sense of smell to choose the right food, the best living space, even the right mate. For us, smell means so much that it has become embodied in our language as a symbolic or inner sense that's applied to situations metaphorically: we smell a rat, we sniff for meaning, we smell trouble, we will even say that we can smell a lie (and, in fact, we can).

So how can a God of the Universe teach us anything meaningful about ourselves—our lives, our bodies, our relationships—if He has

> been effectively deprived of the most basic and essential of our animal senses? For when we make God insensate to odor, then we in turn become the same, and we build a culture of sanitized, genetically modified foods that neither nourish nor entice us with a delightful odor. We also spew poisons into the air and can pretend they're not there, because we have denied, through our Creator stories, our own sense of smell.
>
> This seems to be a problem we need to work on. My first suggestion would be that we simply drop God altogether—flush Him out of our consciousness, individually and culturally. This, however, may meet with a certain resistance in most parts of the world; so my second-best alternative is this: let's give God back His sense of smell. Give Him back his nose.

As in the first Potter book, where the encounter with the magical "Mirror of Erised" brings Harry face-to-face with his personal ancestry, or in Book Two, where Harry is pulled through an enchanted diary into a distant but living past, the outer action of the story is suspended for a moment of reflection, in which perspective is obtained and insight added upon what has gone before, to inform what is to come. Here, in the scene where he encounters the Pensieve, Harry is again drawn into an unknown past, which he must clearly perceive in contemplation before he can be ready to undertake the challenges that lie ahead. Error will be a part of this process, just as it was for Harry when he obsessively studied the images of his family in the mirror of Book One, or when he misinterpreted the scene of his friend Hagrid's past in the diary scene of Book Two. For error, when it is led by humility and the insight of recognition, becomes the spiritual seeker's true guide; it is only when error is ideologically hardened into Sin, or else is completely mistaken and labeled "Truth" or "Reality", that it becomes or leads us into what is known as Evil. This, in essence, is the understanding that Harry achieves within the Pensieve.

This is a transformative moment of learning for Harry, yet he does not explore *his own* memory in the Pensieve—he instead enters the memory of *another*, his mentor, Albus Dumbledore. In this context, Harry's experience moves past the conventional setting of modern psychotherapy and into a deeply personal and primordial realm. He is not receiving treatment, but *initiation*. But it is not initiation into a particular culture or ideology, but an introduction to his unique destiny, through a lens upon the past. This is the induction of the youth into manhood, in which he finds his place within his world through the teaching memory of the elder—this is the moment of the encounter with the sacred spring that Robert Bly describes in the story of Iron John. The Pensieve, with its crystalline depths, runic decoration, and magical allure, is Rowling's version of that sacred spring: it is where Harry experiences the interior transformation that will further his outer life, and support him through the challenges that await him. Just as the boy of the Iron John story discovers his true nature through contact with the spring's water (the metaphor is of his hair and finger being turned golden through touching the water), so also does Harry receive a glimpse of his destiny through being immersed in the Pensieve. In the following chapter, he will enter upon the third and final task of the triwizard tournament, a journey through a maze which will end in his being transported to the graveyard-realm of Lord Voldemort. There, the insight that he received within the Pensieve will serve him well, for it is in the courtroom-flashbacks of Dumbledore that Harry is presented with a vision of the fundamental weakness of evil.

    The well of memory that Harry falls into within the Pensieve is of a series of trial scenes, in which alleged "Death Eaters"—the accomplices of Lord Voldemort—are brought before a court of justice. They are guarded by black demons known as dementors, and indeed a demonic consciousness fills this courtroom, infecting both the accused and their judges. In a montage of scenes, Harry is presented with a convict who turns informant against certain members of Voldemort's circle, then a popular sporting figure who parlays his celebrity into an acquittal, and finally a group of criminals that includes the chief justice's own son. The rot of decadence, like the breath of the dementors, is seen to waft between the condemned and the righteous: Harry is given a visceral illustration of the ambiguity of evil, its incapacity for clarity and its obsession with the noise of its own internal conflict. Indeed, the scene ends with the chief justice's son screaming for mercy; another of the condemned declaiming evangelistically that "the Dark Lord will rise again!"; and the chief justice himself, in a spitting fury, bellowing condemnation upon them all. It is a scene played out today in real life—in our courts, our media, our workplaces, our centers of government, and our homes. Evil cannot hear the quiet voice of insight, because it perpetually shouts it down—sometimes with the self-righteous shriek of human justice.

Harry is led, through the insights drawn from his time within the Pensieve, to the very center of his psyche, where he finds the resources that enable his escape from the demonic consciousness represented in Voldemort and the Death Eaters. The Pensieve within our own lives can be a practice of meditation, a therapeutic experience, a particular creative activity, or any deeply personal psycho-spiritual practice that alchemically merges past and future in the crucible of a continually transforming present. This is the moment of eternal childhood, in which the process of inner growth can freely play ("re-create"). Shunyru Suzuki called it "beginner's mind." It is no wonder, then, that the work of a "children's author" should have so much to teach us here. Throughout the Potter stories, Harry learns that he can safely discard, or separate from, whatever is false to his personal journey—the attachment to the images in the Mirror of Erised, the distortions of a magical diary, the fabrications reported in the wizarding newspaper ("The Daily Prophet"), or the instruments and symbols of Power. In this respect, both Lao Tzu and Professor Dumbledore have the same crucial lesson to teach, which is the way of inner disburdenment:

| Pursuing knowledge: daily accumulation. Following Tao: daily unburdening. Decrease, diminish, deprogram: Continue in this till power is dead. —*Tao Te Ching*, Chapter 48 | "I sometimes find...that I simply have too many thoughts and memories crammed into my mind....At these times," said Dumbledore, "I use the Pensieve. One simply siphons the excess thoughts from one's mind, pours them into the basin, and examines them at one's leisure. It becomes easier to spot patterns and links, you understand, when they are in this form." —*Goblet of Fire*, p. 597 |

This is the process that is spoken of in many spiritual traditions as "detachment." If the seeker's way is, in essence, a process of revealing incipient truth through the disburdenment of error, then in order to know true progress in our lives the only thing we have to learn is *how to unlearn.* Detachment or disburdenment is simply a matter of independently examining all the received beliefs that have seeped into consciousness from childhood onward, and as Dumbledore says, "siphoning the excess." This is how delusion is discarded, and how the mist that clouds one's personal truth is burned away. As Harry discovers throughout his Hogwarts journey, this movement from group-dependence toward individuality does not mean that we are divorcing ourselves from society, just as "learning to unlearn" does not mean that we are spurning our intellectual gifts; what it does mean is that we are making a commitment to draw upon *all* of our inner resources in living our lives. When we join Harry Potter in this process of opening ourselves to all that is real and invisible within ourselves and Nature; when we play freely, joyfully, in the field of consciousness, the quest is fulfilled; the past informs the way forward, and we are perpetually made whole.

Siphoning the Excess: Entering the Pensieve of Meditative Practice

The "unburdening" that Lao Tzu speaks of, and the "siphoning of the excess" that Professor Dumbledore recommends, are best accomplished in the context of a regular practice of meditation. Indeed, Lao Tzu repeatedly encourages us toward such a practice throughout his *Tao Te Ching*, and the Pensieve itself may be considered a vibrant symbol of the experience of meditation. But if you are new to meditation, or better still if you've tried it and found it impossibly difficult, then perhaps there is some "unburdening" to be done with respect to ideas or assumptions you may have received, having to do with meditation. And even if you consider yourself an "experienced meditator" and feel no discomfort or distress about regular practice, it still might be worth going over the following exercise at least once. Many of my clients and students have found it beneficial—not merely in terms of facilitating a natural and health-giving personal practice, but also as an opening to the very heart of natural magic: discarding from within all the conditioning and acculturation of ideologies that obstruct inner growth and prevent us from fulfilling our personal potential. Here, then, is a "meditation for everyone who has been told that meditation is difficult."

    Call it a pet peeve of mine: the idea that meditation should be arduous, difficult, involve long hours twisted up into a painful posture, or that it should lead to some elevated and pristine state of spiritual enlightenment (after, of course, a long period of struggle, confusion, and expense, usually at the hands of a self-appointed "master"). This is the kind of nonsense that keeps people away from a perfectly natural, relatively effortless, and completely healthful form of inner practice. Meditation is the natural and restorative activity of all life: observe how animals, plants, and even some people are able to slow down outer movement, settle into a state of relaxed but aware silence, and simply absorb the regenerative energy of the cosmos. In the ongoing meditative activity of Nature, there is no thought of complexity, struggle, difficulty, or attainment: there is only the practice itself, and the often visible well-being that arises from the quiet openness of one being toward the bountiful energy of the universe. This is how we are meant to meditate; it is nothing special, and in no way should it be a hardship or strain. Indeed, if there is difficulty, then it is not meditation (obviously, we can be *conscious* of difficulty during meditation—we are, after all, not meant to stop thinking or feeling during our practice, because this is impossible; however, to build difficulty into the meditative act itself is simply a distortion of Nature).

    So we must, it seems, begin our practice of meditation with an act of inner separation from falsehood and error—a separation that the *I Ching* calls "Retreat", in Hexagram 33. We must say an inner No[30] to the idea that meditation is a difficult process that can only be engaged by our "higher" or spiritual nature, at the expense and often the abasement of our "lower" or bodily nature. This act of retreat from these incorrect ideas will become our first meditation: we will begin by preparing ourselves to say an inner No to such false notions.

1. Find a quiet place to sit or lie down. Go with what feels comfortable and settling to your own inner sense. You don't need a cushion, altar, icon, incense, or any special environmental trappings, unless any of these feel natural and comfortable to you: all you really need is a quiet place where you can be with your inner self and the cosmic energies that flow through us when we are in a silent and receptive inner place.

2. Get into a comfortable position where you can be relatively still for a few minutes. Listen to your body: let it tell you what position allows you to settle down and open to your inner life. There are no special rules: you do not have to keep your back ramrod-straight and stiff, you do not need to cross or twist up your limbs, and you do not have to lock your hands into a "mudra" or make any special noises to place your body into the optimal state for receiving cosmic energy. Just find a position in which you are comfortable and still aware.

3. Take a few simple breaths in awareness of your own body. Again, there is no need to breathe in a particular way (deeply, shallowly, forcefully, or anything else): just be aware of what happens within when you breathe. At the beginning, it is best to gently close your eyes for the meditation; this may be adjusted or varied in later sessions.

4. Now inwardly ask the helping energies of the cosmos to help you in discarding false ideas about meditation. Once again, let your body ask for this help: perhaps your request will center around the area of your heart, perhaps it will come from the back of your head or neck, or maybe you will feel it most in your stomach. Let your body be a part of the act of requesting this help, because after all, the transformative energy received in response to our inner No will come through our bodily cells.

5. Repeat the phrase that seems to best capture or summarize the mistaken ideas about meditation, quietly to yourself, and offer that phrase, sentence, or image to the universe. If any of the ideas mentioned above resonate with you, or if some other expression occurs to you, go with that. Let's say

you choose the sentence "meditation must lead to spiritual enlightenment, and to do so it must be painful and arduous." Speak that sentence in silence to yourself, and then see it being removed from you—*physically taken out of your body* and offered to the cosmos for correction. Some folks like to imagine the phrase or words being "deleted" before them, or painted over in "cosmic white-out"; others might see the "paper" on which the phrase is written crumpled up and tossed into the garbage—that's fine, too, if such images naturally occur to you in the moment.

6. Now say an inner No, three times, to the phrase. Let your entire being, body and psyche, say "No, No, No, to (the idea that meditation must lead to spiritual enlightenment, and to do so it must be painful and arduous)." Some people actually feel the phrase being eliminated from their heart, abdomen, brain, or other organ or body system; other folks just sense a kind of inner relief, a lightening of their load, sometimes with images of lights or other sensations taking the phrase out of their being, carrying it away. All you have to do is follow your unique experience as the cosmos takes away the phrase or image to be discarded and transformed.

7. Finally, once you feel that the inner No has been completed, thank the cosmic helpers for their assistance. Then you may continue to meditate and absorb the cosmic energy that your inner No has activated. Or you may simply get up and carry on with daily living.

If you have never meditated before (or never thought you had, or could meditate), and you have tried the little seven-step practice above, then congratulations—you've just practiced your "first meditation." It may have taken all of three, five, or ten minutes—the time does not matter. What matters is each experience, and your feelings of each experience. If you are new to meditation, try this simple practice each day for about a week (this ensures that the benefits of the inner No are enduringly realized), and then you can work on deepening your experience with meditation—if you like, you may go on to try some of the other meditations described in this book. As you continue your meditation practice, try varying the place, time, and length of your practice, until you arrive at the general routine that is most natural, comfortable, and effective for you.

Another Exercise in Unburdening

Here is a practice that I've adapted from an exercise taught to me by a Feng Shui practitioner who helped me in doing some space-clearing exercises on my apartment[31]. It is meant to further your ability to "siphon off the excess" of belief and attachment that separates us from our true nature. Like the meditation exercise above, it involves the releasing of conditioned learning, but adds a potent interactive element that many people find refreshingly purgative.

Harry emerges from the Pensieve and its mist of the past with clarity and a certain detachment, which enable him to meet the challenges in his future. We will draw upon a similar perspective, yet with the help of a different element, in separating from the attachment to the past. In this exercise, we will use the written word, along with fire, to clear the mists of our own Pensieve of memory.

Begin in a quiet, undisturbed setting, as you did for the meditation exercise, and have a pen and paper handy. You will be writing down phrases from the ego-noise of your past: it can be from childhood, from school or work experiences, from societal or religious training, teachings absorbed from books or other media, from a spouse or other family member, or any other marked ego-influence from your personal past. In fact, it can be from all of these, or any combination—it is often helpful to order such influences according to their place in your life's past, as in the table below, offered as an illustrative outline from which you can create your own diagram of such phrases.

Source	Demands, ideas, phrases, beliefs transmitted
Parents	"Don't get smart with me." (okay, I'll be stupid instead)
	"I punish you because I love you." (a rationalized deceit that contains one of the most pervasive and destructive societal delusions of Western parenting, captured in the ridiculous phrase, "tough love")
	"Don't ask questions—just do as you're told." (you've heard of the golden rule—this is the iron rule)
	"Can't you ever listen?" (i.e., "obey")
	"When you behave well, you get nice things." (a rather devious means of enforcing obedience, through what Lao Tzu called "inner commerce")
	"I'm so proud of you!" (a claim of ownership with an implied threat—if you ever betray that pride, look out)
Spouse or ex-spouse	"What will people think about us if we do that?" (obsession with appearances)
	"You never pay attention to me." (a global demand for "inner payment")
	"You always give me that excuse." (another demand, couched in an accusation of insufficiency)
Teachers	"Follow instructions or you will fail." (blind obedience means more than truth)
	"I don't want to hear questions—I want to see results." (again, obedience is the only measure of success)
	"I don't care how you feel about it—problems are solved with logic." (the repression of feeling-nature and the isolation of intellect)
Priests, ministers, religious leaders	"You are made in God's image—live up to it." (a demonic self-image statement that puts the soul under an impossible burden)
	"In the beginning was the Word, and the Word was with God." (the defining and distinguishing attribute of humanity—language—came to us as a special gift from an external divinity)
	"Thou shalt have no other gods before me." (another demonic spell that reinforces divisiveness and exclusivity)
Books/TV /News- papers, etc.	"Heroes die for their country." (a spell that binds the individual to the ideology of sacrifice and the parochial allegiance to a state)
	"Miserable weather ruins holiday." (how often is rain— one of the most nourishing and cleansing gifts that the universe brings us—demonized as "miserable" by the media? Such public projections can have alarmingly negative inner consequences)

You can take a few sittings and some repeated effort in producing what you feel is a representative listing of conditioned ego-beliefs: there is no hurry. Just remember that this exercise can be done time and again throughout your life, and so it never has to be exhaustive, because to attempt that would be, well, exhausting. Therefore, don't look to write an "autobiography of ego"; just get a few things down and then go to the next stage of the exercise.

Read the list of phrases over, as if you were about to separate completely from all that these beliefs represent (*you are*). When you're ready, take the paper into a safe area—a fireplace, a sink, a concrete patio with no flammable objects or material nearby—*and then burn it*. Just light it up and watch it burn into ashes. Hold in your awareness the movement of consciousness represented by this series of acts: the transfer of false belief and negative emotions from your body-consciousness to the paper, followed by their transformation into the elements of fire, smoke, and ashes. As the paper burns, offer up the obstructive ideas that you have incinerated to the cosmic whole, and ask that all the ego-noise represented on that piece of paper be taken up and transformed by the teaching energy of universe. Finally, thank the helping energies of the cosmos for their part in this exercise of "burning away" the growth-inhibiting beliefs of the past. Once again, you may repeat this exercise as often as you feel is necessary to effect a comprehensive clearing of your inner space; you can also try it in concert with some of the other exercises and meditations described in this book.

Chapter 4: The Boggart in the Wardrobe: Defeating Fear Through Humor

> "It's always best to have company when you're dealing with a Boggart. He becomes confused....The charm that repels a boggart is simple, yet it requires force of mind. You see, the thing that really finishes a boggart is laughter. What you need to do is force it to assume a shape that you find amusing."
> —Professor Lupin speaking, in *Harry Potter and the Prisoner of Azkaban*

We find ourselves within the Defense Against the Dark Arts classroom, along with the third-year students of Gryffindor House. In the truly ingenious vignette that comprises Chapter 7 of *Harry Potter and the Prisoner of Azkaban*, we are drawn through a delightful lesson in facing our fears and thereby undermining the illusory power of ego. The appearance of this lesson within the story is appropriate to its context: Harry is daunted by the ominous news of the escaped convict, Sirius Black, who is reported to be obsessed with finding and killing Harry. But this threat is rather tame compared with the beings sent by the bureaucratic government of the wizard world to *protect* Harry and the other students from Black—the dementors, creatures who turn summer days into winter nights. Thus, the entirety of *Prisoner of Azkaban* can be considered a reflection on fear, and the power of ego to freeze our souls in the seemingly endless, relentless realm of emotional night.

> "So, the first question we must ask ourselves is, what is a boggart?"
> Hermione put up her hand.
> "It's a shape-shifter," she said. "It can take the shape of whatever it thinks will frighten us most."
> "Couldn't have put it better myself," said Professor Lupin, and Hermione glowed. "So the boggart sitting in the darkness within has not yet assumed a form. He does

not yet know what will frighten the person on the other side of the door. Nobody knows what a boggart looks like when he is alone, but when I let him out, he will immediately become whatever each of us most fears." (p. 133).

The parallel with ego could scarcely be more precise than this: indeed, ego is a shape shifter, which relies on provoking our fears, social anxieties, cultural inhibitions, and the insecurities bred by guilt and pride. Its "natural shape" is unknown to us as well, and this is because it has none. It is shadowy and inherently unbalanced—indeed, instability is its life's blood. In his own description of ego's behavior, Lao Tzu wrote:

> If ego had a scrap of wisdom,
> It would seek to walk the path of Tao.
> But the problem is that ego tends to wander.
>
> The Cosmic Way is straight and easy,
> But people seem compelled
> By distraction and complexity.
>
> The palace in the capital
> Is bathed in opulence,
> While the fields without lie barren,
> And the granary is left untended.
>
> They array themselves in lustrous gowns
> And gleaming weapons at their sides.
> They eat, but are not nourished;
> They drink, yet thirst consumes them.
> Their lives are bloated with the stuff of wealth.
>
> Extravagance is a thief,
> The true self is its victim:
> Is this the way of Tao?
> I doubt it.
> (Chapter 53, *Tao Te Ching*)

Ego, then, is a parasite of sorts, which spreads instability through a delusory sense of complexity. Being a delusion—a distortion of natural consciousness—it has no substance of its own, but preys on the substance of anyone who is subjected to the touch of its toxicity. In Rowling's story, the first child chosen to take on the boggart is Neville Longbottom, a timorous little boy whose journey of inner growth over the course of the Potter stories is equally inspiring as Harry's: Neville's greatest fear is represented by the icy and glowering Potions master, Professor Snape—it is his form that the boggart will take.

If, either in our distant childhood or in our recent life, we have had painful experiences with authority, then ego will assume the foreboding visage of Authority—as an external, demanding, punishing god[32], as a draconian boss or ruler, as a tyrannical, threatening parent, teacher, or minister, or in perhaps its most terrible and unforgiving form, Morality or the Law. It is no coincidence that this last of ego's demonic shapes was referred to by Freud as the embodiment of "super-ego."[33] It is ego in its most Absolute and uncompromising mutation—a forbidding labyrinth walled with guilt, shame, and the fear of retribution. It is the voice of a distant and artificial god that says, "you are a sinner by nature and must therefore pay the toll of repentance until you are ultimately punished with death;" the voice of a monumentalized Morality, or Law, that says, "you are criminal by nature and must be vigilantly watched and hemmed in with restrictions at every turn."

It seems there is no way out of this trap: one can only accept one's place in it and walk in the mud of sin that covers its floor. "But," ego adds in its institutional voice, "if you will sacrifice your individuality, your independence, your deepest true nature, to my illusion, then you will be rewarded—both in this life and the next." This is ego's deal: accept the ideological taint of being alive, and you will receive the privilege of a delusory security, a place within the collective. But, in its typical muddling of figure and ground, ego further demands that you must renounce your own inner truth or suffer irreparable consequences.

Returning now to our Hogwarts class, we find that Professor Lupin is about to release the boggart. He reminds his students that they will be dealing with a volatile force, which will infect anyone who is not prepared; thus, he leads them all through a brief meditation:

> "When the boggart bursts out of this wardrobe, Neville, and sees you, it will assume the form of Professor Snape," said Lupin. "And you will raise your wand—thus—and cry 'Riddikulus'—and concentrate hard on your grandmother's clothes....If Neville is successful, the boggart is likely to shift his attention to each of us in turn," said Professor Lupin. "I would like all of you to take a moment now to think of the thing that scares you most, and imagine how you might force it to look comical...."
>
> The room went quiet. Harry thought....What scared him most in the world? (pp. 135-136).

It is implicit, of course, that the boggart will respond to each person's greatest fear of that moment—but ego's power lies in its ability to evoke, through whatever real or imagined stimuli it may be reached, the most basal and primal fear of humanity, which the psychologist Joan Borysenko describes for us in *Fire in the Soul*:

> The most basic fear of every human being is rooted in the helplessness of childhood, the time before we are capable of surviving on our own and must depend on the protection of powerful others. It is the fear of rejection and abandonment. This instinctual terror arises from the part of the mind that thinks not in words but in feelings and images. The common nightmares that children have about being chased and devoured by monsters—nightmares that occur even in children who have never been exposed to the idea of a monster—are the expression of a primitive fear that has its roots at the dawn of human history when abandoned children were, indeed, chased and devoured by wild animals. (pp. 82-83)

Now Harry's greatest fear has entered the picture: we are now faced with the black ice of the dementors—the poisonous breath of depressive illness. For Borysenko goes on to point out that the destructive effects of emotional abandonment are every bit as devastating and life-threatening as physical abandonment: isolation sickens and eventually kills its host. Lonely children fail to grow naturally; adults trapped in isolation have significantly greater incidence of heart disease, depression, and immunological illness. Borysenko is referring directly to the fear of abandonment within the family or human society, but her description also implies a related and equally primal fear—that of the abandonment of one's true self. This, too, is isolation—the loneliness that comes of separation from the source of our being. This is the isolation that befalls us when, under the influence of a group ideology, we project an intrinsic fault onto Nature, and thus onto ourselves. Lao Tzu describes it this way:

> The only real misfortune
> Is to look at Nature and see affliction.
> When the treasure is split from its source,
> Body and nature become a well of sorrow.
> (*Tao Te Ching*, Chapter 13)

This is the shape-shifting boggart at work—the mutation of ego, distorting the very treasure of our being, our bodily nature, into a demon—a well of guilt, shame, and fear. The monsters that threatened us physically in the pre-historical times that Borysenko describes above have now become the dragons of a twisted consciousness that bestializes our very nature! Here, the boggart of ego operates at its most insidious level—transmuting Nature itself into our most primitive fear. When ego is successful in this trick, and we accept the delusion, then we are trapped in a suspicious and self-referential persona, a brittle mask of tremulous self-confidence which represses our personal truth in a bitter and vindictive display which Freud called a "reaction formation." Every abuse of power, every criminal act, every aggressive and violent impulse that we feel and observe, can be traced to this distortion and damnation of what is most deeply and enduringly genuine within ourselves and our universe.

How, then, can we kill the boggart, how can we reverse or escape the hideous position into which ego has placed us? Professor Lupin advises his students that there is a charm that will work, activated by the word, "Riddikulus!". But, he adds, that is not all—indeed, it is not the half of it. The charm-phrase itself is the right word, the expressive symbol of the spirit that must guide the process, which is a focusing of the mind and heart toward a gentle and humorous inner separation from the distortion represented by the boggart. Lupin here teaches a crucial lesson: the boggart cannot be defeated by outer force, domination, or rigid opposition; it can only be routed through a retreat from the same brooding, fearful self-consciousness that the boggart itself feeds on. Lao Tzu agrees:

> Modesty acts through renunciation:
> It abandons identification.
> In exploding the image,
> It liberates the self.
> In dropping comparison,
> It inaugurates autonomy and lets loose joy.
> (*Tao Te Ching*, Chapter 23)

    This, indeed, is exactly what Neville and the other children do in the wonderful scene that follows: they "explode the image" and thereby "let loose joy." Ego, for some reason, does not respond well to laughter. Amid laughter, ego becomes confused, as does the boggart in the story when it is subjected to the students trained in the application of the "Riddikulus" charm: with each successive mutation, it is further exposed by the joyful concentration of the students whose hearts will it, by turns, into a grim authority figure dressed up in the garish pretension of an old maid; a mummy that trips over its own wrappings; a screaming banshee with a sudden case of laryngitis; and a giant rat that begins chasing its tail like a kitten. After a dozen or so such transformations, the boggart explodes and disperses in "a thousand tiny wisps of smoke," amid the joyful cheers of the students.

    Why? How does simple laughter totally rout such a forbidding and powerful presence as ego? How could Norman Cousins announce to the world that laughter could not only dispel fear, but also heal a chronic, severe, and most painful physical illness?[34] The answer seems to lie in the ability of humor to reflect and express our true nature: life without the oppressive weight of ego is delightfully funny. Laughter nourishes and humor heals, because they are expressions of the fundamentally creative and transformative process of Cosmic Reality, beyond the obsessive self-consciousness of ego.[35]

Another aspect of this has to do with the relinquishing of control: ego is an abstraction based on control. Wherever we let go and release the compulsion to control—ourselves, another person, or a situation—then we have let go of ego, too, and thereby at the same time undermined the props of its existence. This is the way of Modesty that Lao Tzu described above. Humor leads us away from an attitude of dominion and back toward the spontaneity of our true nature. The wonderful (and very funny) Zen philosopher Shunyru Suzuki expressed it this way:

> It is the same with taking care of your everyday life. Even though you try to put people under some control, it is impossible. You cannot do it. The best way to control people is to encourage them to be mischievous. Then they will be in control in its wider sense. To give your sheep or cow a large, spacious meadow is the way to control him. So it is with people: first let them do what they want, and watch them...just watch them, without trying to control them.[36]

Finally, joy is an essentially social emotion: it cannot exist in a vacuum of isolation. As Professor Lupin says, "it's best to have company" when you're dealing with ego. Joy and humor can most easily prevail where there is company, an inner connection among kindred spirits. As we have seen, ego lives and breeds off loneliness and isolation, but weakens in the face of the lighthearted focusing of the whole being that is characteristic of humor. This principle applies in spite of what outer appearances may indicate: we may brood amid a roomful of other dark-hearted souls, but our essential loneliness is just thereby exacerbated: existentialism in a nutshell. Yet if there be a moment of laughter and sincere joy, even in seeming solitude where one's only company is the invisible energy of Cosmic Presence, then all of Nature smiles along, and the boggart of ego airily implodes.

Dispersing the Boggart: Practical Steps in Separating from the Realm of Ego

> ***Let yourself be guided to understand precisely what manifestations of ego are affecting you.*** In Rowling's story, the students are first advised to look within and discover exactly what image represents their greatest fear. We can follow the path indicated by Joan Borysenko, and turn within to find the answer to the question, "how, and to what extent, is the fear of rejection and abandonment working in me now, or what shapes has it taken in the past?" If you can begin to articulate how this particular fear has manifested itself in your life, and especially in your relationships, then you are well on your way to overcoming the boggart. As I often tell my counseling clients, *recognition alone is 80% of the work of healing*. It has been my experience that, for virtually everyone, the simple act of identifying specific ego-obstructions, through words and images, is enough to release the healing and transformative energy of humor. To borrow a metaphor from another famous children's story, when we clearly perceive that "the Emperor's new clothes" are indeed empty fabrications, our fears and self-consciousness suddenly dissolve amid gales of laughter. In the *I Ching*, this reaction of humor to the exposure of error is referred to in Hexagram 51, Shock, in the Judgment: "oh no! Laughing words—ha ha!" Thus, the focus of the exercise becomes the victory over loneliness. If you have like-minded friends who wish to try this exercise and some of the others described in this book, then by all means turn your living room into a Hogwarts classroom. However, if you are by yourself, remember that, as mentioned earlier, you can be utterly alone amid a swarm of "company" (this occurs very often among the wealthy and the socially powerful); you can also be more deeply engaged in the conversation of solitude, where we nurture the communication between inner truth and its loving Source, than in any human party. Thoreau wrote, "I never found the companion that was so

companionable as solitude."[37]

> *Say the inner No to obtain help from the Cosmos in disburdening yourself of those phrases or images that are harming or inhibiting your own inner growth.* The students at Hogwarts use a "charm-phrase" as a way of drawing magical help to dispel the boggart; in the way of natural magic, we draw Cosmic help in freeing ourselves of ego through saying the inner No to ego in all its manifestations. I can speak from experience—both my own and that of my clients: the benefits of the inner No can scarcely be over-estimated. It works to further the process of enduring transformation in life through engaging functionally-specific Cosmic energy patterns—what the *I Ching* refers to metaphorically as "Helpers"—in liberating our true selves. Let's go through another sample session of the inner No to illustrate how this works.[38]

1. *Identify the obstructive phrases and images, and write them down.* It is not enough to say "No" to the fears that haunt you; *you must separate from the ideas and images that support and perpetuate the fears.* For example, you may have discovered that your fear of loneliness is fed by an idea that "there is no help available to me except what I can get from people and their group-institutions." This is the "boggart phrase" that you will explode under the inner No.
2. *Say No to the phrase or image that you've identified.* There can well be more than one, but we'll stay with the sample phrase we've identified above. In a brief meditation along the lines of the instructions from the previous chapter, visualize the image or repeat the phrase in your mind. In this case, we will "see" the phrase "there is no help available except what can be had from people and their institutions." Then say "No" to it, three times, in a non-judgmental way, as if you were merely throwing out a piece of trash. Then say No, again three times, to the source of the phrase—the ego. Finally, say No three times to *yourself* for having ever accepted the belief contained

in that phrase as true. This last one may seem odd, but it points to the conditioned support of ego—the phrase has not come *from* you, it has come from something you've been forced to learn, probably at an impressionable age when you were too small to feel comfortable in questioning or separating from false teachings. This last step both confirms your innocence and clears the cellular detritus that false belief leaves in our bodies.

3. *Ask for help from the Cosmic Origin in clearing the phrase from your true self and healing whatever destructive effects it may have left in your body.* Simply ask that the effort you have just put forth in saying the inner No be completed with the help of the dissolving and restorative energies of the universe. Then ask that the residue of the belief represented by the phrase be released from your body.

4. *Thank those invisible presences for responding to your call for help.* Please don't be put off by the repetition of this one piece of advice throughout every exercise presented in this book. Once you experience the effect of a simple expression of gratitude to the invisible realm, you will appreciate its deeply transformative potential.

➢ **Let your experiences guide you further along your individual path of inner growth.** There is no prescribed or "authorized" way of achieving or expressing your inner truth: each person's experience is unique. You will, no doubt, discover your own way of inner release and understanding: every experience is drawn from the understanding received from the one before it, and informs the one to follow. Each person's fresh understanding adds to the organic and unending process of discovery, and furthers the whole. This is a far more practical approach to improving society than relying on the group-defined Authority of a guru, priest, Master, doctor, or political leader. When each individual can feel free to be led by his own inner light, then there is a natural benefit created for all. When people can live in true independence, then how can that not improve the Whole?

> *To help yourself in your learning, keep an "inner journal" in which you can record your experiences:* poetry or other contemplative writing, personal art, consultations of an oracle, dreamwork, experiences in meditation, and insights that occur to you along the way. There is a certain strength of endurance in recording one's experiences; it seems to develop and add energy to the learning process itself. Whatever for format, the very act of creating the record deepens the learning. It can be a sketchbook, a computer file, a recording, or a notebook. Go with whatever outer means feel natural and convenient to you; but do try recording your experiences. You are likely to find that the benefits will far outweigh the modest effort involved.

Chapter 5: The Cloak and the Mirror: Self-Images of the Individual Ego

> It was a magnificent mirror, as high as the ceiling, with an ornate gold frame, standing on two clawed feet. There was an inscription carved around the top: *Erised stra ehru oyt ube cafru oyt on wohsi.* —*Harry Potter and the Sorcerer's Stone*, Chapter 12

Christmas break is approaching at Hogwarts School of Witchcraft and Wizardry, and Harry Potter is a cauldron of shifting and frequently aggressive emotions. He has just lived the greatest triumph of his young life—the capture of the "golden snitch" in his first competitive Quidditch game—but he is also troubled by his glowering Potions master, Professor Snape, who seems to have carried some sort of personal grudge into his relationship with Harry. There is also the increasingly annoying problem of Draco Malfoy, the school bully who is developing into Harry's personal nemesis among the student body. "I hate them both," Harry says of them, "Malfoy and Snape." Fortunately, Hagrid is there to call him back to the joy that has marked this time of renewal and discovery for Harry, ever since he had been rescued from the torpid superficiality of his oppressive boyhood home to attend this wondrous school where magic is ordinary and where his very name inspires respect.

Yet at this point, he remains trapped in a realm of oppositional thinking, where there are only friends and enemies, for and against, loyalty or hatred. Of course, this is as much as he's been exposed to at the odious home of the Dursleys, with whom he was raised. But he is now in this wondrous academy of natural magic, where he will learn how to unlearn the ideology of opposition with which he has so far been conditioned. This is the beginning of a transformative path toward self-understanding. The way of this unlearning process will be marked by Harry's discovery of certain means of self-insight, as well as the formation of several relationships that will teach him that, no matter what appearances may seem to dictate, evil does not always sit at the same table, conveniently marked with a large green banner decorated with a great silver snake. To help him through this process of inner growth, Harry will be given a number of metaphorical gifts—transformative objects, experiences, and messages—that will gradually lead him to the recovery of his original autonomy. In the first book of the Potter series, a number of these gifts will be introduced in the images of the letters from the magical world (and the owls that bring them); the marvelous train ride which becomes a part of every one of the subsequent stories; the grounds, buildings, and atmosphere of Hogwarts; and the two central metaphors of this "solstice phase" of Harry's inner development[39]—the invisibility cloak and the Mirror of Erised.

The cloak is a Christmas gift—one of the first of Harry's life, since he was never given any by the Dursleys—which comes to him from his dead father through his mentor, Dumbledore: the unsigned note which accompanies the cloak only says, "your father left this in my possession before he died. It is time it was returned to you. Use it well." The invisibility cloak is a magical (and therefore metaphorical) object of immense value and beauty: it is "fluid and silvery gray...strange to the touch, like water woven into material." Clearly, Rowling did not write this in a vacuum: this is a metaphor of great historical depth and psychological meaning, particularly within the mythology of England and Ireland:

> In the story Tochmarc Etaine (The Courtship of Etain), the god of the Otherworld, Midir, demands in compensation for the loss of an eye in a brawl, a chariot, a cloak, and the most beautiful maiden in Ireland as his bride...This was a cloak of invisibility (like Siegfried's tarnkappe in the Nibelungenlied) and of forgetfulness...The god Lug wore a similar cloak which enabled him to pass through the entire Irish army without being seen when he came to aid his son...To put on the cloak is to show that you have chosen Wisdom (the philosopher's cloak). (Jean Chevalier and Alain Gheerbrant, *The Penguin Dictionary of Symbols*, pp. 205-206).

The invisibility cloak is an image of transformation, and not of self-obliteration, depersonalization, or disembodiment. For Harry, his body is still manifestly there—he can feel it, and so can others if they bump into him (indeed, this is part of the challenge in using the cloak). Whenever he wears the cloak over the course of the five stories, Harry's physical and intuitive senses seem to become more acute and penetrating: he becomes more open and alert to experience than when he is visible. The cloak's virtue is to take him to, and through, the experiences that will contribute to his inner growth—indeed, it is an active metaphor of the practices involved in the development of the true self. These include inner movements of one's total being—the intuitive, feeling, and spiritual capacities of our nature, that live and glow in quiescence beneath the often-repressive monarch known as intellect.

Harry discovers this the first time he uses the cloak: he goes to the library, thinking that this is where he "should" go, in order to obtain information. But he quickly discovers that he is being called beyond the realm of "should" and "ought," once he has put on this cloak—that he is being called to penetrate deeper regions of the psyche than he can reach through the symbols and instruments of intellect. This message is brought to him very quickly: the library is said to be "pitch-black and eerie"; the books "didn't tell him much," because they are written in "words in languages Harry couldn't understand." Finally, he comes to a book that screams into the night as soon as he opens it, and that drives him out of there, toward the place where a more potent image of self-discovery lies, which will engage his entire being. In his retreat from the images of intellect and the representatives of Authority (the caretaker Argus Filch and Professor Snape, who come looking for him), Harry encounters exactly what he needs to further his inner learning: the Mirror of Erised.

Mrs. Rowling leaves no question about what Harry is being presented with here: as many readers of the Potter stories have discovered, the inscription on the Mirror, read in reverse (ignoring the spacing) says, "I show not your face but your heart's desire." Harry looks into the Mirror and sees his family—

several generations' worth of family[40]:

> The Potters smiled and waved at Harry and he stared hungrily back at them, his hands pressed flat against the glass as though he was hoping to fall right through it and reach them. He had a powerful kind of ache inside him, half joy, half terrible sadness. (p. 209)

Harry abandons himself to this experience: in the following days, he shows no mind for food, physical comfort, games or sport, or even for his best friend, Ron (Harry drags him the next evening to the Mirror, in a rather imperious and evangelical display; then, after Ron retreats from the Mirror's danger, Harry's isolation becomes complete). Finally, Harry is even careless of external danger in going to the Mirror: on the third night, "he was walking so fast he knew he was making more noise than was wise, but he didn't meet anyone." The Mirror—its images, its presence, its identity—has become his very life, his obsession. Then, he is brought back to his senses by Dumbledore, who suddenly appears, armed with questions: "you've realized by now what it does? Can you think what the Mirror of Erised shows us all?". But Harry has not paused to question the real meaning or function of this Mirror; he believes that he has found his Answer, and only wants to immerse himself in its static but poignant images. But Dumbledore presents him with a new perspective on the Mirror:

> "It shows us nothing more or less than the deepest, most desperate desire of our hearts. You, who have never known your family, see them standing around you. Ronald Weasley, who has always been overshadowed by his brothers, sees himself standing alone, the best of all of them. However, this mirror will give us neither knowledge or truth. Men have wasted away before it, entranced by what they have seen, or been driven mad, not knowing if what it shows is real or even possible.
> The Mirror will be moved to a new home tomorrow, Harry, and I ask you not to go looking for it again. If you ever do run across it, you will now be prepared. It does not do to dwell on dreams, and forget to live, remember that." (pp. 213-214)

It is no mistake that, a few pages after this lesson has been imparted and somewhat grudgingly accepted, Harry experiences (after a purgative physical workout on the Quidditch field) a coincidence which provides him the exact knowledge he'd been seeking in the library—the key to the meaning behind the name of Nicholas Flamel (as the possessor of the Sorcerer's Stone). This helps to illustrate a principle which can be experienced time and again in our own lives: *inner clarity leads to outer accomplishment*; because wherever clarity exists, expectation and projection are absent. This is the lesson that the Mirror of Erised brings to Harry; it is a lesson that we can benefit from today.

The psychologist and relationship counselor, John Welwood, has independently articulated Professor Dumbledore's lesson, in his book *Love and Awakening*:

> When we are young, our parents reflect back to us certain pictures of who we are in their eyes. Lacking our own self-reflective awareness, we inevitably start to internalize these reflections, coming to see ourselves in terms of how we appear to others. This is akin to looking at ourselves in a mirror and then taking that visual image, rather than our immediate, lived experience of embodied presence, to be who we are...When seeing ourselves in terms of an image, we treat ourselves as an object. We become an object of our thought, rather than the subject of our experience. And this prevents us from knowing ourselves in a more direct, immediate way.
>
> The problem here is that we take the reflections of ourselves in others' eyes to represent who we are, whether we like them or not...we fixate on these images, giving them more weight and credence than our own direct experience of ourselves. This makes them into soul-cages...we grow up seeing ourselves in ways that separate us from our true nature and its full range of powers and potentials. (pp. 36-37)

These false and limiting reflections, carried forward through our inner life into adulthood, become traps that close upon our true selves and keep us from the experiences we need to really grow. Worse still, when these conditioned self-images become what Welwood calls "the unconscious templates" in which relationships are formed and communication within them managed, then vast pools of inner resources are abandoned and left dry and poisoned, like the well in line 1 of Hexagram 48 in the *I Ching*.[41] This is the time of estrangement, conflict, and divorce, when we have completely separated from the helping energies of the cosmos through our own obsession with the wooden images of self. The poet Robert Bly, himself drawing upon metaphors from the *I Ching*, expresses this loss as follows:[42]

> The wagon behind bouncing,
> breaking on boulders, back
> and forth, slowly
> smashed to pieces. This crumb-
>
> ling darkness is a reality
> too, the feather
> on the snow, the rooster's
> half-eaten body nearby.
> ("Visiting the Farallones," from *The Man in the Black Coat Turns*)

This is the wasteland of opposition, where so many of our relationships founder and die. Welwood refers to this dynamic as the "self/other setup", in which there is a dreary, stultifying swing between conflict played out in stereotyped, scripted noise and strife, broken by periods of withdrawal and icy fear. It is what happens when the fantasy-images of those old reflections so far repress our present experience of life that we may as well be dead—and indeed, *we are*. For Harry before the Mirror of Erised, this mood takes the form of that self-absorbed withdrawal into fantasy that is characteristic of the schizoid personality.[43] Despite the instruction given by Professor Dumbledore, this mood will re-appear sporadically to Harry, in some form or degree, for years to come, as his learning unfolds. There is a certain learned rigidity—something like what Freud called the "repetition compulsion"—that tends to keep us locked in our "soul-cages." It is the images, and the narrow roles in which they imprison our true selves, that comprise the identifying noise of ego, where its societal and individual expressions intersect:

> The ego can be heard as a voice within the personality, in the speech modes of the character or the role it is playing. Thus, when a person says to himself, 'I am a father,' he then takes on the role of the father in whatever way the idea of a father is defined by his group...So long as he identifies with the role, it dictates his life, for his inner voice is constantly checking to see if he is fitting the role, and whether others are recognizing him as such...All self-images are character-masks that live their 'lives' at the expense of the true self. The true self is thrust aside, gagged, and locked up in an inner prison cell, where it leads the life of a slave.
> (Carol Anthony and Hanna Moog, *I Ching: The Oracle of the Cosmic Way*, p. 62)

For young Harry, the array of roles and images into which he has been, and continues to be locked is dizzyingly diverse. From infancy, the Dursleys filled him with images of unworthiness, dependency, and of his mere existence as a burden to others; from the point of his entry into the wizarding world, he has been fed self-images of the sacrificial victim turned survivor, the living miracle, the princely orphan, the magician, and that most destructive and confusing of all self-images, the hero. He is saddled with the relics of his parents' accomplishments and sacrifices, some of which exist even within the grounds of Hogwarts (such as the plaque in the trophy room which commemorates James Potter's heroics on the Quidditch field, and the stories told all over the school of his parents' heroic deaths). This cult of heroism, which distorts the true meaning of his parents' gift of protection, is what the magical objects and messages of the stories, along with the teachings of Dumbledore, are calling Harry to discard from within. This is a living, practical teaching, applicable to our own lives: whenever we are able to rid ourselves of the fixed and derived images of self and others, we are instantly freed to preserve and treasure the pure and abiding love of true nature—our own and that of the people we have loved and lost. This is the love that exists within and beyond the realm of death.

But Harry is particularly haunted by this image of the

hero: he has been tabbed as the death-defying man-wizard, the vaunted defender of Good; he has been placed on a pedestal of fame and aggrandizement, from whose artificial heights he can only move by falling. Otherwise, he is frozen to the image, incapable of growth or exploration. Think of how often you have found yourself in this very predicament! Perhaps you have been trapped in the role of the ideal father or mother, the perfectly dutiful child, the flawlessly efficient or self-sacrificing employee, the straight-A student, the devoted, selfless, "unconditional" lover, or the faithful and submissive spouse: these are all heroic roles in which we are confined, and woe betide us should we place a toe across the rigid boundaries of their claustrophobia-inducing definitions. The further we become connected with these roles, the more vigilant must we become in supporting the connection, until the energy we pour into the effort of remaining balanced on that pedestal simply exhausts us, and we collapse into mute withdrawal, or the private hells of mental illness, abuse, chemical dependency, or perversion. Then, when our inability to sustain the image is finally exposed, we fall into disgrace and anonymity, with the all-too-frequent consequence of suicide. Once the true self has been effectively murdered, the act of physical self-destruction is a relatively small final step.

Sometimes, it seems we must come to the brink of such an extreme in order to realize that the outward-gazing fixation on the heroic, the god-as-other, can no longer be justified. Joseph Campbell recognized this, even in his own literary celebration of the mythology of heroism[44]—he concludes this marvelous book by finding that the mythic hero of ancient, monumental spiritual belief needs to be pushed off the stage of our ever-diminishing, ravaged planet. At last, he calls upon each of us to recover the precious autonomy of inner life, "in the silences of his personal despair." He urges that the modern person "cannot, indeed must not, wait for his community to cast off its slough of pride, fear, rationalized avarice, and sanctified misunderstanding." (p. 391).

This is the realization to which Harry Potter is led through his years at Hogwarts: Harry, when read as a heroic character, is a literary dinosaur, as much a relic as the totem gods of antiquity. But when we see him as a person on the journey of inner discovery, as a spiritual child seeking the way to true growth through the identification and disburdenment of the acculturated self-images within—as a person, in Campbell's words, "through whom the ego is to be crucified and resurrected" as an undiluted self—then Harry has something to teach every one of us.

Meeting Lord Voldemort

At the climactic end to this first story in the Potter series, Harry once again encounters the Mirror of Erised—as indeed, Professor Dumbledore had obliquely predicted he would. This is also his first meeting with Lord Voldemort.

As we have seen, Lord Voldemort is portrayed throughout the series as a parasite—an essentially dead entity with no independent or autonomous existence. In Lord Voldemort, we see a derived, artificial reality, which is the inevitable consequence of the feudal and tribal religiosity of centuries—a seemingly formidable pyramid of lies, built to conceal the hollowness of inner death that lies within its walls.

The institutional group-lie is the symbol of death—the death of Nature and of human nature, the only death worth fearing. Voldemort's character as the authoritarian liar is revealed in his first conversation with Harry: he tells him first that "your parents died begging me for mercy," and then almost immediately reverses himself: "I always value bravery...your parents were brave" (thus the title of the chapter in which this scene occurs: "The Man with Two Faces"). In this encounter, he also announces his essential insubstantiality: "see what I have become? Mere shadow and vapor...I have form only when I can share another's body...but there have always been those willing to let me into their hearts and minds."

Meanwhile, the host to the parasitic Voldemort—Professor Quirrell—cannot understand the Mirror of Erised except as an object which appears to "contain" what he desires. This is a fundamental error of the cult follower, especially in religion: the reification of the metaphors associated with inner life and growth. When we mistake an image for an object—*the object*—of our quest, then what begins as a helping insight becomes monumentalized as The Truth; and every form of murder, depredation, and tyranny will be perpetrated in defense of this act of reification. Quirrell cannot appreciate the Mirror as a transformative device, because he is (quite literally, in this case) possessed by the institutional lie; nor can Voldemort connect with the Mirror as the instrument of inner alchemy, though he does suspect that Harry has the ability. So, unable to manipulate the Mirror's images to present him with the desired object (i.e., the physical reality of the Sorcerer's Stone), Voldemort directs his host to "use the boy."

Indeed, Voldemort is right: Harry has the stone, *but only because he does not want it*, and does not want to use it. This, as we learn in the epilogue to the story, is Dumbledore's act of magical protection that he endowed to the stone. This beautiful piece of narrative insight brings closure and completion to the vision of Desire-as-attachment, which is embodied in the very name of this Mirror: the only person who is able to receive the stone is the one who has no ego-desire for it. Dumbledore's earlier oral teaching has now been realized in the field of Harry's experience; this, indeed, is where true learning is fulfilled for all of us.

An Insight Meditation: Experiencing Invisibility

Throughout the Potter stories, Harry—often accompanied by his friends Ron and Hermione—is brought to increasingly deeper levels of experience and understanding with the help of his invisibility cloak. The cloak represents an insight guide for her characters, to which they turn in times of challenge and crisis—you might say that it performs the role of an oracle. That's why it is so interesting to find the following text in the *I Ching*, from Hexagram 52, "Keep Still":

> He keeps still
> And is not taken captive.
> They pass his house
> And he is not seen.

> He escapes harm.
> (from the translation by Greg Whincup)

This hexagram (and, I believe, the image of the cloak in the Potter stories) is a metaphor that teaches us how we may effectively separate from the invasions of ego—especially from the ego-invasions of others upon our inner space. This is the meaning of "they pass his house," where one's "house" is the psyche or inner truth. When we are able to "keep still," we cannot be seen by others as an object, an enemy, an idol, or a hero; thus, our independence is preserved and protected (the meaning of "he escapes harm"). To "keep still" means to retreat from acting out of impulse or aggression (which would only feed negative energy to the individuals or groups that place themselves in opposition to us); what it does *not* mean is that we become frozen in a state of passivity. To keep still is to let inner clarity catalyze outer action; this is the experience that Lao Tzu describes as *wu-wei*, or unforced action. Once it is practiced and the results experienced in real life, one realizes that there is scarcely a more pragmatic approach to daily living. When we are able to "keep still" within, we hold to our center of being, as Lao Tzu expressed in Chapter 42 of the *Tao Te Ching*:

> Each compressed form bears yin behind
> And holds yang before it.
> At the still point in the center
> These complementary energies merge,
> And harmony is thus realized.

Lao Tzu emphasizes the image of merging energies in this verse, to remind us that "keeping still" is not passivity, but simply action of a different and more subtle, comprehensive kind. Consider a pond, or even a glass of water: how still it appears, though we know that if we were to place a drop of it under a microscope we would discover a world of movement and energy.[45] This is the stillness that the *I Ching* and Lao Tzu encourage us to learn and adapt, each to his or her own unique personality and circumstances. Like Harry's cloak, this stillness takes us out of the realm of opposites—"mind over (versus) matter"—and into the center of being, where death and life, yin and yang, male and female, self and other, are no longer experienced as opposites, but rather as *complementary* energies. This understanding is the "realization of harmony" that Lao Tzu describes in his poems.

Here, then, is a brief meditation to help you in "putting on your invisibility cloak." This meditation has many benefits, which are best discovered through experience rather than suggestion, but one that deserves to be mentioned is the way it assists in re-balancing energy within the body, creating reduction where there is excess, and replenishment where there is scarcity. This meditation has also been found helpful in working through feelings of fear and anxiety. Finally, as an aid to concentration, emotional balance, and that clarity, discussed earlier, which is fundamental to successful action, this meditation will provide benefit even if practiced for a few minutes per day.

Begin by getting in touch with your body. Take a comfortable position in which you are relaxed and aware; if you are sitting, feel your spine become straight yet without stiffness, and your shoulders relaxed. Sense the weight of your body where it contacts the floor, chair, or cushion that you're sitting on; feel the connection between your feet and the floor. Note the sense of the clothing on your skin, the feel of the ambient air around you, any sounds that reach you in the moment, and the light and images before your eyes (whether they are open or closed). Feel each of these sensations in turn, and then the movement of your body-breath, in and out, without making any attempt to control or direct the experience.

Now begin feeling yourself—your whole being—as energy. From this point, let the experience become uniquely your own: see which of the following sensations or metaphors brings you the most benefit.

♦ *You could feel an "invisibility cloak" passing over your body, and let its aqueous material reveal your light-body. As the cloak covers you, feel the transformation of your body from matter to energy.*

- *You may find that a feeling-image of movement is helpful: nebulae in motion, wind blowing through trees or high grass, microscopic cellular activity, radiant heat, clouds moving across the sky, osmotic movement between cells, an aura or energy field; or you may have a flowing sensation, as of moving water.*
- *Remember that the basic idea is to experience yourself as energy—activity, motion, formless, kinetic being without any particular material reference point. Consider the "stillness" referred to by the I Ching in Hexagram 52, and by Lao Tzu in his teaching poems. You are living the experience of your body in its vital and enduring Cosmic presence—as a dance of complementary energies, the yin and the yang commingling formlessly, effortlessly, and timelessly in a harmonic that Lao Tzu compared with the coalescing flow of the breath of lovers.*

The variations, again, are seemingly infinite: one client of mine who regularly watched "Star Trek" found herself either in the "beam-up" energy transfer mode (matter to light) or as "becoming" (or sometimes simply feeling) the soft, blue light emitted by the "tricorder" mechanisms in those stories. You may find that any of these images, a combination of them, or still another not mentioned here that best suits you, will bring you the feeling of energy-presence, and the accompanying practical benefits.

I do not want to project anything onto your personal experience of this meditation, so I'll add no more about what I or others have experienced in this practice, except to note, in general, that most people have found this to be refreshing, insightful, often transformative, and always—in the spirit of Black Elk—a *fun* meditation.

Looking into the Mirror of Erised

Earlier, we discussed how the size of objects and creatures at Hogwarts is part of the metaphor of the Potter tales. Ego likes to make things big and imposing, so as to inspire awe, fear, or reverence. Size, used to this advantage, can prevent people from asking unpleasant questions. The Mirror of Erised is an enormous thing—it is said to reach all the way to the ceiling, and thus would be at least seven or eight feet high (maybe more, considering the general spaciousness that pervades at Hogwarts). Its size and magical qualities would seem to make it an intimidating presence indeed—especially to an eleven year old boy—yet it is, after all, "just a mirror." Professor Dumbledore helps to bring this point home to Harry: "the happiest man on earth," he says, "would be able to use the Mirror of Erised like a normal mirror..." Later, Dumbledore adds that, when he looks at himself in the Mirror, he sees himself "holding a pair of thick, woolen socks...one can never have enough socks." The Mirror, then, merely reflects us as form; what we project onto the reflection is another matter entirely.

Thus, it seems that the focus of mirror-gazing as inner work would need to be on the projected images—what they are, how they look, and how they look back at us.

The notion of looking into a mirror as an insight practice is not at all new or unusual. The Tibetan spiritual teacher, Akong Tulku Rinpoche, describes such a practice in some detail in his book, *Taming the Tiger.* He describes a very helpful meditation, which you may wish to try for yourself. It involves looking into a mirror and allowing images and emotions to arise from within, and then "moving" these into the mirror on one's every out-breath. He then asks that we perceive the negative and positive qualities, traits, and emotions that pass into the mirror and then "take back" those we wish to keep within ourselves. While this approach will undoubtedly have value to many, I personally prefer a more loosely-structured practice, and I do not see the need to "take back" anything, since whatever is intrinsic to our true nature will never leave us or be lost. What is important is that we get rid of all that is alien to the true self.

- Take a few minutes to position yourself comfortably as described in the beginning of the energy field meditation described above. Remember to have a small mirror available. An interesting variation is to use a webcam on a computer. You can do a little centering and relaxation with your eyes open or closed before you begin working with the mirror.
- Remember, you want to sense what judgments or other projections are coming back from the glass and its images. We spend a great deal of our time and energy thinking about how we appear to others. This exercise is about following your own spontaneous impressions of the face that looks back at you from the glass. Look into the eyes: are you repelled or attracted; are they warm or cold; are you interested, intrigued, or bored? See whether any words or associations occur to you as you look at that person; be particularly alert to emotions such as fear or revulsion.
- This should be a time for revealing your masks—the images that you have been taught to wear for others. Examine the reflection inwardly for the presence of such images. T.S. Eliot wrote that "there will be time to prepare a face to meet the faces that you meet..."[46] He was talking about the masks that are worn in society, which prevent others from seeing us as we are, and which inhibit our self-realization. This is why, in the following lines from the same poem, Eliot describes "the works and days of hands that lift and drop a question on your plate..." I am encouraging you not to wait for Fate or trouble to intervene, but that *you* be the one to "drop a question," so that you do not wind up living behind the mask, while every day you make "a hundred visions and revisions before the taking of a toast and tea." The ego, with its capacity to steal our inborn creative energy, has devised a number of masks for all occasions—there is the corporate mask, the parental mask, the mask of piety, the mask of patriotism, a mask of asceticism and sacrifice—the list has been steadily growing for a few thousand years. If you see or otherwise sense any such masks in your contemplation before the mirror, ask for help from the cosmic realm in firmly dispersing them from

your psyche, and use the "inner No" method described in the earlier chapters to help you further in releasing this inner excess.
- It may become necessary to apply some destructive energy to the task at this point. If you feel uncomfortable with this, by all means refrain, and continue to ask questions instead (of your feelings of hesitation, fear, or revulsion, for instance). Masks and images, after all, must be destroyed. Let your feelings guide you in the process, and allow spontaneous perception to lead you from there. Some folks decide to see the masks burned; some "shoot them" with the weaponry of inner release; some simply throw the self-images of ego out a "cosmic window" where the dissolving and healing energies of the Cosmos can completely clear them from the field of consciousness—in effect, "kill them." This is the activity of what Robert Bly refers to as "the interior warrior."[47]
- Finish by separating from the mirror and its contents (what you saw in it). As Tulku Rinpoche says, it's important "to realize that what you see is not at all solid." Let it become a pane of glass once more, and ask the Helper of Meditation to call you back to your center once more. Then, as always in completing a practice of your inner life, thank the universe, the helping energies of transformation, or whatever personal metaphor you invoke in your conversation with the invisible realm, for the help and insight you have been led to in this experience.

Chapter 6: Priori Incantatem: Engaging Cosmic Protection[48]

> "The golden thread connecting Harry and Voldemort splintered; though the wands remained connected, a thousand more beams arced high over Harry and Voldemort, crisscrossing all around them, until they were enclosed in a golden, dome-shaped web, a cage of light, beyond which the Death Eaters circled like jackals, their cries strangely muffled now."
>
> (–*Harry Potter and the Goblet of Fire*, from Chapter 34, "Priori Incantatem")

We now find Harry trapped in a graveyard, to which he has been magically transported in one of the darker moments from the Potter series—a scene in which Harry's fellow competitor in sport and love (Cedric Diggory) has been murdered, and Harry himself cruelly tortured. He is now in a desperate and seemingly hopeless confrontation with Lord Voldemort, who has, with the help of a twisted rite of transubstantiation, been revived to a skeletal semblance of a human form, and he is intent on destruction. Harry assumes himself defenseless against his antagonist, but decides that "he was going to die trying to defend himself, even if no defense was possible."

Harry thus enters into his first armed encounter against his nemesis in a human body. Harry resorts to the only defense he has learned, the charm designed to disarm an opponent ("Expelliarmus"), while Voldemort employs his trump, the killing curse ("Avada Kedavra"). The red light of Harry's pure anger meets the cold green death-trail of Voldemort's termination mania, and together they synergize into a golden laser beam of kinetic electromagnetism.[49] It is from this composite gold energy that the web described above is formed. Voldemort, obsessed with the notion of completing the kill himself and thus fulfilling his revenge on Harry, orders his servants, the Death Eaters, not to intervene. Meanwhile, Harry simply holds on, trusting in the protective dome around him. Indeed, he has no alternative, but his trust is quickly recognized and affirmed by the invisible realm:

> And then an unearthly and beautiful sound filled the air....It was coming from every thread of the light-spun web vibrating around Harry and Voldemort. It was a sound Harry recognized, though he had heard it only once before in his life: phoenix song. It was the sound of hope to Harry...the most beautiful and welcome thing he had ever heard in his life....It was the sound he connected with Dumbledore, and it was almost as though a friend were speaking in his ear....(*Goblet of Fire*, p. 664)

The light-energy of this cosmic web does more than protect Harry; it also inspires him with its radiant music and *communicates with him* on a level of pure feeling. It is this communicative function of the web, its ability to touch the heart with wordless energy, that helps to answer the question, "why doesn't the web protect Harry from *Voldemort*, as well as from his followers?"

The answer lies in the metaphor: this encounter with Voldemort is another stage in Harry's journey of inner learning that started four years earlier. Here, the lesson begun within the Pensieve continues: Harry is being led to understand the illusory nature of evil, its fundamental depravity as energy stolen from Nature. Evil draws its power not from its own storehouse of life-force, for it has none—but via inner thievery from the essence of living beings. Thus, Lord Voldemort, who has previously appeared as a parasitic infection in the back of a man's head and a pale memory from a darkly enchanted diary, comes now in the form of a ghoulish, wasted fragment of humanity—a skeleton with a snake's head.

It is the inevitable fate of all evil to separate itself from humanity; thus, Voldemort becomes a grim caricature of a body, a composite distortion. Metaphorically, Voldemort is this surreal distortion of nature—he is the flag around which nationalists strut in smug exclusion to all others as they aggrandize their insular group, or the God whose vengeful Power is adumbrated to authorize every kind of slaughter and depredation upon all who live outside the sphere of His followers. Voldemort is this empty fantasy that, in every age and always a moment too late, history comes to recognize as Evil.

But Harry is being taught to clearly perceive this illusion for what it is; therefore he needs the experience of facing down Voldemort in single combat. However, he also needs protection from the followers of this evil—the corporate military of human adherents who could do him real harm—the "Death Eaters". Later on, in the fifth book, after Voldemort has returned to human strength, the "Death Eaters," who first appear as ghoulish pranksters and cheerleaders in the fourth book, arise in their fully destructive and institutional state, as punishing priests and crusaders—the army of their corporate God. Robert Bly, in a poem written over 25 years before the appearance of the first Potter story, described this corrupt, "death-eating" consciousness as a deadly amalgam of religious, governmental, and institutional deceit:

> The ministers lie, the professors lie, the television lies, the priests lie...
> These lies mean that the country wants to die.
> Lie after lie starts out into the prairie grass,
> like enormous caravans of Conestoga wagons....
>
> And a long desire for death flows out, guiding the enormous caravans
> from beneath,
> stringing together the vague and foolish words.
> It is a desire to eat death,
> to gobble it down,
> to rush on it like a cobra with mouth open
>
> It's a desire to take death inside,
> to feel it burning inside, pushing out velvety hairs,
> like a clothes brush in the intestines—
> (from "The Teeth Mother Naked at Last", 1970)

Rowling's setting of the confrontation between Harry and Voldemort also contains a lesson for all of us in how we may best deal with the evil represented by Voldemort and the Death Eaters. To start a war against the *followers* of a demonic consciousness (as is typically done by powerful governments in our world, under the banner of a holy nationalism) is an incomplete and inevitably self-defeating approach; it raises enmity among the followers, who therefore only multiply in their fierceness and number, while leaving the ideological source of the decadence intact. Conflict simply pits one fundamentalism against another. It is far more practical to separate inwardly from evil. This is done *within the heart of each individual,* where true transformation always happens. It is the process known as "retreat" in the literature of the Tao:

> Let the fear of God die among the people,
> And they will find their own true guide within.
>
> Do not constrict them in their homes,
> Or oppress them at their work,
> For if the people lack a sense of burden,
> Then they will not feel oppressed.
>
> Thus, the teaching heart of the Cosmos:
> It is a living, dynamic consciousness—
> It draws close to sincerity,
> And retreats from exaltation.
>
> The former it receives,
> The latter it discards.
> (Lao Tzu, *Tao Te Ching*, 72)

When we discard pomposity, self-righteousness, and evil from within, we lead others to do the same, and the monuments of ideology and attachment are isolated—left to lie naked and exposed in their black-hearted delusion. In other words, we can overcome the "Death Eaters" by starving them of their vapid and shadowy sustenance—the rotted meat of opposition.

The song of the phoenix—symbol of the regeneration and timelessness of Life—comes to Harry from the web's golden strands as a confirmation that he is being protected, that he can hold on and remain connected. Harry's response to it may seem familiar to many of us: he grimly orders himself, "don't break the connection," and "no sooner had he thought it, than the thing became much harder to do."

For those of us who have undertaken meditation or a similar practice of inner development, the resonance here is rather harshly amusing. Who cannot recall having struggled "not to think," "not to feel," or "not to wander" in one's pursuit of the elusive avatar of enlightenment or realization? Negative orders from within seem to interrupt the energy connection between the true self and its cosmic origin; they also seem to suck us into a vortex of self-repression that eventually becomes rigidified as Law or Commandment. The response which takes us back to our center is merely to focus on what is directly before (or within) us in the moment—this practice, embodied in the term "perseverance" within the *I Ching*, is all we need to restore the connection.

This is exactly what happens for Harry. He maintains his inner focus, and a new feature appears in the magical stream between his wandlight and Voldemort's: beads of light moving, sliding, along the path of their connection. These beads bring a further message to Harry—that he is not alone in this battle with Voldemort, but that a deep quantum energy is there for him as well. He then realizes that he needs to use his own will to move these beads of light back toward Voldemort, and this becomes the focus of his inner work. Like an athlete in a peak moment of deep performance, or a child simply gazing into a candle's flame, his conscious energy is thus directed away from the realm of "thou shalt not" and into that of positive effort—again, "perseverance." This movement from negativity to directed focus draws the helping energies of the cosmic realm to Harry's side, and they complete the work he has begun. The beads do indeed move back to Voldemort, and the transformation occurs that will deliver Harry from danger.

Wherever there is music, there will be dance: the phoenix-song of Life being played from the web is joined by a Dance of the Spheres: the dead victims of Voldemort's murderous tyranny reveal themselves from the light stream connecting the wands, and each offers encouragement to Harry. The last of these spirits to appear is Harry's father, who instructs him on how and when to break the connection and escape; he then assures him that the spirits will be able to delay the pursuit of Voldemort and the

Death Eaters. This is the invisible realm fulfilling its dual function of protection and insight, for all who will verify its truth and immediacy within the field of their experience. Though the dead may appear to be separated from us, their consciousness can remain with us as helping energy, whenever we open ourselves just a little to the possibility. It really requires such a minimal effort of receptivity to achieve, through one's lived experience, a truly panoramic and regenerative understanding of Life and Death. Harry discovers that the only person Voldemort has really *killed* is Tom Riddle—his own true and original nature. But his murdered victims remain active and vibrant in that quantum realm of formlessness. So it has always been with tyranny: every slaughter begins with an act of inner suicide. Lao Tzu came to the same discovery and described it poetically, in Chapter 31 of the *Tao Te Ching*:

> Of all the instruments of human ego,
> Weapons of war are the most horrible.
> The teaching Heart of the Cosmos
> Turns away in revulsion from these,
> And from those that use them.
>
> The student of the Sage
> Embraces the supple form of truth.
> The student of war
> Hides beneath the stiff shield of delusion.
> The former walks in blessing,
> The latter strides toward Fate.
>
> When the infantile lord descends
> To playing with his toys of war,
> He must be resolutely answered
> With a calm and firm rejection.
> And should he kill and conquer,
> Let him not revel in his hideous slaughter;
> Let him not exult in extermination.
> For he who delights in destruction
> Shall never live in the Way of Nature.
>
> Celebrate the living body of truth,
> Mourn the madness that is power:
> For power is the seat of appearances,

Where the dead figurehead resides.
Let a dirge of sorrow be sung
For the victorious commander-in-chief.
Lament as well the grievous slaughter he has wrought.

Though we may weep for all his seeming victims,
It is the patriot, the power-drunk demon,
For whom the funeral rites must be observed.

The only loss we ever incur is within the graveyard of the spirit: whenever we bury our true nature beneath the loam of appearance, struggle, and conquest, we have separated from Life. To choose tyranny is to choose suicide, for it kills the essence and stops the flow of the life-force within. Life is not about power, domination, or mastery; it is about suppleness and movement—life does not strut or march; it dances, and thus, it endures.

In this sense, the metaphor of the web has much to teach us. The web is golden because it represents the treasure, the essence: it contains and reflects all of life, in all its transformations. Its color is the sun's light, mingled with the brown of Earth. The web represents the universe, the Cosmos, the protecting and nourishing Whole. It represents our home, our origin, our source and destination; it contains both our unity and our uniqueness.

In the Buddhist Pali Canon, there is the inspiring image of the "net of gems." In the net of gems, each being, each moment of compressed consciousness, reflects the light of all the others, just as it is reflected in turn. Every life—no matter how brief or buried in anonymity—is cast within the core of every other, and thus to the Whole as well.

The constellations in the night sky have long suggested the metaphor of the cosmic web or net of gems, as has been recorded in Homeric poetry and Hindu mythology. In our own time, science has responded to this range of metaphor, in its conception of life and matter as the activity and interaction of a sub-microscopic weaving of "strings" or "superstrings" in subatomic physics, along with the new biological models that are being proposed to explain the nature and functions of life at the cellular, genetic, and macro-organic levels of being.[50]

Mathematics, in the form of nonlinear dynamics, is adding to this burgeoning web metaphor within science, as revealed by the popularity of fractal images.

Obviously, computer science has contributed exponentially to these developments, and thus it is no random coincidence that its dominant communication medium is the interconnected consciousness that has come to be called the "world-wide web," or what we may refer to as the "Inter-Net of Gems". Merely to open one's awareness to this web-metaphor is to begin the work of discarding the superstition of the world as appearance and machine, which is one of the fundamental delusions of Voldemort-consciousness.

One feature of all these images and metaphors is worth noting specifically: the web, in both the Potter story and in the languages of myth, symbol, and science, is not a closed system (just as the fractal image cannot be "plotted" according to traditional concepts of point, line, or slope). In other words, it is porous, open, and active. It is receptive as well as protective; indeed, these two functions are simply shifting expressions of its true nature. The web is not a defensive wall, but an open network of organic sensitivity. Fritjof Capra explains this function in the context of a discussion of cell membranes:

> A membrane is very different from a cell wall. Whereas cell walls are rigid structures, membranes are always active, opening and closing continually, keeping certain substances out and letting others in. The cell's metabolic reactions involve a variety of ions, and the membrane, by being semi-permeable, controls their proportions and keeps them in balance. ...All these activities help to maintain the cell as a distinct entity and protect it from harmful environmental influences. Indeed, the first thing a bacterium does when it is attacked by another organism is to make membranes. (*The Hidden Connections*, p. 8)

A wall—as either matter or metaphor—is an inflexible and brittle structure; but a membrane is an organic web that receives nourishment and closes spontaneously to toxicity or encroachment. In Harry's experience, the Death Eaters appear remote to his senses while he is within the golden web, because its function is to seal off that threat. But the nourishing and reassuring phoenix-song comes through loud and clear to Harry inside the web, as does perspective and information about his environment, by virtue of the gossamer, net-like structure of the web. Returning to Lao Tzu, he provides a very precise metaphor on this aspect of the web, in Chapter 73 from the *Tao Te Ching*:

> The Cosmic Whole is like a net—
> So perfectly cast, its open meshes are capable
> Of catching everything.

No wall can possibly protect us as well as can openness and movement; even the famous military strategist of ancient China, Sun Tzu, agreed with this principle.[51] The *I Ching* supports this view as well, with its own insight from Hexagram 7, titled "The Army":

> THE ARMY. The army needs perseverance
> And a strong man.
> Good fortune without blame.

The protection that is engaged through perseverance has already been mentioned: this is the "one-pointed attention" of such contemplative practices as meditation, the tea ceremony, or flower-arranging in the Zen traditions. As for the "strong man" referred to in the *I Ching* verse (and elsewhere translated as "the leader"), this is a metaphor on the true self, which leads the personality when it is released from the distortions of ego. In their commentary to this hexagram, Carol Anthony and Hanna Moog discover a fresh direction for the military metaphor of this hexagram—that of a "*Cosmic* Army." This is an interpretation that appears to resonate with Harry's experience inside the golden web:

> The Cosmic Army's function is to fight, when called upon, transgressions against ourselves, other people, and against Nature in general (animals, plants, and the earth as a whole). When humans try to do this themselves, they only create opposition that strengthens the aggressor, for when the ego is engaged in defending, the other's ego is energized and empowered. (from *I Ching: The Oracle of the Cosmic Way*, p. 138)

The distinction that is implicit in both this interpretation of the *I Ching* and Harry's encounter with Lord Voldemort deserves further thought, for it shows us the psychological difference between *defense* and *protection*. Defense is an ego-referenced activity, which fixes upon aggressive, passive-aggressive, or escapist strategies of coping with a threat or danger; its means are often maladaptive or inappropriate to the situation or challenge being faced. These means typically include denial, avoidance, lashing out, identification with the aggressor, rationalization, or any of the related ego-stratagems that have been catalogued within the Freudian canon under the heading "defense mechanisms." The problem with these is exactly that they are *mechanisms*—they reduce lived experience to a purely mechanical and reactive paradigm of fixed and ultimately inadequate responses. This has the effect of closing off access to a vast storehouse of intra-psychic resources and their protective capacities, which in turn reinforces the urgency and exacerbates the aggressiveness of the defense mechanisms, in an unceasing spiral of further separation from one's true nature.

The way out of this trap is to begin by perceiving *that the obsession with mere appearance has brought us, again and again, to failure*. At the time we encounter him in the graveyard, Harry Potter has already taken this step: he spent the first decade of his life trapped within a shallow pool of appearances, and he felt deeply how meager and insufficient the Dursleys' preoccupation with the veneer of existence was to him and his growth. Once the call from the invisible world had arrived, represented by the letters carried to him by the messengers of intuitive wisdom (owls)[52], Harry was ready and receptive.

The next step out of the trap of the superficial is to

acknowledge *the possibility of experiencing a fresh and holistic perception of reality*, which includes the direct engagement of one's feeling-nature. Harry is open to this as well, and each opening he creates to the approach of natural magic is rewarded with yet another experience of helping energies, which teach, provide, and protect more fully and restoratively than any human or mechanical agency possibly could. Through each such encounter, Harry is brought deeper into his true nature, his personal connection with the Cosmic Whole and its nurturing, protective energies. For Cosmic protection, unlike the defense mechanisms of ego, comes from the totality of consciousness, the web of transcendence that Lao Tzu called *Tao*. This is the Source that can always be relied upon, for it takes us out of the flat plane of appearances and securely into the realm of transformation:

> Sublime, the Cosmic Breath
> That limitlessly pervades and imbues
> Time and space, form and non-form.
> It diffuses in every direction,
> It flows through all being,
> It creates and furthers all,
> But makes no claim and takes no credit.
>
> It is the catalyst of transformation,
> And we do not even know its name!
> It loves and nourishes
> The infinite family of forms,
> But seeks not allegiance or submission.
>
> Eternally free of abstraction,
> Its essence may be sought
> Within the realm of the infinitesimal,
> Though it is the origin and destiny
> Of the myriad expressions of Nature.
> It rejects aggrandizement,
> And thus may be called great.
>
> Just so, the student of the Sage:
> He divorces his ego, repudiates elevation,
> And retreats from recognition:
> Thus his achievement endures,
> And his work is made great.
> (Chapter 34, *Tao Te Ching*)

Meditation: Engaging the Personal Energy of Protection

This work is best done on a regular, perhaps daily basis, and can be fit into normal routines that are part of many people's lives. It can be done during a commute to work on a train or bus; as part of one's preparation for the day's work; during a break or after work; or even in the space of something as fleeting as a ride up an elevator or escalator. This meditation can also be helpful at bedtime, particularly if you're having difficulty falling asleep. It naturally clears out the dross of the day from within and thus permits full and restful sleep. However the timing suits your personality and schedule, try to find a few minutes' worth of room within each day where this meditation can be done, and I am sure you'll soon feel yourself more grounded, centered, and invisibly protected from harm and invasion throughout the day. We can begin with the "energy field meditation" which I have described in the chapter on the invisibility cloak; since it is brief, I will reproduce it here.

Begin by getting in touch with your body. Take a comfortable position in which you are relaxed and aware; if you are sitting, feel your spine become straight yet without stiffness, and your shoulders relaxed. Sense the weight of your body where it contacts the floor, chair, or cushion that you're sitting on; feel the connection between your feet and the floor. Note the sense of the clothing on your skin, the feel of the ambient air around you, any sounds that reach you in the moment, and the light and images before your eyes (whether they are open or closed). Feel each of these sensations in turn, and then the movement of your body-breath, in and out, without making any attempt to control or direct the experience.
Now begin feeling yourself—your whole being—as energy. You could, if you like, feel an "invisibility cloak" passing over your body, though this is not necessary. You might find yourself with an image of energic movement, such as nebulae in motion, wind blowing through trees or high grass, microscopic cellular activity, radiant heat, osmotic movement, an aura or

energy field, or have a flowing, aqueous sensation. The basic idea is to experience yourself as energy—activity, motion— formless, kinetic being without any particular material reference point. Feel your body in its vital and enduring presence—as a dance of complementary energies, the yin and the yang commingling formlessly, effortlessly, and timelessly in a harmonic that Lao Tzu compared with the coalescing flow of the breath of lovers.

This initial phase can be as long or as brief as you need it to be; with a little experience, you can enter this "energy field" center in a minute or so. Next comes the protective aspect of this meditation, which you can engage as soon as you feel your energy field opened and ready—indeed, the one phase leads naturally into the other, so that it's often scarcely possible to differentiate where one phase ends and the next begins.

Now begin to feel a field of light forming around you. It can take any shape, direction, or expression that is natural to you: a web of laser-like beams such as surrounds Harry; an aura that flows from your center outward; or a pulsing, membranous glow of colored energy that radiates around you. No matter what shape it takes for you, a simple, modest glow of luminosity is the most beneficial image, since a harsh, glaring, or piercing light is not protective but instead tends to provoke the ego within others. Remember that you are seeking protection, not display.

Once you can feel your light-field moving, surrounding you, then you can focus on its function. See and feel it as a Cosmic energy filter which catches toxicity—emotional, intellectual, and even physical toxicity—from within and especially around you, and then neutralizes, cleanses, and disperses the poisonous energy. You can also synchronize this protective movement with that of your breath: on the in-breath, feel the membranous web opening to receive nourishing Cosmic light-energy; then on the out-breath, feel the web expelling toxic consciousness, out and away from you. Remain with this feeling of your energy-glow trapping and filtering out the poisons of Ego, and call on the helping energies of Clarity, Detachment, and Purification to complete and support this work of your inner filter of light. As you near the end of the meditation, thank these helping energies and the Cosmic Whole for their presence in your inner work.

Try this exercise for a few days, and adapt it to your personality and inner needs as you go. You may well find yourself increasingly protected from invasion, conflict, stress, and pressure amid all your relationships. As you continue with this meditation, pay attention to the presence of any "holes"—gaps, blank or dark spots in your light-field, or weak areas in the energy pattern. See where these may be emanating from in terms of bodily regions or points that you feel associated with the gaps. The awareness of such points often leads us to an understanding of areas in which we are especially vulnerable or where our life-force is obstructed; these gaps can even be helping us to recognize the presence of an illness of the body or psyche that needs attention.

Chapter 7: No. 12, Grimmauld Place and The Voices of Neurosis

> Pressing a finger to her lips, she led him on tiptoes past a pair of long, moth-eaten curtains, behind which Harry supposed there must be another door, and after skirting a large umbrella stand that looked as though it had been made from a severed troll's leg, they started up the dark staircase, passing a row of shrunken heads mounted on plaques on the wall. A closer look showed Harry that the heads belonged to house-elves. All of them had the same rather snoutlike nose.
> Harry's bewilderment deepened with every step he took. What on earth were they doing in a house that looked as though it belonged to the darkest of wizards?
> —*Harry Potter and the Order of the Phoenix*, Chapter 4

In the opening chapters of the fifth book in the Harry Potter series, the fifteen year-old boy wizard is attacked by a pair of "dementors"—malevolent ghouls with the power to suck one's very soul out with a single "kiss." Harry successfully defends himself from this assault and is then rescued from his Muggle home by a group of his adult friends, who take him to an obscure house in a darkened, low-income neighborhood within London. This house is the headquarters of the "Order of the Phoenix," the social defense association that has been hurriedly re-formed in response to the threat posed by the return of Lord Voldemort.

Nothing about his new environment is particularly encouraging to Harry: garbage is piled up in the street; dirt and filth seem to define the homes at Grimmauld Place, sticking to their exteriors like a gloomy mood. The door to the place is "black...shabby...scratched"; the darkness inside is dominated by a "sweetish, rotting smell" which gives it "the feeling of a derelict building." Gas lamps are lit, which cast "a flickering insubstantial light over the peeling wallpaper and threadbare carpet"; there are other haunted-house features, such as a "cobwebby chandelier" and "age-blackened portraits" on the walls. The question that occurs to Harry, as he walks through the house at Grimmauld Place, seems entirely natural (the name says it all: "grim and old," or "grime and mould"): *what on earth is he doing here?*

The question is not answered for him immediately: he only knows that he is in the headquarters of the Order, that it seems an uncharacteristic place for his friends and allies to be calling home, even if only as a temporary measure, and that its pervasive gloom feels poisonous to him. And from a metaphorical perspective, *it is*, as Rowling swiftly demonstrates in this tour through the realm of the neurotic tenement.

For it is here, at 12 Grimmauld Place, that Harry's smoldering emotions of fear and anger are appropriated by the ego and thus find expression in a completely misdirected outer attack on those closest to him. Why does this happen? Why, after less than a quarter hour within this house and its threatening metaphorical presence, does the ego within Harry explode in a cacophony of bile against his two deepest and most enduring friends?

One answer to this is obvious: 12 Grimmauld Place is decidedly not "a safe place." I am borrowing that phrase from a 1989 book by a Harvard psychologist named Leston Havens. *A Safe Place* is a compact volume of poetic clarity, which reminds psychotherapists that "every theory acts to suppress...the real person who consists of much else," and that furthering another's inner growth is really about offering a safe and open place in which true healing may happen. Havens writes compellingly about the inner requirements for "safe place making:"

> We have to learn how to be still when the other needs to be left alone but asks for intervention, to give confidence when the patient induces despair, to find strength when everything suggests madness and deviance, to bring sobriety to those who would set us afire, and...sometimes to be what the patient needs....(p. 131)

In this respect, young Harry has not been given "a safe place" for a moment during this his fifteenth year of life, and we can all observe from our own lives how common this unfortunate truth is within our culture, especially for adolescents. For Harry, it is only at his school—particularly within Dumbledore's office and Hagrid's hut—that he's allowed the freedom and safety to expose his inner demons to the light of clarity, and gradually uncover his true self. As this story proceeds, Harry will discover that learning and healing are possible beyond Hogwarts, and even within the lugubrious confines of Grimmauld Place—but only after a process of inner cleansing is allowed to unfold. At this point in the story, there is no safe place in which Harry can grow or heal: he has been delivered from the plastic world of Privet Drive, into the frosty but insubstantial air of escape (the broom-flight to London), and finally to this moribund home at Grimmauld Place.

So, Harry is hustled upstairs, into another glowering space ("a gloomy, high-ceilinged room"), left alone by the adults who have important, grownup business to attend to downstairs, and he is then almost immediately excoriating his friends Ron and Hermione with demands, claims of right and privilege, bitter, and paranoid accusations.[53] His bitterness is a function of the fact that a more natural expression of his fear and anger has been closed off to him; it is also a reflection of and response to his environment. As Havens points out in his book, our spaces, in both their outer and inner shapes, will show us whether we will be allowed a healthy and disburdening expression of our distress, or be left with a narrow, restricted, and distorted projection.

To illustrate this principle, let's compare the way Harry accounts for identical actions from his past in two separate spaces, first during his tirade at Grimmauld Place (on the left) and later at Hogwarts (on the right):[54]

...before he knew it, Harry was shouting... "I'VE BEEN STUCK AT THE DURSLEYS' FOR A MONTH! AND I'VE HANDLED MORE THAN YOU TWO'VE EVER MANAGED AND DUMBLEDORE KNOWS IT—WHO SAVED THE SORCERER'S STONE? WHO GOT RID OF RIDDLE? WHO SAVED BOTH YOUR SKINS FROM THE DEMENTORS?..WHO HAD TO GET PAST DRAGONS AND SPHINXES AND EVERY OTHER FOUL THING LAST YEAR?...BUT WHY SHOULD I KNOW WHAT'S GOING ON? WHY SHOULD ANYONE BOTHER TO TELL ME WHAT'S BEEN HAPPENING?" (pp. 65-66)	"Just listen to me, all right? It sounds great, but all that stuff was luck—I didn't know what I was doing half the time, I didn't plan any of it, I just did whatever I could think of, and I nearly always had help—I got through it all because—because help came at the right time, or because I guessed right—but I just blundered through it all, I didn't have a clue what I was doing—STOP LAUGHING!" (p. 327)

Returning to Grimmauld Place, the full impact of the relationship of environment and psychology is revealed as the textural details of this house are drawn. Harry soon understands the necessity of silence and darkness in the entryway to the building, when an accidental noise sets off one of the more intriguing images of the book:

> The moth-eaten velvet curtain Harry had passed earlier had flown apart, but there was no door behind them. For a split second, Harry thought he was looking through a window, a window behind which an old woman in a black cap was screaming and screaming as though she was being tortured—then he realized it was simply a life-size portrait, but the most realistic, and the most unpleasant, he had ever seen in his life.
> The old woman was drooling, her eyes were rolling, the yellowing skin of her face stretched taut as she screamed, and all along the hall behind them, the other portraits awoke and began to yell too, so that Harry actually screwed up his eyes at the noise and clapped his hands over his ears...the old woman screeched louder than

ever, brandishing clawed hands as though trying to tear at their faces.

"Filth! Scum! By-products of dirt and vileness! Half-breeds, mutants, freaks, begone from this place! How dare you befoul the house of my fathers—" (pp. 77-78)

This portrait represents the figure of Sirius Black's dead mother, and now it becomes clear where Harry has landed—in the ancestral home of his godfather's ancient family. Now as tempting as it may be for us to see certain Freudian (specifically, Oedipal) analogies in this concatenation of images and relationships, it would seem more consonant with the development of the story to focus on this metaphor from the perspective of a more human and less ideological psychology.

For we have now entered the metaphorical realm of what Karen Horney called "neurotic pride" and what Carol Anthony and Hanna Moog refer to as "the demonic sphere of consciousness." Kierkegaard called it "the sickness unto death," and specifically "the despair of weakness," which he describes pointedly in terms of false self-perception:

> ...there are essentially two forms of illusion: that of hope and that of recollection. The adolescent's illusion is that of hope, that of the adult recollection. But precisely because the adult suffers from this illusion, his conception of illusion itself is also the quite one-sided one that the only illusion is the illusion of hope...What afflicts the adult is not so much the illusion of hope as, no doubt among other things, the grotesque illusion of looking down from some supposedly higher vantage-point, free from illusion, upon the illusions of the young. (*The Sickness Unto Death*, p. 89)

Horney speaks of this illusory, projected consciousness as the product of a neurotic error, in which "a wish or need, in itself quite understandable, turns into a claim."[55] We may see that Harry himself falls into this neurotic trap: his rant comes from the same inner milieu as that of the portrait of Sirius' mother. Under the influence of ego, his *need* for personal autonomy becomes a *claim* to superiority above others, based on his past accomplishments. This claim is a brand of personal prejudice, which parallels the positively racist tone of the portrait's rant against "half-breeds, mutants, and freaks." Certainly, their noises are very well matched: Harry and the painting are both loud, biting, offensive, and imperious. This is what Horney refers to as "the expansive solution of mastery," in which "the individual prevailingly identifies himself with his glorified self." To do so, however, is to separate from one's own *true* self and its human needs. This inner act of dehumanization springs from the same seed, which condemns others as "the enemy," "the traitors," "the mob," or "the ignorant," and subjects them to oppression and demonization, usually in furtherance of some proclaimed "noble end."

It is this "noble end" that disguises the prejudices that fuel the engine of tyranny. We will meet this smokescreen of corruption again in the seventh and final book of the series, in the phrase "for the greater good" that a young Dumbledore and his friend Grindelwald use to paper over their predatory plans of social tyranny.[56] The corruption underlying this prejudice is revealed during the cleansing of the house at Grimmauld Place, which, as Harry discovers, is more a process of "waging war on the house" than mere dusting and cleaning. In one scene, the children join the grownups in clearing out a collection of glass cabinets that contain some of the relics of "the noble and most ancient house of Black."

These cabinets at Grimmauld Place hold "an odd assortment of objects: a selection of rusty daggers, claws, a coiled snakeskin, a number of tarnished silver boxes inscribed with languages Harry could not understand, and, least pleasant of all, an ornate crystal bottle with a large opal set into the stopper, full of what Harry was quite sure was blood." (p. 106). During the actual clearing of these cabinets, Sirius sustains a bite from one of the silver boxes, Harry is attacked by another object, and everyone present is almost clinically sedated by "a musical box that emitted a faintly sinister, tinkling tune when wound," until Ginny Weasley has the good sense to force the lid shut.

The common theme to all of these threatening objects is their *medieval* character: metaphorically, they are the demons of an ancient, corrupt, feudal racism. They must be dealt with harshly: as each object is removed, it is thrown into a trash bag.

There is the bottle of black, rotten blood of nobility; the silver trinkets of excess; various seals, lockets, and medals won for empty deeds or else bought with money and influence; and finally a massive book entitled "Nature's Nobility: A Wizarding Genealogy".

Now we must be very clear about the reference of these metaphors: though their character is collectively medieval, they represent acutely modern problems—the neuroses of both group and individual consciousness *today*. They are deeply embedded in our culture, our law, our moral codes, our religions, our educational systems, and even in our arts and sciences.

The Noise of Neurosis: Kreacher the House-Elf

The essentially neurotic character of this corrupt realm of depraved nobility is revealed in the physical rot that infests all of the objects in this scene. It is also betrayed in the voices which are heard throughout: the occasional screams of the portrait of Sirius' mother, which pierce the air whenever someone rings the doorbell downstairs, and the muttering, malevolent rant of Kreacher the house-elf. Kreacher, who is the house servant, steals into the room where the children are cleaning. He is a tiny monster, ancient and ill-appearing, with drooping skin, bloodshot eyes, and a hunchbacked gait. But his most alarming trait is his voice—a muttering, psychotic drone "in a hoarse, deep voice like a bullfrog's." His word-salad diatribes croak out of him unconsciously, in schizoid bursts that are clearly audible. The disorganized commentary runs like a subterranean echo to the rant of his former mistress in the painting:

> "Smells like a drain and a criminal to boot, but she's no better, nasty old blood traitor with her brats messing up my Mistress's house, oh my poor Mistress, if she knew, if she knew that scum they've let in her house, what would she say to old Kreacher, oh the shame of it, Mudbloods and werewolves and traitors and thieves, poor old Kreacher, what can he do..." (pp. 107-108)

Hermione alone senses that the old house elf is mentally ill, and intuits the cause (this is later confirmed by Dumbledore himself). The others, including Sirius himself, see only insolence, hatred, and utter depravity in Kreacher; Hermione sees, or rather feels, the demons that have enslaved him, and she only wishes that he could be healed. But Hermione is ignored, and even playfully ridiculed for her insight, and the book ends with the revelation that Kreacher has betrayed Sirius and Harry to Lord Voldemort, causing death to the one and yet another bitter loss to the other.

As Kierkegaard might add, the "sickness unto death" has many faces. It has a face of power-blinded evil, such as we find in Voldemort; it has a face of smug superiority, such as that of the Ministry of Magic; it also has the face of enslavement to the false and feudal ideologies of tyranny, such as we find in the "noble and ancient house of Black" and its servants. The "sickness" that Kierkegaard describes is not one unto physical death, but rather unto the only death that need be truly feared—the death of one's true and natural self:

> Finitude's despair is just so. A man in this kind of despair can very well live on in temporality; indeed he can do so all the more easily, be to all appearances a human being, praised by others, honoured and esteemed, occupied with all the goals of temporal life. Yes, what we call worldliness simply consists of such people who, if one may so express it, pawn themselves to the world. They use their abilities, amass wealth, carry out worldly enterprises, make prudent calculations, etc., and perhaps are mentioned in history, but they are not themselves. In a spiritual sense, they have no self, no self for whose sake they could venture everything, no self for God—however selfish they are otherwise. (Kierkegaard, *The Sickness Unto Death*, p. 65)

Silencing the Demons: An Approach to Healing

> Let us suppose that a certain individual shows no inclination whatever to recognize his projections. The projection-making factor then has a free hand and can realize its object—if it has one—or bring about some other situation characteristic of its power. As we know, it is not the conscious subject but the unconscious which does the projecting. Hence one meets with projections, one does not make them. The effect of projection is to isolate the subject from his environment, since instead of a real relation to it there is now only an illusory one. Projections change the world into the replica of one's own unknown face. In the last analysis, therefore, they lead to a...condition in which one dreams a world whose reality remains forever unattainable. —Carl Jung, from *Aion*, CW 9, ii, par. 17

Jung was able to show how every person seems to create a parallel world of his life, through the projective activity of an aspect of personality that Jung called *shadow*.[57] Now my own feeling is that there is no particular psychological entity as shadow (especially as a universal and timeless entity, or archetype), and that what Jung was really referring to is what I have consistently called *ego* throughout this volume.

Ego has arisen out of error, out of something that we have *done*, rather than something that we *are*. It is a wandering maelstrom, whose energy—stolen from our true nature—adopts the kinetic shape of a hurricane, around whose stillness a storm of destructive and distorted energy swirls. The solution to the problem of ego is in the act of returning to that silent "eye of the hurricane," for that is where the pure energy of natural being may be discovered and experienced, in its deep and original clarity; that is the "safe place" of which Leston Havens writes. To get there, we must "silence the demons," and like Harry and his friends, clear our inner cabinets of false thoughts and negative emotion, by breaking the inner bonds of feudal belief. Later in the same novel, after Harry has had another outburst of paranoia and self-righteousness, his ego is stopped dead in its tracks by a remark from Ginny, who had been possessed by Lord Voldemort during Harry's second year at Hogwarts. Ginny's reminder delivers another measure of clarity to Harry at 12 Grimmauld Place, and he responds by admitting his mistake. Moments like these occur in every life, and we must squeeze them for all they're worth: they are the doors to true learning, where ego is frozen and the natural self is set free.

When, like Harry during his Dursley upbringing, we are conditioned as children to deny our natural selves, then we become, as the psychologist John Welwood expresses it, "an open hand that gradually starts to contract and close:"

> Although clenching the hand into a fist may be a fitting response to immediate threat, it would obviously be inappropriate to walk around that way for the rest of our life. Yet this is exactly what happens in our psyche! Our first response to emotional pain is to flinch, which is not a problem in and of itself. But then we start to take refuge in this contraction, and identify with it. It feels safer to be a closed fist than a vulnerable open hand. This protective tightening becomes installed in our body/mind as a set of chronic, rigid defenses that cut us off from our feelings and thus shut down our capacity to respond to life freely and openly. In our attempt to say no to the pain, we wind up saying no to ourselves instead. In this way, we inflict on ourselves the core wound that will haunt us the rest of our lives. We start to separate from our own being. —John Welwood, *Love and Awakening*, pp. 12-13

Our choice, of course, cannot be to say No to the pain—for pain (as Jung recognized) is a messenger designed to provide helpful information—our choice must be to say No to the ideas, beliefs, and images that perpetuate the pain, *that are its actual source*. When understood correctly, we find that pain is pointing, very specifically, to someplace. If we can identify the destructive beliefs and attitudes that were drilled into us during childhood, we have an excellent chance of pulling down the inner pillars that support the ego and the disease it brings us. As Welwood points out, it is the body in which these false defenses, with their supporting belief systems, are trapped; to rid the body of their cellular detritus is to free the psyche from their illusory power.

Chapter 8: The Black Door, the Circular Room, and Dreams of the Present

> "It is *my* fault that Sirius died," said Dumbledore clearly. "Or I should say almost entirely my fault – I will not be so arrogant as to claim responsibility for the whole...you should never have believed for an instant that there was any necessity for you to go to the Department of Mysteries tonight. If I had been open with you, Harry, as I should have been, you would have known a long time ago that Voldemort might try and lure you to the Department of Mysteries, and you would never have been tricked into going there tonight. And Sirius would not have had to come after you. That blame lies with me, and with me alone." —from Chapter 37, "The Lost Prophecy" in *Harry Potter and the Order of the Phoenix* (pp. 825-826)

We are now with Harry near the end of the fifth story, amid the epilogue to the most painful and emotionally ravaging scene of his young life. His godfather, Sirius Black, has been killed in a battle which was brought on, in part, by Harry's impulse to reify the images of a dream, and act the role of hero. By this point in the story, he knows he was duped, and he is agonizingly aware that he has made a horrible error, which could have been averted—if only he had been still enough within to be clear before deciding to act. Dumbledore, however, is not a mentor who teaches through recrimination (how many so-called teachers in our own Muggle world could learn from that alone?); nor does he believe in applying the sticky balm of pity to open wounds of the heart. He teaches through the strength of a natural empathy which does not parade its inherent compassion. He has learned himself what few seem ever to learn: that pity is as obstructive to healing as pedantry is to learning. This is a lesson that we can hear in an old Zen story, as told and explained by Philip Kapleau:

> Once the governor of a province in ancient China spent several days in the mountains with his Zen teacher....As the governor was preparing to depart, the master asked him, "When you return to the capital, how will you govern the people?"
> "With compassion and wisdom," replied the governor.
> "In that case," commented the master, "every last one of them will suffer."
> A truly generous person doesn't boast of his generosity nor an honest man of his integrity....True love lays no claim to loving. It loves silently, spontaneously, like a plant turning to the sun.[58]

Dumbledore does not deny or cover up Harry's blame; he shares it, and thus obliquely reveals to him the way of healing, which is the removal of guilt—not through forced acts of repentance or confession, but through a calm, firm, and open acknowledgement of error, and the sharing of remorse. In *The Book of Loss*, novelist Julith Jedamus has one of her characters declare that "absolution isn't a reward. It's a gift."[59] Dumbledore quietly teaches Harry that this gift requires no payment in punishment, repentance, or any other currency of self-abasement that is demanded of us from the pulpits of ideological spirituality. He teaches instead that when we are able to share blame through an open and inner connection with others, then guilt is transformed into remorse, and from remorse comes the true learning that promotes growth. Through this lesson, Dumbledore is also able to show Harry the way to understanding and accepting the gift of inner vision, which has brought him to this painful turning point in his process of growth.

For Harry does appear to have a challenging gift, which he is still struggling to understand: he can receive impressions of the thoughts, actions, plans, emotions, and desires of Lord Voldemort, to the point where he can viscerally experience Voldemort's consciousness—specifically through the scar on his forehead that is the mark of their mutual connection. This scar is, of course, the remnant of a wound left on Harry's body by Voldemort's murder attempt on him, made while Harry was still a baby. Now, some 14 years later, the scar remains, and so does Voldemort—as a lurking, parasitic presence with no seeming life of its own except what it steals of the life-force of others. Virtually for as long as he can remember, Harry has felt the presence of this Voldemort-consciousness, in one form or another: passing visions, stinging, burning pains, fleeting emotional sensations, and of course, the dreams.

They begin in the first story, before Harry is even aware of his "magical" status: he has dreams and somnolent visions of a green light, sometimes accompanied by the sound of icy laughter. Once at Hogwarts, he feels a stinging in his scar, which he mistakenly associates with the brooding Potions master, Professor Snape. These experiences recur sporadically in the stories that follow, until the fourth book opens with a scene in which Voldemort murders an old caretaker at his boyhood home, from long before he became "the Dark Lord." Harry is a dream-witness to this murder. Later in this story, he dreams again of Voldemort in the act of torturing one of his followers, and Harry rushes to Dumbledore's office for help. The information from these dreams is so precise and self-consistent that Dumbledore is able to draw conclusions about Voldemort's activity, based on little more than the details provided through Harry's visions.

This trend gathers even more momentum in the fifth story, *Harry Potter and the Order of the Phoenix*. Here, the premonitory visions center around a recurring dream in which Harry sees himself walking down a corridor to a locked, black door that, he later finds, leads into a dark, circular room. The first of these comes to him the night before he is to return to Hogwarts. But before Harry has this dream, something else happens that is itself rather nightmarish: he watches as a Boggart mutates into the dead bodies of Mrs. Weasley's husband and children, right before her. After seeing the Boggart appear as (among others) his *own* dead body on the floor, Harry suddenly feels that "without warning, the scar on his forehead seared with pain again and his stomach churned horribly."

As in so many other similar scenes, there is a prominently visceral aspect to these visions that Harry experiences. It is not just his forebrain (the scar) that is involved; he feels these premonitions "in his guts," as it were. Of course, we are all familiar with the deep sensitivity of our stomachs to stress, anxiety, and painful emotion—the pervasiveness of chronic nausea, ulcers, irritable bowel syndrome, and more serious gastro-intestinal disorders is nearly endemic in our culture, and this is obviously no coincidence. Emotional pain, fatigue, stress, and psychological toxicity are often more manifest in our bellies than our heads. Even early on in the fifth book, Harry is viscerally affected by the poison of Voldemort's consciousness within the body cells of his physical center, the abdomen.[60]

There are, of course, ominous signs coming from everywhere, and seemingly everything, from the very beginning of this fifth book. Upon his arrival at Hogwarts, Harry has his first encounter with certain eerie, reptilian equines—creatures later identified as "thestrals", which can only be seen by a person who has witnessed death. During the opening feast, the popular "sorting hat" sings broodingly of strife, warfare, and division amid the wizarding world, and Harry remains deeply troubled at the remoteness of Professor Dumbledore. It's as if every dark corner of his life is closing in on him, while at the same time, the influences he has to this point relied on as secure and supportive are becoming distant.

In light of this, it should come as no surprise that people in therapy have been known to refer to depression as "an attack of dementors." These are just the kinds of circumstances where depression's icy black grip becomes truly deadly; for this is where we are viscerally reacting to the poisonous ideas and influences that are the seeds of depression, which by now have penetrated our bodily cells— this is where it "gets under our skin," as the expression goes. Indeed, this is precisely what happens to Harry next in this dark fifth year: he falls afoul of the odious Professor Umbridge in his first classroom experience with her, and is punished with that Kafka-esque torture which we will be discussing in more detail in Chapter 9—the needle-writing that penetrates Harry's skin with its message of hatred and violent emotional toxicity. Here again, Harry has another remote-sensing encounter with Voldemort:

> She moved toward him, stretching out her short be-ringed fingers for his arm. And then, as she took hold of him to examine the words now cut into his skin, pain seared, not across the back of his hand, but across the scar on his forehead. At the same time, he had a most peculiar sensation somewhere around his midriff. (p. 275).

Once more, the trauma comes as pain and discomfort in both the head and the abdomen, as this new delusory influence grips him.

Umbridge is a truly demonic character: she evokes the image of the dutiful Nazi who practices torture as a mere form of bureaucracy. I was reminded of Hannah Arendt's well-known expression, "the banality of evil."[61] Indeed, Umbridge is merely a different kind of "Death Eater": a ponderous, two-dimensional bureaucrat with no other mission in life than to enforce a credo of oppression and ideological dehumanization, backed by the illusory power of the state and its inevitably hideous means of enforcement. Harry's deep physical response to her touch is the natural revulsion of true being to the icy illusion of Evil. If Voldemort, as has been suggested throughout this book, represents the vengeful, destructive gods of institutional religion who hungrily slaughter all those who retreat from the stinking breath of group-hatred, then Umbridge symbolizes the concomitant inner corruption and depravity of the State.

Harry's self-insight with respect to his empathic ability waxes and wanes over his time at Hogwarts: he recognizes, fairly early on, that he has a connection with Voldemort, and that it involves the ability to *read the consciousness of the moment*, rather than foretell the future. He is able to articulate this understanding in a conversation with Ron:

> Harry was thinking himself back. He had been looking into Umbridge's face...his scar had hurt...and he had had that odd feeling in his stomach...a strange, leaping feeling...a *happy* feeling...
> "Last time, it was because he was pleased," he said. "Really pleased. He thought...something good was going to happen. And the night before we came back to Hogwarts...he was furious."

> He looked around at Ron, who was gaping at him.
> "You could take over from Trelawney, mate," he said in an awed voice.
> "I'm not making prophecies," said Harry.
> "No, you know what you're doing?" Ron said, sounding both scared and impressed. "Harry, *you're reading You-Know-Who's mind...*"
> "No," said Harry, shaking his head. "It's more like...his mood, I suppose. I'm just getting flashes of what mood he's in...Dumbledore said something like this was happening last year...He said that when Voldemort was near me, or when he was feeling hatred, I could tell. Well, now I'm feeling it when he's pleased too..." (pp. 381-382)

This is very much like the workings of an oracle: while it *appears* to "divine the future," what is really happening when we use the *I Ching* or Tarot cards, for example, is that an *active consciousness of the present* is being read for us, but from a broader, more encompassing perspective than we can typically obtain from the position of individual awareness. To use an oracle is to obtain access to the natural magic within us, and to understand that what is so often deemed "mystical" or "paranormal" is really the expression of abilities that we all possess: remote sensing is simply an ordinary aspect of our animal nature.

So now we should emphasize that we are no longer in a realm of fantasy-magic in which charmed sticks are waved at objects, to make them fly or move or otherwise perform: the experience that we are now discussing is something that most of us have probably felt in our own lives and relationships, though we are also taught to rationalize or repress such experiences. Yet we can *feel* deeply when something about a situation, a relationship, or an anticipated encounter is wrong or ominous—when, to use Shakespeare's expression, "the time is out of joint." It cannot, however, be explained or accounted for on a rational level, because its promptings arise from whole-body senses that surpass the realm of mere intellect. Nevertheless, anyone who avows such feelings for what they truly are—transpersonal experiences of the consciousness of a person, group, or situation—is instantly labeled an attention-seeking fraud, or else pathologized with one or more of the brand-marks of conventional Western psychiatry ("derealization," "paranoid schizophrenia," "psychosis"). In her book *Fire in the Soul*, the psychologist Joan Borysenko provides some perspective on this clash between subjective experience and cultural conditioning:

> Data from studies conducted by the National Social Survey based at the University of Chicago indicate [that] visionary experiences are not the province of mentally ill people or misinformed, fanatical weirdos. Furthermore, they are not rare. Fully 35 percent of the American people have actually seen a vision—a dead relative, an angel, an apparition of light, an entire scene from another level of reality. Fearful of ridicule, a majority of these people keep their experiences to themselves...
>
> The general public is currently far more accepting of these experiences than my psychological and scientific colleagues are. Since visions and voices can also be symptoms of psychosis, in which a person is unable to separate everyday reality from hallucinations, there is certainly reason for caution. Visionary experiences, however, are quite different from psychotic hallucinations. Whereas psychosis usually leads to losing touch with this reality (not being able to tell what is real and what is imagined) and to dysfunctional behavior, transcendent visions lead to an expanded appreciation of this reality and to more adaptive, healthy behavior. (p. 38)

While Harry's experiences can hardly be called "transcendent" (in the sense of visionary or beatific), his psi abilities serve a positive purpose—they are the same talents that police departments have been known to call upon to help solve their most difficult cases. In general, Harry's experiences in this regard are not atypical of those heard in real-life accounts of people describing so-called "psychic" or transpersonal encounters. His capacity for reality-testing generally remains intact, even in those moments when his judgment is impaired; he is able to work through his feeling-visions in memory on a conceptual basis; he comes to a burgeoning understanding of both the challenges and the benefits of his gift; and he must of course endure the calumny of fools who brand him either a charlatan or a lunatic.

Thus, Harry develops a relationship with his ability, which might be termed a "gift/curse" relationship, somewhat on the plane of the more proverbial "love/hate" model. I have worked with empaths myself, and have seen and heard the same thing. Harry must find his way toward seeing this often physically painful, emotionally agonizing, and socially stigmatizing sensitivity as a *natural* gift, rather than as either the detritus of an evil branding or some special dispensation of Providence. A turning point in this path comes in his vision of an attack by Lord Voldemort's pet snake (named "Nagini", after "naga," the snake-symbol of immortality in Hindu mythology) upon Ron's father, Arthur Weasley. Harry has a dream in which he *becomes* this snake, and from within its body he has a direct, visceral experience of biting Mr. Weasley, as if with venomous fangs that were his own. Upon awakening, Harry instantly recognizes that this was not "just a nightmare," but a remote-seeing experience of an actual event, and so he raises the alarm. Fortunately, this is heard and understood by the adults of Harry's world (in this case, Professors McGonagall and Dumbledore), and action is taken to rescue Mr. Weasley and get him to the hospital. The emotional consequences of this event for Harry will lead us to a greater understanding of the meaning of empathic ability, but first we must take a closer look at the actual metaphor of this attack, for seeing the inter-relationship between the clairvoyant event and the perceiver will help us toward a fresh view of this ability, beyond the pale of the "gift/curse" dichotomy.

Voldemort's obsession, throughout the Potter stories, is with immortality.[62] It is an obsession that makes appearance into Reality. Voldemort accepts the lie that death is an ending, and the other falsehood that says unending physical life is eternal life. Thus, he is dragged further and further into the muck of delusion and failure. Since Harry is receiving the emanations of this demonic consciousness, he is led into depression and the neurotic outbursts of ego, to the point where he must re-learn each lesson that Dumbledore and the other teaching influences within the stories present him. We have already seen this process at work in the episode of the Mirror of Erised. In the fifth book, the situation is no different in kind, but becomes more complex in degree. Harry's connection to this twisted, stolen life force of Voldemort's undermines his true being, and takes him out of his center of inner gravity. We experience this in our own lives when we inadvertently or unquestioningly allow latent religious, cultural, or institutional commandments to influence us, distorting our self-perception and poisonously infecting our relationships with others.

The conflict-obsession that seems to define neurosis is itself fed by the emotional toxicity of guilt and self-blame. This, indeed, is exactly what Harry experiences in the aftermath of the attack on Arthur Weasley: he overhears the grownups talking about his vision, and the possibility that Harry is being possessed by Voldemort. One of them, Mad-Eye Moody, actually says, "there's something funny about the Potter kid, we all know that." (p. 491). From this point, it is a short but regressive step for Harry to arrive at the conclusion, "I am unclean":

> Was this why Dumbeldore would no longer meet Harry's eyes? Did he expect to see Voldemort staring out of them, afraid, perhaps, that their vivid green might turn suddenly to scarlet, with catlike slits for pupils? Harry remembered how the snakelike face of Voldemort had once forced itself out of the back of Professor Quirrell's head, and he ran his hand over the back of his own, wondering what it would feel like if Voldemort burst out of his skull.
>
> He felt dirty, contaminated, as though he were carrying some deadly germ, unworthy to sit on the underground train back from the hospital with decent, clean people whose minds and bodies were free of the taint of Voldemort. He had not merely seen the snake, he had *been* the snake, he knew it now. (p. 492)

"Dirty and contaminated" is *exactly* what Voldemort would want Harry to feel: this is the guilt that allows the Voldemort-consciousness of our culture to perpetuate and increase in power. It is the power of the unfounded accusation, couched in terms of Original Sin, Evil Nature, or the Dark Side of humanity—the disease whose truth-killing pathogens are always at hand, ready to spring and bite deep into the true self, whenever we should even *think* of disobeying or questioning the Commandments, Vows, Laws, or Statutes of religion or state. All have sinned, so all must be punished, and there is no more exquisite or Sisyphean punishment than guilt, for it is the pain that is recurrently applied through self-infliction; thus it is the very foundation of all punishment. Rowling's metaphor could hardly be more pointed than this, and she goes on to lead poor Harry through a positively inane logical argument, which goes from one ridiculous conclusion to another—all of it framed in the grimy plastic artifice of Guilt. The inner dialog runs as follows: Voldemort must be seeking followers through the means of possession; he is after a secret weapon that is contained in the Ministry's Department of Mysteries; I (Harry) am the weapon (here Rowling adds that "it was as though poison were pumping through his veins"); Voldemort is an animagus and that's how he can possess me, transport me to remote places and use me to complete his evil plan.

Even as this absurd argument courses through him, Harry is vaguely aware of its madness, yet not enough to return to a clear center of perception; therefore, he makes a decision that many people come to when under the intolerable burden of guilt—he decides to run away. In making this decision, he recapitulates the insidious dogma of the culture he was raised in: the burden of guilt leads us to condemn and renounce ourselves, just as a certain couple did when they allowed themselves to be expelled from Paradise because one of them had eaten an apple. Fortunately for Harry, a figure in a magical painting—Phineas Nigellus, of the supposedly-evil Slytherin house—is there to help. In a comical dialog, Phineas feeds Harry's fallacious logic right back to him in the form of mildly acidic satire: "Oh, I *see*, this is no cowardly flight—you are being *noble*." He then peremptorily delivers a message from Dumbledore—"stay where you are"—and departs with a curmudgeonly dismissal: "I have better things to do than to listen to adolescent agonizing." (pp. 495-496).

Yet Dumbledore, through Phineas, is only able to keep Harry from *physically* fleeing his guilt; otherwise, "the feeling of being unclean intensified," and Harry retreats into isolation, as many people do when their deepest and most reliable intuitions have been demonized as madness or charlatanism, their true selves stung with the poisoned darts of guilt and blame.

For Harry, the solution is simple, direct, and rejuvenating: the arrival of feminine, or feeling-energy, to re-awaken a sense of clarity. Hermione arrives to draw Harry out of his self-absorbed, monastic seclusion in the attic at Grimmauld Place, and to prepare the ground for a renewal: she has prepared a setting replete with food, warmth, and non-judgmental, loving companionship—in short, the energies of Earth itself. Ron's sister, Ginny, completes this restorative gathering of feminine influences, and provides the crucial insight that opens Harry's understanding (she has been herself possessed by Voldemort in a previous story, and thus is able to prove to him, based on the contrast between their experiences, that Harry has not been possessed). This feminine presence is able to patiently endure, yet firmly expose, Harry's false self-imagery and his toxic emotional noise, until the work of insight has been completed. Lao Tzu speaks of the healing influence of this type of energy throughout his *Tao Te Ching*, perhaps most lyrically in Chapter 28:

> Acknowledge the masculine
> And be one with the feminine:
> Let the river of your being flow
> Into the valley of eternal Nature.
>
> The path of Modesty is true and complete:
> Ever returning to the origin,
> As a child returns to its mother.
>
> Acknowledge the white,
> But trust in the black:
> Let Nature be the mold
> Into which you pour
> The liquid energy of your being.
>
> Let Modesty guide you;
> Perseveringly return to the Source
> Of limitless serenity.
>
> Be aware of your influence,

> Yet act from humility:
> Let your action be drawn from
> The valley's fertile depths,
> And Modesty will be furthered.
>
> Returning to your perfect nature,
> You may be shaped and arrayed—
> Honed to a sparse and simple beauty.
>
> Thus do the Sage and the Cosmic energies
> Create completion and fulfillment—
> Not through division and reduction—
> But through transformation.

To complete this metaphorical picture of the feminine influence in healing our inner wounds and clearing the taint of false belief, it should be added that this all happens at Christmas time, and thus represents another "solstice moment" for Harry (see Chapter 6, "The Cloak and the Mirror"): the day of the longest darkness is followed upon immediately by the arrival of increasing light and the promise of spring and its feminine principle of transformation through birth and growth. In the *I Ching*, the month of the Solstice is represented by Hexagram 2, *K'un*, which is variously translated as "Earth" or "Nature."

The common-sense, feeling-oriented resolution provided by the feminine energy of Hermione and Ginny is soon afforded its contrast in the decidedly "masculine," or manipulative plan that is presented next to Harry as a means of understanding and managing his empathic abilities. This solution comes to Harry through lessons in "Occlumency" with Professor Snape. It is designed to provide protection against the destructive encroachment of malevolent consciousness; but Harry has already experienced a far more natural and effective protection against such dangers, in the magical web of light that forms around him during his graveyard-encounter with Voldemort at the climax of the fourth book. But Occlumency is merely a contrived and artificial response to a threat or challenge: Snape describes it as the "branch of magic [that] seals the mind against magical intrusion and influence."[63] It is an absurdly impractical stratagem, which involves "closing the mind," "emptying oneself of emotion," and "stopping thoughts." It also appears to involve physical pain, to judge by Harry's actual experience of Occlumency.

In all, Occlumency is not unlike certain spiritual practices or meditation techniques that are taught among various disciplines, both religious and secular, all fed by the bizarre belief that inner life should be forced, painful, expensive in terms of both one's time and money, damned-near impossible from a practical standpoint, and always rigidly disciplined. I would like to encourage all who read this, that if you are ever approached by any guru, master, priest, shaman, or self-professed spiritual teacher with a message that meditation is about stopping thought, stilling emotion, and enduring physical pain, just briskly turn about and run away, and don't look back. More people have been driven off from what is truly a natural and healing activity of one's whole being, just because some fraud has filled them with such horsefeathers about using "discipline" to stop up the mind.

Snape brings to Occlumency the same error in orientation that underlies his approach to his principal subject, Potions. In his opening address to the first-year Potions class in Book One, Snape praises "the delicate power of liquids that creep through human veins, bewitching the mind, ensnaring the senses." (Professor Snape is obviously not aware of the epidemic problems created in our Muggle world by such mind-numbing "potions" among alcoholics and drug addicts.) He carries this cursory understanding to the problem of successfully managing empathic ability: Occlumency, he explains, involves the capacity to close one's mind and feelings to external penetration, though he does a very poor job of further explaining how this is practically accomplished, except through the inflexible rigors of what he calls "discipline." As an illustration, Snape describes how "Legilimency," which is the soul-reading capacity of Lord Voldemort that infects Harry in his dreams and visions, is combated through Occlumency:

> The Dark Lord, for instance, almost always knows when somebody is lying to him. Only those skilled at Occlumency are able to shut down those feelings and

memories that contradict the lie, and so utter falsehoods in his presence without detection. (p. 531)[64]

Harry's response to this is inner retreat: "Whatever Snape said, Legilimency sounded like mind reading to Harry and he did not like the sound of it at all." It is an appropriate response which, in our world, is reinforced by experience and study: it is well known that sociopaths are almost always able to "pass" (i.e., fool) lie detector tests, and of course, deceive people. Clearly, neither we nor Harry are being asked to perceive our natural empathic abilities in the context of a sociopathic tendency; nor can we be expected to experience inner life through stopping thought, drowning emotion, or submitting to the absurd rigidity of mind-control or "mental discipline." Empathic feeling, or "psi" ability, cannot be successfully stopped, discarded, or refuted, any more than it can be flaunted or displayed.[65]

In spite of the rather superficial approach that Snape brings to Occlumency, there is some practical value in a little of his teaching.[66] He instructs Harry that having empathic abilities is not "mind reading":

> "The mind is not a book, to be opened at will and examined at leisure. Thoughts are not etched on the inside of skulls, to be perused by any invader." (p. 530)

This is actually a helpful insight, which counters the popular belief that clairvoyance, remote seeing, and telepathy are all about "reading others' minds" or "seeing into the future." The ability to sense the feelings and attitudes of others is not a key to their deepest, most private selves, nor does it present a deterministic picture of someone's future behavior. What it does show us is how a person's (or a group's) consciousness is directed and arrayed at the moment, in terms of their intentions (malevolent or helpful), the presence of any hidden agenda, positive emanations that we may constructively engage in a relationship with them, the relative trustworthiness of the person or group, and whether their attitude in general is influenced by ego or by receptivity. To be sure, such empathic sensing of another may *seem* to reveal (and, retrospectively, to have predicted) future behavior or the outcome of a situation; but this is more a reflection or sense of the rigidity of the other person's attitude than of any foresight that the empath may be presumed to possess.

This one useful piece of instruction from Professor Snape provides Harry, and us, with insight that can lead toward a more balanced understanding of empathic ability. As I suggested earlier, we are not meant to look upon psi abilities as special gifts endowed to only a few, nor as curses visited upon us by a malevolent or indifferent Cosmos: they are simply meant to be understood as natural abilities that we all are born with, though they may vary in their particular form or direction according to the individual personality. They are gifts that have been given to us to be used but not displayed; trusted but not idolized; shared but not broadcast; kept confidential but not repressed.

As his fifth year progresses, Harry gradually discovers that others have empathic abilities, and that he is not alone after all. He finds that Hermione, Ginny, Luna Lovegood, and of course Professor Dumbledore have certain abilities that involve the inner sensation of consciousness coming from people, animals, or objects in their environment.[67] This recognition, combined with the gratifying realization that his vision had almost undoubtedly saved a man's life, brings Harry to a certain poised, if wavering acceptance of his gift, though to the very end of the story he falls just short of making that further step of understanding—in part, because he must also come to associate the gift with the death of his godfather. Whether and to what extent it must be ascribed to youth, pride, impulsiveness, the deceit of others, inexperience, the lack of an appropriate teaching presence, or to the destructive effect of Voldemort's consciousness, Harry is led to the error that brings him the greatest pain that has so far occurred to him since his entry into the wizarding world.

Harry's final dream of *The Order of the Phoenix* occurs during a slumber that overtakes him in the midst of a tiresome examination in "History of Magic". In this dream, he sees Voldemort torturing Harry's godfather, Sirius Black, within the Department of Mysteries corridor that has been the scene of many of the dreams to this point. He instantly and impulsively assumes that this dream, like the one in which Arthur Weasley was bitten by the snake, is a remote seeing of an event that is actually occurring in the present moment. He arrives at this conclusion in spite of the fact that Snape had warned him, during his Occlumency training, that Voldemort could likely be plotting to send him a false vision based on whatever knowledge he could obtain of Harry's emotional weaknesses; in spite of the differing features of this dream (Harry is a witness rather than the surrogate agent of the action); and in spite of Hermione's own intuition that this dream was not truly representative of a real event, and her warning against surrendering to ego's hero-impulse. In short, he acts without clarity, and there is no trusted adult available to balance his impulse with insight.[68] This leads him into the flight to London and the battle scene at the Department of Mysteries, in which Sirius is killed. The fight ends with an encounter between Dumbledore and Voldemort, in which the latter is put to flight, while several of his followers are left behind and captured.

Before he flees, Voldemort makes one last attempt at spiritual occupation: he (or his snake) possesses Harry and challenges Dumbledore to kill them both. Like many who have reached the limit of their endurance with the toxic soul-infection of institutional evil, Harry wishes death upon himself, and lovingly longs for a reunion with his dead godfather. As soon as this loving thought desire for the return to the Origin arises within him, Harry is freed—Voldemort cannot abide for a moment that consciousness which Rumi called "the longing for union with the Beloved." Once it is over, Harry is magically transported back to Hogwarts, to the safety and quiet of Dumbledore's office. But as soon as he arrives and has a moment to reflect, Harry is assailed with grief and guilt that exceed any torment he has ever felt before:

> It was his fault that Sirius had died; it was all his fault. If he, Harry, had not been stupid enough to fall for Voldemort's trick, if he had not been so convinced that what he had seen in his dream was real, if he had only opened his mind to the possibility that Voldemort was, as Hermione had said, banking on Harry's *love of playing the hero*.... (pp. 820-821)

How disabling guilt can be in the presence of grief! How easily is it transmuted into hatred—often against those whom we have the least reason to hate. Harry instantly and overwhelmingly feels the gnawing, leaden poison of this immense inner burden:

> The guilt filling the whole of Harry's chest like some monstrous, weighty parasite now writhed and squirmed. Harry could not stand this, he could not stand being Harry anymore. He had never felt more trapped inside his own head and body, never wished so intensely that he could be somebody—anybody—else. (p. 822)

Then, he turns on Dumbledore in a writhing fury, until he is destroying his office. At last, he attempts to escape, but Dumbledore has locked the door and will not let him out. Nothing at all will freeze Harry's guilt-driven rage until Dumbledore clearly and courageously shares the blame for the death of Sirius Black. This admission alone stops Harry, and causes him to listen.

> "You see," continued Dumbledore heavily, "I believed that it could not be long before Voldemort attempted to force his way into your mind, to manipulate and misdirect your thoughts, and I was not eager to give him more incentives to do so. I was sure that if he realized that our relationship was—or ever had been—closer than that of headmaster and pupil, he would seize his chance to use you as a means to spy on me. I feared the uses to which he would put you, the possibility that he might try and possess you...On those rare occasions when we had close contact, I thought I saw a shadow of him stir behind your eyes. I was trying, in distancing myself from you, to protect you." (pp. 827-828)

This is the first step in the long process of healing to follow for Harry. After his interview with Dumbledore, other inner windows of understanding and acceptance are opened for him—in the encounter with the mascot-ghost of his school house, and again in a brief conversation with Luna Lovegood.[69] These discussions open his awareness, first to the possibility that death is not the ultimate termination that Voldemort assumes it to be; and second, that there are other people, spirits, and animals in this world who feel and have suffered, and that some of them can share with us in the mistakes and the pain that can accompany even our most precious and natural inner abilities. It is this sense of community that Harry takes into the summer with him; it is this that will support him in his continuing grief, as he realizes in silently bidding his friends good-bye at the train station:

> Harry nodded. He somehow could not find words to tell them what it meant to him, to see them all ranged there, on his side. Instead he smiled, raised a hand in farewell, turned around, and led the way out of the station...(p. 870)

Unlocking the Black Door: Nurturing Communication on the Inner Plane of Being

It is the kind of experience that all of us have had—many of us quite frequently: we happen to be thinking of someone, and soon the phone or the doorbell rings (okay, now the "you have mail" guy's voice might come out of your computer, too). Or you may feel, from quite a distance, that someone is looking at you, or sense an oncoming conflict well before it becomes manifest. Or you may have a positively visceral, synchronous feeling-moment with another, which is later confirmed as to its mutual timing and depth. Of course, it's a theme with countless variations, yet many of us remain closed to the signals that such ordinary events of the life of natural magic are sending us, or we rationalize them away with the dull knife of logic. "What a coincidence!" we may cry out, but there is little further reflection beyond that momentary exclamation. Still, for all but those who are inexorably locked into a reductionistic view of life, the teaching presence of the Cosmic Reality continues to tap softly and regularly at the door of consciousness, as it did for Carl Jung:

> The problem of synchronicity has puzzled me for a long time, ever since I was investigating the phenomena of the collective unconscious and kept on coming across connections which I simply could not explain as chance grouping or 'runs.' What I found were 'coincidences' which were connected so meaningfully that their 'chance' concurrence would represent a degree of improbability that would have to be expressed by an astronomical figure....I do not imagine for a moment that this will induce anybody who is determined to regard such things as pure 'chance' to change his mind...[yet] meaningful coincidences usually present themselves in practical life.
> —from "Synchronicity: An Acausal Connecting Principle" (CW 8, pars. 843-5).

Jung attempted to "explain" what he called synchronicity, and to tie it into various psychological and scientific theories; perhaps you would not be surprised to learn that the effort was, in effect, rather self-defeating. The hard-soled boots of logic tend to slip amid the watery substance of our feeling-senses; yet that doesn't imply that the two are naturally incompatible. Wherever we perceive and use these elements of the psyche as equals, we will find that the natural footwear of our cerebral cortex is very well adapted to a watery environment. So the first step to take in nurturing our "psi abilities" is to bring Reason down from its pedestal and invite it into the welcoming company of our physical, intuitive, and feeling senses.

Returning to the world of Hogwarts, we have seen how Hermione Granger was able to discover and nurture this harmony between her intellectual gift and her feeling-nature. Over the course of the five stories, Hermione finds that Reason serves practical ends that further life and promote inner growth, when it is allowed to work cooperatively with intuition and sensation. Hermione's magic is a way of accomplishment, in which intellect dances with the other aspects of her psyche—here following, there leading—always, however, in a position of mutual balance and equality. What we have called "natural magic" in this book is simply the transformative effect of that dance amid those aspects of the psyche that are so often divided in the hierarchical paradigms of religious, scientific, and cultural ideologies. Here, then, is a meditation, offered to assist you in restoring the balance and unity of your body-mind. It is adapted from a Taoist practice that I learned at the Healing Tao Center of New York City.[70]

Prepare yourself as you've learned to do from the meditations in the previous chapters—in a quiet place, settling yourself into a position that allows you both comfort and the inner alertness of relaxed attention. Now focus your awareness on your heart, and see if you can feel its energy—the rhythm of its systole and diastole, the feeling of its regular movement. Then, let that feeling merge into an image of an energy-pulse of whatever color or shape seems natural to you, and once the image has become alive to your awareness, gently begin to direct it downward through your abdomen, as a pouring stream of light that moves from your heart through your abdominal organs. As it descends, note how its glow vibrates omni-directionally within and around your body; feel it now enter your pelvic floor, pass under and through your genitals as it sends light-pulses into your legs. Now feel this stream move into your lower back and begin to rise up and around the spine, ascending like an energy-thermometer. Let it rise as quickly or as slowly as necessary for you to feel its presence touching each segment of your spine and vibrating with a pulse that can be felt in your kidneys, back muscles, lungs, shoulders, and spreading out into your arms. Now it ascends into the back of your neck and through the top of your head, over into your forebrain. Perhaps it pauses there, rests, gathers itself, and then begins its descent back toward your heart—passing through the brain, where its energy-stream joins the forebrain, midbrain, caudate brain in the back of your neck, and pours downward, back into your chest and heart. Take this tour of your body-being two or three times again, and then rest in the regenerative energy that this practice has brought you.

When you've finished this meditation and are ready to reflect on the experience, ask yourself whether you had any sense of division or hierarchical relationship between your heart, abdominal organs, spine, forebrain, or caudate brain. Try to remember whether any awareness of the "right brain/left brain" division occurred to you during the meditation (this persistent cultural prejudice remains one of the more obdurate "New Age" distortions inspired by various scientific half-truths; it is a misunderstanding that is being gradually dispersed, in part with the help of new research findings from neurobiology). Recall how each area of your being felt or "looked" as you directed your heart-energy stream through it: if a particular organ or inner space appeared blotched, out-of-balance, or disproportionately large or small, note that sense to yourself. When you come to try the meditation again, first ask for help from the helping energy of the Cosmos in correcting the imbalance; then see how you experience that same area. Most people who have tried this meditation have found that after a few repetitions, they are led to an experience of increasing balance, clarity, and a sense of unity and equality amid the various aspects of being as "body-mind" or "heart-mind." In addition, when it is done while lying down, this meditation is an excellent sleep-aid for those who have occasional difficulty with insomnia.

In the context of the topic of this chapter, this meditation is meant to nurture and promote our sensitivity to our feeling-nature and its ability to provide us with information that the physical senses or intellectual capacities in isolation cannot. So as you continue with this practice (which will take all of about ten to twenty minutes of your time each day), note to yourself any "odd feelings" that seem to lead you to a helping coincidence, or any fresh awareness of the moods or presence of others around you that you had missed or overlooked before. See whether your dreams become clearer and more easily recalled, and if any flashes of insight or recognition occur to you that had been lost or repressed before you began this practice. Such insights arise from the awakening of previously dormant natural senses that you have always had. You may find yourself recalling similar sensations from childhood, and even how such experiences were "trained out of you" by the forces of cultural conditioning, or else simply rationalized in a kind of pseudo-scientific prattle. If any such recollections occur to you, follow them to their source, and devote one or two meditation sessions to saying a firm inner No to the rationalizations and their source. The perseverance of mild effort in this practice is all that is being asked of you: after a few weeks' worth of exercising your inner senses, you will find yourself rewarded with an awakening that is the regenerative and self-renewing energy of natural magic.

Chapter 9: The Ministry of Magic: Bureaucracy and Other Ideologies of Fear

> They were standing at one end of a very long and splendid hall with a highly polished, dark wood floor. The peacock-blue ceiling was inlaid with gleaming golden-symbols that were continually moving and changing like some enormous heavenly notice board. The walls on each side were paneled in shiny dark wood and had many gilded fireplaces set into them...Halfway down the hall was a fountain. A group of golden statues, larger than life-size, stood in the middle of a circular pool. Tallest of them all was a noble-looking wizard...Grouped around him were a beautiful witch, a centaur, a goblin, and a house-elf. The last three were all looking adoringly up at the witch and wizard. Glittering jets of water were flying from the ends of the two wands, the point of the centaur's arrow, the tip of the goblin's hat, and each of the house-elf's ears. — *Harry Potter and the Order of the Phoenix*, Chapter 7

Harry Potter has arrived for a disciplinary hearing before the "Wizengamot," a sort of Supreme Court of the wizarding government, or Ministry of Magic. He is being prosecuted for practicing wizardry as a minor performing magic outside of school, although his offense seems perfectly defensible (two weeks earlier, he had magically repelled an attack by two dementors on himself and his Muggle cousin, Dudley). Yet he has been suspended from school and threatened with expulsion on these grounds; it is under this dark cloud of litigation that he first encounters the opulent hallways of the Ministry of Magic.

Up to the point in the Potter series, Ms. Rowling has portrayed the Ministry of Magic in gradually more severe tones, beginning with the blunderingly benign government of the first book, continuing with the more alarming misjudgments of its functionaries in the second and third stories, and into the profile of outright corruption that begins to appear in the fourth.[71] To be sure, Harry's mentor, Professor Dumbledore, is often seen clashing with the Ministry and its predilection for interfering in the affairs of the school, often under the sway of money and influence. But here, in the fifth book, the pretense of the Ministry's purposes and agenda is finally blown clean off, and Rowling's trenchant perspective on the monumental architecture of the institutional ego is drawn with an alarmingly modern clarity.

The primary impression of the Ministry's capitol building (which, interestingly, is underground) is formed through the many references to its preening, glaring opulence. Here, the hyperbole is obviously intentional: the ceiling is "gleaming golden"; the walls "shiny...gilded"; the floor "highly polished"; the statue "golden and glittering." Thus is the metaphorical façade of the institutional ego: it is the artifice of excess that lures the individual into its ideological snare, while averting attention from the inner reality of its lurking depravity.

But Harry gets a dose, full in the face, of both aspects: his subsequent hearing takes place in a dungeon set deep in the bowels of the Ministry, far below the sparkling dome of the Capitol. Once he is presented with the punitive face of the government of his adopted world, Harry finds himself in a place with "walls made of dark stone, dimly lit by torches," where "many shadowy figures" loom over him in the glowering mists above, their voices cold and condemning, their collective visage imperially distant. It suddenly seems as if Harry has stumbled into the midst of Hate Week in Oceania—and the Orwellian parallel extends itself throughout the remainder of *Harry Potter and the Order of the Phoenix*. These two aspects of the Ministry reflect the description of the collective ego, given by Carol Anthony and Hanna Moog in their book, *I Ching: The Oracle of the Cosmic Way*:

> The collective ego has set itself up in competition with the Cosmos, both in its visible and invisible aspects. Through this competition, it has created a parallel reality, which like the Cosmos, also has visible and invisible sides. The invisible side of the parallel reality is the negative consciousness called 'the demonic sphere of consciousness'. It is negative because in every way its ideas negate the Cosmic Reality. It is demonic inasmuch as every false work, image, and idea takes on a demonic form

in a person's psyche. These forms can be seen in meditation, dreams, and the fantasized reality that occurs in schizophrenia....The visible side of the parallel reality consists of the institutions that are based on the collective ego's concepts, and those natural social forms that it has turned to its purposes...[which] include the family, community, nation, and cultural institutions in whatever ways they are devoted to serving the ideas and purposes of the parallel reality.[72]

Like every false construction of empty display, the "parallel reality" separates us from our spontaneous, inborn connection with Nature, while it infects us with the slime of its soft underbelly—the "demonic sphere of consciousness" and its negative view of life and humankind. This "collective ego" arises from certain fears and forced vanities that are in turn perpetuated by a warped belief in the insufficiency of our natural self to live successfully. The physical and ideological architecture of such beliefs, and the systems built from them, "costs more than it comes to," as Thoreau points out in *Walden*:

> A simple and independent mind does not toil at the bidding of any prince. Genius is not a retainer to any emperor, nor is its material silver, or gold, or marble, except to a trifling extent. To what end, pray, is so much stone hammered? Nations are possessed with an insane ambition to perpetuate the memory of themselves by the amount of hammered stone they leave. What if equal pains were taken to smooth and polish their manners? One piece of good sense would be more memorable than a monument as high as the moon.[73]

The natural equipment we are given to live our lives will be found more than adequate to its purpose, if we will but allow it the freedom from trumped-up notions of forced order, power, and institutional affiliation. Like Lao Tzu, Thoreau advocated poetically for a life of separation from the monumentalism of institutional excess—in thought, speech, material possessions, and spiritual life. He concluded that when it comes to the institutional ego, "the mainspring is vanity," in the sense of excess. As have we earlier observed[74], it is excess that feeds the collective ego, that drags its minions further into the mire of delusion.

In Harry Potter's world, this influence of excess is portrayed in the characters most frequently associated with the Ministry. Cornelius Fudge, the Minister of Magic from the first five Potter stories, is described as a corpulent, anxious, distracted sort of fellow, who is often seen dressed in a ridiculous agglomeration of cheap opulence, rather in the manner of a used car salesman. There is a superficial, preening quality to the appearance of many of his hangers-on, as well—the character of Percy Weasley, brother of Harry's best friend at school, is an example of this. Then there is the bloated, prissy, absurd, but dangerous toad-like figure of Dolores Umbridge, who eventually attempts, and temporarily succeeds at, a takeover of the administration of Hogwarts School, while styling herself (in a chilling medieval analogy) as "High Inquisitor." In her, Harry will find the "demonic sphere of consciousness" described by Anthony and Moog, joined with its repressive institutional mask.

Attributes of the Ministry of Magic (and other fear-based institutions)

Throughout Book Five, Rowling delivers for us a rigorous portrait of the collective ego and the forces that manipulate its ideologies and institutions. It may be worth reviewing the attributes of the Ministry of Magic as we find it in this novel, for that will likely lead us toward a strategy for freeing ourselves from the influence of similarly repressive ideologies as may be found in our Muggle world.

The Ministry exists in a realm of opposition, which continually leads it into false judgment. In the second of the Potter books, *Harry Potter and the Chamber of Secrets*, Harry is blamed when Dobby the elf practices magic at Privet Drive. Later in that story, Fudge sends Hagrid to prison on a vague suspicion based on racist prejudice and misinformation. In the third book, *Harry Potter and the Prisoner of Azkaban*, the Ministry again issues a false conviction—this time against an animal, the hippogriff Buckbeak; and then it persists in attempting to execute Sirius Black, even after testimony in support of his innocence is heard. This kind of repetitive error arises from the "you're either with us or you're against us" mentality that is characteristic of the institutional ego. In our time, it can be seen in the division of nations among the "coalition of the willing" and the "axis of evil."

It is, of course, easier to divide every issue along the dichotomy of opposition, and act accordingly. But we live in a time when, as Professor Dumbledore would say, we need to choose what is right over what is easy. Yet to the institutional mindset, there is no greater good than action—no matter how rash, ill considered, predatory, or falsely grounded—to act is to evade the exposure that reflection would otherwise provide. Thus, Emerson complained that "people are diseased with the theological problems of original sin, origin of evil, predestination, and the like...We are full of these superstitions of sense, the worship of magnitude. We call the poet inactive, because he is not a president, a merchant, or a porter. We adore an institution, and do not see that it is founded on a thought which we have." Then he offers us an alternative perspective, that "real action is in silent moments...I will not meanly decline the immensity of good, because I have heard that it has come to others in another shape."[75]

The Ministry is comprised of a forced, rigidly layered hierarchy of bureaucratic forms, departments, and titles. Throughout the Potter series, Rowling gleefully lampoons the bureaucratic aspect of the collective ego, in her portrayal of the labyrinthine nesting of departments and functionaries. In reading of the "Improper Use of Magic Office" or the "Misuse of Muggle Artifacts" department, one is reminded of the "Ministry of Silly Walks" of the Monty Python program. In Chapter 7 of the fifth book, this keelhauling of the bureaucratic is brought to an amusing apotheosis in Harry's elevator ride through the Ministry (which, in an evocation of Lewis Carroll, goes to higher-numbered floors as it descends). At each stop, a disembodied female voice announces the proximity of such entities as the "Official Gobstones Club," "Ludicrous Patents Office," the "Broom Regulatory Control," the "Department of International Magical Cooperation" (a swipe at the U.N. or the E.U.?), the "Pest Advisory Bureau," and "the International

Magical Trading Standards Body" (WTO? World Bank?).

The author also rakes the very concept of hierarchy, emphatically noting how incompetence and ranking are discovered to be in direct proportion within the collective ego's institutional forms. Fudge, the Minister of Magic, is a doddering fool who obtained his post only because another high official lost the appointment when his adolescent son was discovered to be a criminal, in league with Voldemort. Fudge's inner circle is comprised of petty, vindictive, power-drunk functionaries, and it is only in the relatively lower echelons of the Ministry's organizational structure that one finds any semblance of competence or humanity.

The portrayal of the Ministry and its drones strikes a blow at the very foundation of the pedestal of institutional hierarchy. The proof of this is to be found in the contrasting social structures to the Ministry that she offers. The first of these alternatives is the "Order of the Phoenix" itself, a grassroots-style, community-oriented, and loosely structured social order, which has been formed to provide defense for the wizarding nation and its moribund and decadent official government. The Order of the Phoenix is comprised, in part, of a falsely-convicted criminal (Sirius Black); a variety of social outcasts which includes a werewolf (Lupin); a pair of half-giants (Hagrid and his consort, Madame Maxime); a paranoid neurotic (Mad-Eye Moody); and a common thief (Mundungus). The Order is firmly but fluidly led by Dumbledore, but otherwise there is no discernible hierarchy among its members.

The second of these alternatives to the Ministry forms spontaneously at the school, as a reaction to the incompetence of the Ministry-appointed teacher; this gathering is called "Dumbledore's Army," and is comprised of a small and diverse assemblage of students who wish to truly learn their art—through experience rather than arid theory. These spontaneous and mutually supportive social structures represent Rowling's depiction of what Anthony and Moog describe as the "natural social order:"

> The existence of a natural social order is neither a myth nor an ideal. It can be seen to exist in certain

situations, as when shock causes individuals' egos to temporarily freeze. The natural social order is more obvious when shocking events occur on a large scale, such as in wars, earthquakes, etc. It emerges when people are temporarily free of the egos within them. Then they relate heart-to-heart as they spontaneously see and respond to each other's needs. (pp. 54-55)

The Ministry deals in a cult of self-imagery, which is fed by the strategies of misinformation and manipulation. Rowling is a writer with an acute awareness of the problem of self-images, particularly group self-images. In the trial scene referred to above, she carefully portrays a monumentalized group self-image, and then just as meticulously exposes its shadowy reality. We are referring, of course, to the maudlin statue in the main hallway of the Ministry, with its gilded human figures and the adulatory "sub-humans" beneath them. This statue is not just a representative self-glorification of wizard-kind, but of *humankind*, as is most tellingly clarified in the account of the denouement to Harry's hearing. After he is cleared (thanks to the intervention of Dumbledore, who appears with the only eyewitness to the incident under investigation), Harry encounters Lucius Malfoy in the company of the Minister. Only Harry and Malfoy know the latter's true identity as a member of Voldemort's inner circle—to Fudge, Malfoy is a source of money and influence, the magical equivalent of a corporate PAC leader. Harry can sense that Malfoy is there for no other purpose than to weaken the Ministry by softening its leader with money and lies. But there is nothing to be done about it for the moment; even in the aftermath of his triumph at the hearing, Harry is filled with revulsion at this appearance of the man whom he had last seen in a graveyard, cheering while Voldemort tortured Harry. So, with this emotional background laid, Rowling takes Harry back into the hallway, before that statue, and the self-image of the Ministry is chillingly exposed:

> He looked up into the handsome wizard's face, but up close, Harry thought he looked rather weak and foolish. The witch was wearing a vapid smile like a beauty contestant, and from what Harry knew of goblins and

centaurs, they were most unlikely to be caught staring this soppily at humans of any description. (p. 156)

Much later in the story, that statue will be physically blown to pieces in the final battle between Voldemort and Dumbledore; but in this early scene, it is far more effectively destroyed through reflection. Harry's contemplation of the statue is a more potent demolition of the group-image than any physical act. When we monumentalize our species, our race, our nation, our religion, our social ideology and its human figureheads, then we expose ourselves to the only kind of death worth fearing—the death that comes from the rotting away of our true nature from within, in which we are destroyed from our core by the parasitic legions of ego's superficial and delusory abstractions.

Since a cult of self-imagery is misinformation against oneself, it leads inevitably to a parallel cult of misinformation against others—whenever we are false to ourselves, the lie will be projected onto the world around us. In the case of supporting a group self-image, such as is commonly seen in government, this manifests itself in the manipulation of the press. Throughout the fourth and fifth books of the Potter series, Rowling lets loose some of her most scathing satire upon the press and its cloying servility towards government. It really is delightful: for this aspect of her work alone, Rowling's books deserve to be read and enjoyed. Though we might, on a cursory reading, mistake the hilarious character of Rita Skeeter, prominent in the fourth book, for a mere gossip columnist, there is no mistaking the broader scope of Mrs. Rowling's satire in the fifth book. The primary voice of the wizarding press, the "Daily Prophet" newspaper, is quickly revealed to have been spending the summer holidays spreading malicious "reports" on the psychotic delirium affecting Harry and Dumbledore, and it only gets worse from there. Finally, Rowling shows the Daily Prophet reveling in the creation of the "Hogwarts High Inquisitor"—an appointment which provides "the Minister with on-the-ground feedback about what's really happening at Hogwarts." (p. 307). As if this blast isn't enough, Rowling later inserts the phrase "fair and objective" into the newspaper's account of this development, in a pointed barb at a modern multi-billion dollar News Corporation particularly well known to American television viewers, but also quite infamous in Britain as well.

The Ministry enforces uniformity through a ritualization of language and behavior. Is any group of workers more renowned for its universal sense of resigned misery and plodding, monotonic conformity than government employees? Rowling has fun with this as well: amid the description of the glorious statue in the hallway, she finally notes the presence of the people arriving for work—hundreds of them—"wearing glum, early-morning looks."(p. 127). But what else can be expected of people who have turned over their individual autonomy to a group juggernaut? As we have observed several times throughout this book, our language leads us inwardly, determining our behavior, our moods, and our sense of self. If we express ourselves in the formulaic drone of a vocabulary of conformity, then we will find that there is nothing personal to speak of—except perhaps the weather. All our natural creativity, spontaneity, and feeling are smothered under a mountain of gray verbiage. The repression becomes so complete that it comically warps the most basic elements of human communication: observe the language of the official letter of expulsion that Harry originally receives after the incident with the dementors:

> The severity of this breach of the Decree for the Reasonable Restriction of Underage Sorcery has resulted in your expulsion from Hogwarts School...Ministry representatives will be calling on your place of residence shortly to destroy your wand...As you have already received an official warning for a previous offense under section 13 of the International Confederation of Wizards' Statute of Secrecy, we regret to inform you that your presence is required at a disciplinary hearing at the Ministry of Magic...
> Hoping you are well,
> Yours sincerely...
> (pp. 26-27)

Note as well the message being imparted amid this arid formality: when you are separated from a group, from any collective body, you are not merely deprived of your membership, but *of your identity*. Harry is not only told that he is no longer a student, but no longer a wizard; but he is to take comfort in the fact that the poisonous punishment of expulsion is served up with the stiff pleasantry of institutionalism.

This attitude is repeated, though rather more grimly, in the "educational decrees" of Dolores Umbridge, the Ministry mole at Hogwarts, and again as she applies her needle-writing torture to Harry's hand—she speaks to him in an archaic, feudal moralism of banal oppression. Like so much of the language of government, it deals in shapeless formulae of expression stripped of human feeling.

The Ministry locks people into cubicles of specialization. This is more than a parable on the physical boxes of corporate life or the stuff of Dilbert comic strips; this is about the *inner compartmentalizing of human beings*.[76] Yes, the employees at the Ministry are stuffed into cramped offices, with desks overwhelmed by paperwork and minutiae (even the crowded elevators fill at every stop with magically flying memoranda); but Rowling pays equal attention to the claustrophobia that overtakes the *inner* lives of those subjected to the bureaucratic enslavement known as specialization.

For the employees of the Ministry, work is no longer a vocation; it becomes an indentured compulsion. The effects are seen in the shallow characters that move through the Ministry, and also in the fates to which they are often led. In the fourth book, the cold, official zealot, Barty Crouch, descends to madness and death after his son becomes a murderer and his wife a suicide; in the fifth book, young Percy Weasley willfully divorces his loving family when he marries himself to his official ambition and adherence to the collective. How many marriages have been undermined, how many families dispersed, how many lives ruined, through someone's obsessive affiliation to a job or a company, and his willing submission to its claims upon his inner truth?

The Ministry condemns and attacks anyone outside its narrow boundaries of belief. As noted earlier, an institutional ideology will accept no challenge from without, nor even a modest course of questioning; thus the Ministry attacks and demonizes those it brands as enemies of Truth—its fixed and monumentalized truth. Dissent is ruthlessly met with threats and punishments—this is true of both the Ministry and of Lord Voldemort and his church. In our own culture, they may be expressed in any of a seemingly numberless variety of forms: entire books have been written cataloguing the "science of torture" alone. Murder is, of course, still a big one: capital punishment at home, and mass slaughter abroad, persist as favored solutions to social and international challenges, particularly among so-called "developed" nations. Confinement is perhaps the most popular choice of them all—the promise of more prisons and harsher conditions with longer sentences is a staple of every politician's social agenda at campaign time. At the corporate level, intimidation is a favored means of oppression, over a vast array of forms and techniques. But whether it appears as slander, misinformation, spying, financial intimidation, or a corporate "annual review," what it all amounts to is merely another specific variety of torture—inner torture. The collective ego relies on the power of three principal abstractions to reinforce and concretize its cyclic program of threat, submission and punishment: guilt, blame, and dread.

Weapons in the War on the True Self: Guilt, Blame, and Dread

> The false limitations exercised by the collective ego, through its feudal power structure, seek to press all individuals into its molds, since conformity is the only way it can maintain its order. Tremendous pressure is put on individuals who do not fit into these molds, to cut out of themselves whatever does not fit. This [is] the process by which the growth of humans and of Nature is limited...
> —Carol Anthony and Hanna Moog, *I Ching: The Oracle of the Cosmic Way*, from Hexagram 60, "Limitation".

Where conformity is the end, any means—however violent, malevolent, or oppressive—are justified. With respect to individuals, the psychological fuel that drives the engine of oppression within the collective ego is guilt. Through its power, group blame is given the freedom to attack or reward at its whim and leisure, while dread, the axle that turns the wheels of this juggernaut of inner oppression, is given its perpetuating force from the synergy of guilt and blame within the psyche. The way out of this destructive cycle will be discussed a little further along; but first it is important to understand what we are dealing with here.

Guilt: The "High Inquisitor" of the Psyche

It does not seem to be any coincidence that Rowling has chosen a brutal, medieval image for the title adopted by the odious Professor Umbridge and the power of the magical government behind her. In literary terms, the obvious evocation is of that haunting chapter from Dostoyevky's novel, *The Brothers Karamazov*, in which "The Grand Inquisitor," the Catholic Cardinal of Seville, having just returned from the day's mass burning of convicted "heretics," encounters Christ himself, silently performing miracles among the people. The Inquisitor intervenes and orders Christ arrested, and then visits Him in His prison cell. The Cardinal proudly proclaims to Christ that his church has turned against Him, "corrected His work"—taken freedom from the hearts of the people and replaced it with Authority. Then, he informs the Savior that tomorrow, He will burn at the stake of the auto-da-fe, and the people who today worshiped Him will tomorrow, at the order of the Cardinal, stoke the coals beneath the flames that burn Him. At last, the Inquisitor's speech is over, and Christ, who has listened in silence all the time, now rises and kisses the old Cardinal on the lips. The Inquisitor opens the door to the cell and warns Him: go and never return again. Pressed for an epilogue to his story, Ivan Karamazov, who is the narrator, explains the Inquisitor's fate: "the kiss glows in his heart, but he adheres to his idea."

The ideologies of religion, science, and society—personified in Dostoyevsky's tale as the Grand Inquisitor—offer each person who will follow them the security of their protection, the comfort of a forced order, and the glossy sheen of their entitlements, but only at an incalculable price: that of the sacrifice of one's true, autonomous, and unique self. This is, in reality, a classic inner shakedown—the original bait-and-switch scheme. The need for the sacrifice has been manufactured via advertisement; the market is concocted. There is, in fact, no *natural* danger, disorder, or inner failing that requires the sacrifice demanded of the individual. Of even more concern is the consequence that the price of self-sacrifice conceals: a hidden tax or surcharge which will make it inevitably intolerable to the purchaser. This tax is the precondition of guilt; it is the ideological smear on one's true being. All have sinned, so all must repent (the religious embodiment of the tax); all of us are brutal, predatory, evil animals, and so must submit to the rule of a forced Code of Law in order to live peacefully with one another (the moral embodiment of the tax); all of us are lacking, incapable of living successfully out of the inner resources that Nature has provided, and so we must gain the additional support of institutionally-provided sustenance and social standing (the governmental embodiment of the tax).

Implicit in every one of these formulations is the threat of punishment. If you don't repent, you'll be punished (and according to some religious ideologies, you will even if you do repent, though not as badly or eternally as you would be if you didn't); if you disobey or question the code of conduct prescribed by the collective, you will be punished; if you attempt to live independently, according to the inborn means and social skills that Nature has given you, and without regard to the personal restrictions established by the ruling authority, you will be punished.

But mere physical punishment, while temporarily or sporadically effective, has proven itself to be an incomplete means of oppression, so the abstractions of guilt and blame were projected beneath our hearts by the collective ego—very much like the fires of the Grand Inquisitor's auto-da-fe. Through thousands of years of deep, behaviorist-style programming, these concepts have been driven deep into our psyches, forming a vast architecture of damnation. It has evolved into quite a massive structure, so perhaps a brief walk around this monument will help us as we prepare to destroy it.

Guilt is a blanket of blame thrown over all of human nature, and even over Nature itself. If you are human, you are guilty—to the collective ego, the proof is in the perpetuation of the delusion: "doesn't everyone feel guilty at one time or another?" it asks. If you are alive, you are stained; if you dare to reject, or even to question, the dogma that casts this blot on your being, then you are branded as one in denial, and you are threatened with "correction"—i.e., punishment.

Therefore, guilt is a part of *your* identity—you are forced to acknowledge that culpritude is a part of your nature—as an individual and as a representative of your species. Even God, in His human transmutation, was a sinner, and he admitted it! If God Himself was a sinner and therefore guilty, how much more so are you?

Guilt is an admission of the fact that one deserves to be punished by a vengeful God or an indifferent Cosmos (take your pick), and its human, self-appointed representatives. Many ideologies add to this axiom the codicil that the more painful and brutal the punishment, the better—this is the doctrine of asceticism in a nutshell. Again, God got himself nailed to a cross and only complained a little, right near the very end, so we may as well accept our punishment with open arms, whenever it falls our way.

Guilt is not only natural to humans, but also often perfectly justified. Many therapists will ask a client or patient who is feeling guilty about something, "is the guilt logical?" What they mean by this is, "did you do or say something for which you *deserve* to feel guilty?" They never stop to wonder whether the client should rather be undertaking an inner revolution upon the very idea of guilt itself, because they have accepted the reified notion of guilt that has been programmed into them by their culture—and even by their "science" (Freud believed that guilt was a perfectly natural consequence of the Oedipus complex, in which a child combined a sexual desire for its opposite-sex parent with a murderous wish against the same-sex parent).

Guilt is one of those spots that never washes clean. In America, the recidivism rate of ex-convicts released from prison hovers around 70 percent, closer to 90 percent in many areas. Their unemployment rates are also enormous—to have been deemed legally guilty in this society is a life sentence, whether you are within or outside of a correctional facility. This derives from our religious ideologies, which presuppose that sin can never be washed clean in this lifetime (which in turn, by the way, lies at the root of many obsessive-compulsive disorders).

Separating from Guilt: Banishing the High Inquisitor

In Rowling's story, Professor Umbridge is eventually driven out of the school after the climactic battle with Voldemort. Once the government has been presented with the proof of Voldemort's return, Dumbledore is restored to the leadership of the school. Harry is also vindicated in his clear vision of the danger, and he is finally given the credit of his convictions in the Ministry's public voice, the wizarding press; though this official absolution is, according to the institutional ego's habits in this respect, merely temporary and superficial.

Still, we are led to feel that Harry will inevitably come to a clear view of what he needs to learn in order to enduringly free himself from the influence of the Ministry and its insidious programs of demonization and intimidation. We, however, will not have to wait for future volumes of the Potter series to arrive, in order to come to a similar understanding through the teaching energy of the Cosmos—the solution to the problems of group adherence and its costs in guilt, blame, and dread, are directly before us. Indeed, they are within each of us. The following are merely a few suggestions to help you get started on this path of inner clarity.

Say an inner No to the validity of guilt as a principle of human nature. In a brief, daily meditation, ask for help from the hidden world and firmly, yet without bitterness or hatred, say the word "No" three times to *the idea of guilt as a natural aspect of your being.* Say a further No to any group ideology, pseudo-scientific theory, religious belief, or social doctrine that arises to your awareness as a source of the belief in guilt as a natural human trait. Ask the cosmic teacher and the helping energy of dispersion to dissolve the notion of guilt from within you. Finish each meditation with an expression of thanks to the cosmic energies that are thus clearing you of these destructive attachments and prejudices against your true nature. Many people have found this to be an extraordinarily restorative and cleansing exercise, and the best part of it is that it costs you almost no outer effort and only about two or three minutes out of each day.

Identify the areas in your life where you are bound by group affiliation, and sever the ties on the inner plane. In Hexagram 59 of the *I Ching* ("Dispersion"), Line 4 has this poem:

> He dissolves his bond with his group.
> Supreme good fortune.
> Dispersion leads to accumulation.
> This is something that ordinary men do not think of.
> (from the Wilhelm/Baynes translation)

Let this insight lead you to reflect on the aspects of your life—work, national affiliation, an academic, social, religious, or other group allegiance, and even family life—that need to be examined for the limitations they may be imposing on your true nature and the fulfillment of your individual uniqueness. Many of us have spent much of our lives trying to live up to the group self-images projected upon us by collective ideologies—the obedient child, the good and sacrificing husband/wife/parent, the loyal, hardworking employee, the patriotic citizen of a particular nation. The fact is that children naturally behave as adults would like them to, when obedience is not beaten into them as an ideological imperative engraved on the stone of an institution's moral code; we are all of us more natural, loving, and enduring marriage partners when we are allowed to live independently, even as we maintain the inner connection with our beloved, free of the darkly threatening decree to "honor and obey" another; we become more loyal, supportive, and nurturing parents when we give up the lugubrious self-consciousness of "sacrificial duty" towards our children; we are more productive and creative workers when we are liberated from that obsessive and vaguely paranoid attachment to the institutional ethic of "hard work"; and we are far more beneficial to our community and our nation when we consider ourselves as citizens of the Cosmic Whole, rather than as parochially allied to some tribe, clan, or state and its prevailing ideology of the moment.

So consider which of the institutionally-programmed self-images of the collective ego are most limiting you in your inner growth as an individual, and work on releasing these bonds, in the knowledge that you are truly benefiting the natural family, community, business organization, and nation by doing so.

Be led to a more accurate and personally viable understanding of error and its place in our lives. In the *I Ching*, there is no direct mention of guilt, because, as we have discussed, guilt has no basis in cosmic reality. However, it is understood throughout the oracle's text that error is natural to growth, and so the *I Ching* speaks in many places of "remorse" or "regret." This, indeed, is how we are meant to understand the role of error in our lives. In contrast to what the collective ego and its ideologies would have us believe, there are no spots that won't wash out: our bodies, after all, are 75% water—*the basic element of the baptismal ritual is already within us in abundance*! So when you have said or done something which you regret, and that you recognize as an error, a temporary separation from your true nature, try the following steps in a brief meditation:

- Ask for help from the Cosmic realm in understanding the cause, nature, and the correct resolution of your mistake, and apologize to the Cosmos for the error, in a free and open inner expression of remorse that is unstained by guilt, self-blame, or bitterness.
- If it is an interpersonal issue, then apologize to the person you believe you have wronged, on the inner plane. Simply let your consciousness speak to that person and express your regret sincerely, as if they were right beside you in the room. This practice has a far greater transformative effect than most people would be willing to acknowledge, *until they experience it for themselves*.

- Finally, ask the Sage, the teaching energy of the Cosmic Consciousness, to guide you in understanding what, if anything, must be done, in addition to the above, to resolve the effect of your mistake and return you to harmony with the principle of *Te*, or Modesty. You may use the *I Ching* or other oracle, or simply attend to the messages you receive in meditations, in dreams, or through your own reflection. If you feel that any action or communication on the outer plane would be helpful in completing the resolution of your error, ask for help in learning the correct approach. And remember this: *the capacity to say from your heart, "I am sorry" reveals an ability of such greatness as the leaders of the most powerful nations on earth completely lack.* As with any meditation, finish by expressing your thanks to the Cosmos for its help in guiding you through this process of self-understanding amid an awareness of remorse.

If guilt, blame, and fear are severely troubling you, seek help from a professional. The guilt and self-blame that are engendered by our futile efforts to live up to the institutional ego's monumental self-images lie at the root of many depressive and anxiety disorders. We are not born to live in an inner state of slavery, ever fearful that we will be deemed insufficient to the self-images that cultural laws, moral codes, religious beliefs, and societal norms define for us and program into us. Your need for help is not a manifestation of something aberrant or weak in your true nature. You can find a counselor, therapist, or other professional through talking to family and friends, or via professional organizations that offer referrals based on your needs and resources.

Chapter 10: Inside the Department of Mysteries: Time, Death, and the Search for Truth

> This room was larger than the last, dimly lit and rectangular, and the center of it was sunken, forming a great stone pit some twenty feet below them. They were standing on the topmost tier of what seemed to be stone benches running all around the room and descending in steep steps like an amphitheater, or the courtroom in which Harry had been tried by the Wizengamot. Instead of a chained chair, however, there was a raised stone dais in the center of the lowered floor, and upon this dais stood a stone archway that looked so ancient, cracked, and crumbling that Harry was amazed the thing was still standing. Unsupported by any surrounding wall, the archway was hung with a tattered black curtain or veil which, despite the complete stillness of the cold surrounding air, was fluttering very slightly as though it had just been touched.
> —*Harry Potter and the Order of the Phoenix*, Chapter 34

By now, you may have noticed that we've been paying a lot of attention to the cycle of events that begins with the graveyard scene of Book Four and continues through the close of Book Five. To me, this only seems natural, especially if you happen to be trying to draw certain psycho-spiritual lessons from these Harry Potter stories. The battle scenes that provide the climax to Harry's fifth year are particularly important in this sense, because so much of the metaphor of the entire series is compressed into these events. They all happen in a place called the "Department of Mysteries," where Harry comes face to face with symbolic images of the three great riddles of human consciousness in the world of form: Time, Thought, and Death.

It is not only a climactic narrative moment; it is the stem of the metaphorical funnel into which all the transformative symbols and allegory of the stories to date have been poured. It is a point at which Harry will be made to look beyond appearances more deeply and penetratingly than he has ever had to before. By the end of it all, he will be at the brink of an understanding that would suggest a major passage—a point in life where the movement from dependence to autonomy has been nearly completed; where feeling is joined to sensation and thought; where the fog of ego begins to clear before a deepening insight; where out of the boy, a man is formed.

This transformative passage will be defined more by inner growth than outer adventures: Harry will learn that even Professor Dumbledore is a human like himself, with weaknesses and the capacity for error. As the bond between them deepens from the wounds they have incurred and the responsibilities they bear together, so will the uniqueness of each be further realized. Harry will soon understand that in the way of natural magic, there are no Masters, but only guides; he will also perceive that growth proceeds not from a clutching obedience, but from the insight born of letting go. He will be led to perceive that death, which has been a part of his life since he was an infant, is not quite what he may have thought it was. He will soon understand that the ghosts of Hogwarts are not merely the benign and friendly spirits that talked and joked with him at the dinner table; he will be inexorably called to a fresh and personal way of seeing the deaths that have occurred in his young life—the deaths of his past and those yet to come.

Time seems to take a particularly central place in this scenario: its presence is felt in the hourglasses and bell jar in one room; it is also suggested in the death-veil; finally, throughout the battle scenes and into the emotionally-charged denouement in Dumbledore's office, there is the image of the prophecy that appears to link Harry and Voldemort in time. What must be remembered, however, is that the scenes in the "Department of Mysteries" occur within the basement offices of the shallow, decadent and inept bureaucratic government of the wizarding world. The images of time, thought, and death are set in their institutional context, so as to contrast this view with a broader perspective to which we and Harry are being led. Let us look more deeply into these images, and see what can be discovered on our own journey through the "Department of Mysteries."

The first overall impression from this part of the story is of Mystery itself—a forced, reified, and medieval obscurity, an awful but dust-covered secrecy which seems vaguely discordant to a truly magical understanding of reality. In Chapter 9, our discussion focused on bureaucracy and systems of group belief, especially as they relate to the domination of our inner life via ideology. Whether it is packaged as religion, law, nationalism, scientism, skepticism, or the "anti-belief" of nihilism or anarchism, a collective ideology of any sort tends to become evangelical in its pretensions. It will aggrandize its knowledge or insight in a manner that closes off the possibility of alternative understanding or future discovery, and will archly imply that its system contains the key to the door of Mystery, which it nevertheless holds firmly closed against independent inspection. Whenever it is questioned, however, by some courageous inquirer, the defenders of an ideology will bark in alarm that the sanctity or consistency of their system is being assaulted, and will circle their wagons while perhaps temporarily adopting the role of the misunderstood iconoclast.

This is an attitude that Plato exposes in his *Euthyphro*, in which the doctrinal possessor of Mystery is personified in the character of Euthyphro. He alone owns the understanding of piety and impiety, of good and evil, of justice and crime; and he says so, telling Socrates that this is why he is so widely misunderstood and ridiculed by his fellow citizens. Plato was not simply painting a portrait of some isolated nut-case in the person of Euthyphro: he was showing us the very silhouette of the institutional ego and its ideologies. It is no mistake that this dialogue finds Euthyphro and Socrates outside the Athenian court of justice, the one as prosecutor (of his own father) and the other as defendant in separate cases—in the very place where the justice of the gods was believed to be manifested in the affairs of men.

Socrates was executed because he penetrated too far (and too publicly) into the Athenian plutocracy's "Department of Mysteries." He showed that the separation from the collective ego may be said to begin with an inner rejection of its tendency to *claim ownership on the basis of secrecy*. Once again,

Rowling's governmental metaphor is chillingly exact to this point, as can be seen today from the behavior of certain governmental entities toward any who would question their motives or actions—they suppress and even condemn such free inquiry, on the basis of "intelligence" which they claim to possess but will not reveal. This is precisely what religious, scientific, and media-driven group entities do to us as individuals on the path of self-understanding: they tell us that we must accept on faith whatever it is that they claim to possess, but refuse to disclose. *This is precisely what we must question*; this is where our work of disempowering the bureaucracy of Mystery begins.

Lao Tzu described the vast benefit of this questioning attitude in Chapter 6 of his *Tao Te Ching*:

> The valley is ever open and alive;
> It is the mother of consciousness.
> Amid night-flower darkness,
> The bounty of Nature is concealed—
> Until, looking within, we see
> The Mystery extinguished, the curtain drawn
> From the heart of the Mother of the Cosmos.

"Mystery" is not, after all, a natural attribute of the Cosmos, nor of ourselves! The cult of Mystery is nothing but the casting of a shroud onto Nature, and though we may sometimes find, as does Harry, that the process of cutting through that ideological shroud is marked with peril, pain, and even grief; the inner clarity and self-assurance that the journey brings tends to reward our courage in facing those dangers.

One reason to question the monuments and relics that represent institutional leadership, whether of the sacred or secular variety, has to do with their essential fragility: they are old, worn, dust-encased, and rigidified symbols of a frozen past. As Lao Tzu reminds us[77], whatever is rigid is brittle and easily broken; the shards that fly throughout the Department of Mysteries in Rowling's story comprise another illustration of that principle.

> The jet of red light flew right over the Death Eater's shoulder and hit a glass-fronted cabinet on the wall full of

variously shaped hourglasses. The cabinet fell to the floor and burst apart, glass flying everywhere, then sprang back up onto the wall, fully mended, then fell down again, and shattered— (*Harry Potter and the Order of the Phoenix*, p. 790)

A little further along, the aforementioned Death Eater is knocked into a bell jar by a stunning spell:

> He collapsed backward...his head sank through the surface of the bell jar as though it was nothing but a soap bubble and he came to rest...with his head lying inside the jar full of glittering wind. (p. 790)

Instantly, the man's head morphs into that of an infant, and then back into its former state, and again into infancy. "It's time," mutters Hermione, in a tone of uncharacteristic awe. We feel sure that once her mind clears from the heat of battle and she is allowed a moment's reflection on this, she will realize her error. For these images are a parody of Time, even a metaphorical "anti-time" which switches itself between two dichotomous states (broken and repaired; adult and infant). It really is a rather pathetic banality, of the same sort we've seen before from the Ministry of Magic consciousness, and it crumbles beneath the most casual examination. All we have to do is ask the question, "what about *Now*?" We can ask it in much the same way as Jon Kabat-Zinn does in his guide to meditation, *Wherever You Go, There You Are*:[78]

> To find our way, we will need to pay more attention to this moment. It is the only time that we have in which to live, grow, feel, and change. We will need to become more aware of and take precautions against the incredible pull of the Scylla and Charybdis of past and future, and the dreamworld they offer us in place of our lives. (p. xv).

The polar caricature of time found in the Department of Mysteries scene may remind us of Stephen Hawking's discussion in Chapter 9 ("The Arrow of Time") of his *A Brief History of Time*, in what he refers to as "the cosmological arrow of Time." This is a picture of the universe as a system in a state of progressive expansion (since the hypothetical Big Bang of creation), whose inherent disorder is revealed and accentuated throughout this expansive period. Theoretically, Hawking explains that the expansion must, in ten billion years or so, slow and then cease entirely, reversing its direction to contract back toward a state of primordial order or compression. Hawking spends part of this chapter in debunking one aspect of this theory, although he was unable to retreat entirely from it—and he certainly does not attempt the bold and humorous keelhauling that Mrs. Rowling applies to the linear and dichotomous view of Time.[79]

But such a refreshing perspective is emerging among scientists today: it may be seen in an accessibly articulate form in the popular work of Brian Greene, whose engaging mixture of ebullience and humility brings the most recondite ideas to life. In his recent book, *The Fabric of the Cosmos*, he offers us the following reminder[80]:

> A common misconception is that the big bang provides a theory of cosmic origins. It doesn't. The big bang is a theory...that delineates cosmic evolution from a split second after whatever happened to bring the universe into existence, but *it says nothing at all about time zero itself*. And since, according to the big bang theory, the bang is what is supposed to have happened at the beginning, the big bang leaves out the bang. It tells us nothing about what banged, why it banged, or, frankly, whether it ever really banged at all. (p. 272).

So how can science pretend to predict the future along the arrow of Time, if it can't even reliably tell us what's already happened—or even *if* it happened at all? Greene's response is that Time is unique among the dimensions of lived experience in that, unlike space, it is "asymmetrical," meaning that past and future cannot be experienced or even conceived (it appears) in a balance of proportions. You can push an egg off the edge of a countertop and watch it fall to the floor and splatter, but you can't see it "unsplatter"—come back together and hop back up onto the counter, whole and nicely ordered once more. But you can *predict*, with varying degrees of confidence, that something will happen in the future, given certain circumstances (if you push an egg over a smooth surface with nothing to stop its momentum, it will likely fall and break once it hits the floor).

Which brings us to the Prophecy: the little, dust-covered glass ball, pulled off a shelf among rows and rows of other such shelves, stacked to the ceiling of a vast, darkened room in the bowels of the Ministry's back offices. From the very beginning of the Potter tales, Rowling has gleefully lampooned everything having to do with the "art of the inner eye," or foretelling the future. Long before the introduction in Book Three of Professor Trelawney, this comical theme was appearing in the vapid distraction of the centaurs gazing into the heavens for portents (in *Sorcerer's Stone*). Suffice it to say that the art of prophecy has received some hilariously rough treatment from Ms. Rowling, and the Prophecy in the Department of Mysteries scene is *physically* manhandled. It is fought over; pushed and pulled; its companion prophecies residing on those shelves are destroyed by a trapped group of adolescent children; it is thrown about, chased, passed from hand to hand, and finally shattered near the end of the battle, its small voice smothered amid the cacophony of war.

But as is made abundantly clear by the end of *Harry Potter and the Order of the Phoenix*, there are messages of truth contained in that small voice of oracular insight—but as a *guide to the present* rather than a map to the future. In a few instances throughout the Potter stories, a true reading of consciousness is delivered—even through the hapless Professor Trelawney—that is subsequently verified by experience. Perhaps, then, divination is on some level valid—a worthy, ancient, well-practiced and esteemed art, is it not? As Professor Dumbledore might say, "yes...and no." I rely on the *I Ching* for both personal insight and help in working with my counseling clients; others rely on astrology, runes, the Kabbalah, or the Tarot. Is Rowling merely playing both sides of the fence, or is she pointing us with the unconscious clarity of art, toward a more precise and balanced understanding of what a true insight practice can be, by exposing cultural distortions about what an oracle is, and does?

I feel that Rowling is taking us on the latter track, showing us again the difference between perception and pretense. What she is really ridiculing—especially in the character of Professor Trelawney—is the interpersonal commercialism of self-display, as well as the elitist snobbery of the cults of Mystery. In fact, the teaching potential of an oracle is no more meant to be the exclusive province of magical specialists than is human law intended to be the special domain of judges, attorneys, and politicians. In every field of human experience, exclusivity is the footman of corruption.

Those who approach an oracle with an expectation of "seeing their future" will be either disappointed, forced into a net of contrivance, or simply left frustrated and scornful (as are Harry, Ron, and Hermione after some experience with Professor Trelawney). But if we work with an oracle as an insight guide—a Cosmic reflector of the consciousness of a moment, which can lead us toward a clearer, broader perspective on the present— then we will discover the truly practical benefit of relying on an oracle to support successful action in daily living. This approach to an oracle—as a gateway to a holistic understanding that encompasses past and future within the embrace of a Cosmic *Now*—far surpasses any advantage to be gained from fortune telling and its egotistical projection of a predetermined future along an arrow of linear time. An oracle, properly used, is about learning what we need to know about ourselves, our lives, and the lives around us, in order to *self-create a future* that is in harmony with Nature. It is much more meaningful to feel our present transformed than it is to have a lowdown on some chain of events which are to transpire in a deterministic future.

Why, however, do the *I Ching* and other oracles, *appear* to "tell the future," to predict what is often later proven to have been ahead of us in life and time? I think the answer to that question lies both in our limited conception of Time, and in the distortions often prompted by interpretation and that backward projection known as "20/20 hindsight" (which, as Greene shows us in his reflections on the big bang, isn't so clear-sighted after all). To illustrate this point, it may be helpful to review the last two hexagrams of the *I Ching*, which may be said to represent a composite view of Time, from the perspective of the teaching energy which speaks through the oracle. The Ritsema/Karcher translation presents them as follows:

Hexagram 63: Already Fording	**Hexagram 64: Not-Yet Fording**
Already Fording. Growing: the small. Harvesting Trial. Initially significant. Completing: disarraying.	Not-yet Fording, Growing. The small fox, a muddy Ford. Soaking one's tail: Without direction: Harvesting.

Hexagram 63 may be seen to represent Hawking's "Cosmological Arrow of Time" in its portrait of an aboriginal stability ("initially significant") progressively followed by an endgame marked by increasing chaos ("completing: disarraying"). But that's how Time may appear when we have already made our crossing (the "fording" of the river) and are now looking back; this is how we may see, via retrospect, how an oracle could "foresee the future." This is life on the linear plane of Time, and its scope is narrow indeed—both for oracles and for those self-fulfilling prophecies of science known as statistics.

We have been led to assume, by the proponents of exclusivity, that an oracle, a corporate vision statement, a scientific prediction, a political agenda, or indeed any guide to human action, must point us toward the future. Yet in certain Western insight practices, such as psychotherapy, this structure is reversed, and is dedicated to achieving a clear and cathartic view of the *past*—as if such a practice were designed to "retrospect the past" rather than "foretell the future." It is all a matter of one's point of orientation, an insight which is also arrived at in Brian Greene's discussion of quantum mechanics:

> Whereas human intuition, and its embodiment in classical physics, envision a reality in which things are always definitely one way *or* another, quantum mechanics describes a reality in which things sometimes hover in a haze of being partly one way *and* partly another....This, plainly speaking, is weird. We are unused to a reality that remains ambiguous until perceived. But the oddity of quantum mechanics does not stop here...quantum mechanics—if taken at face value—implies that something

you do over here can be *instantaneously* linked to something happening over there, regardless of distance. (p. 11).

There is, in fact, nothing "weird" about it: as Jon Kabat-Zinn would remind us, this "oddity" of quantum mechanics (or of the experience of meditation, or the act of consulting an oracle) points us within, *to the immanent Present*.

This insight would seem to be leading us toward the perspective obtained in Hexagram 64. Now one would expect that the final chapter in a book like the *I Ching* would have something significant to tell us, and it does. It says, in effect: *live in your moment, with all your being*. It teaches us that our holistic experience of Time is only "muddied" by our culture's repression of feeling and the inner senses: this is the meaning of "the small fox soaking its tail." The "tail" is a metaphorical reference to the caudate (Latin for "tail") brain, wherein our primordial feeling senses are centered within our nervous system—to submerge these feeling senses in favor of the monarchical intellect (the "small fox," or evolutionary adolescent that is our forebrain) is to suppress that part of our being which serves us best in intuiting a broader and more inclusive sense of Time. Greene, Kabat-Zinn, and the final line of the Judgment in Hexagram 64, seem to be encouraging us to recall and to validate this feeling aspect of our nature, so we may discover that in our intimation of "the directionless" there is the potential for both deeper insight into ourselves and an expanded perspective on Nature, which is the "Harvest" promised in the *I Ching*. To discover this capacity within oneself is to enable the inner release of the grasping, controlling, anthropocentric vision of Time. When we are able to arrive at such an inner perspective, it becomes palpably easier to still live and grow within the illusory paradigm of rational, linear time.

During his adventure within the Department of Mysteries, Harry is presented with this lesson as well: as he pursues the killer of his godfather, he is assaulted by the seething, pickled brains that had also attacked his friend Ron:

> She aimed a curse over her shoulder. The tank rose into the air and tipped. Harry was deluged in the foul-

smelling potion within. The brains slipped and slid over him and began spinning their long, colored tentacles, but her shouted, "Wingardium Leviosa!" and they flew into the air away from him. Slipping and sliding he ran on toward the door. (p. 809).

It is how the trap of thought works in all of us: the reified thought-forms of the forebrain attack with tentacles of intellect, which wrap themselves in a burning grip upon their victim—the whole self given us by Nature—constricting the movement of our entire organism and cutting off life itself. This, in essence, is how intellect isolated from its whole and natural setting limits us, whenever we allow it—by choking off our feeling senses and repressing the inner resources we truly need to live fully and successfully.

Yet how can we re-connect with our feeling nature, with this inner sense of the directionless—how can we release what appears to be an entirely natural and necessary linear orientation when it comes to the experience of Time? It is a matter of loosening our inner grip on this purely intellectual perception of reality; of coming to an understanding led by *the totality of one's being*, that, in the words of the Greek philosopher Heraclitus, "An unapparent connection is stronger than an apparent one...the unity of things lies beneath the surface."[81] There may be no more direct path to a deeper understanding and experiencing of Time and reality than to wander in the realm of Death; this is exactly where Harry and his friends are taken next.

Katabasis: *Journeying Beneath the Surface of Death*

When Harry and his friends approach the room in which the archway and its mysterious veil lie, their minds are not on death, or certainly not focused on an effort to understand death. They are on a mission to save a life instead: they have come to the "Department of Mysteries" to rescue Harry's godfather, Sirius Black, from the room where Harry believes that Sirius is being tortured by Voldemort. Harry has driven his friends to this point with an obsessive urgency and a certain imperiousness—the total force of his will has been directed toward the completion of this mission, and he will tolerate not the slightest delay. Thus, it is all the more notable that Harry not merely pauses, but positively forgets what he has come so far to accomplish, as soon as he is presented with this room and this dark, fluttering curtain hanging from a dilapidated archway.

> Harry scrambled down the benches one by one until he reached the stone bottom of the sunken pit. His footsteps echoed loudly as he walked slowly toward the dais. The pointed archway looked much taller from where he stood now than when he had been looking down on it from above. Still the veil swayed gently, as though somebody had just passed through it. (*Order of the Phoenix*, p. 773)

Those familiar with the ancient literature of the encounter with death-realms will recognize that Harry has arrived at another point of *katabasis*, the Greek phrase meaning "going down or under," and indicating the descent beyond the surface that is required for new understanding to emerge. Harry and his friends have experienced *katabasis* before, most notably in the first book, amid the descent through the trapdoor guarded by a Cerberus-like hound, on their way to Harry's encounter with the delusion that seeks to conquer death through a fixed vision of immortality, represented by Voldemort and his pursuit of the Sorcerer's Stone. It happened again in the second book, amid a deep fall through the plumbing and into another realm of false magic, guarded by a powerful snake-dragon in the Chamber of Secrets. These involved symbols of inner death; now, however, he is going down again, to approach a different symbol of death, which is not protected by any beast or magical object. In doing so, he is repeating the experience of numerous literary figures throughout history: Odysseus and Aeneas amid the shades of Hades, and Dante's Pilgrim within the Inferno. Perhaps because he has already explored the realm of *katabasis* before, Harry is not intimidated, but remains frozen in fascination as he faces this worn and degraded symbol of the Formless. His friend Hermione, however, senses danger—perhaps she recognizes the cracked, corrupt institutional aura of the archway and its stone pedestal. In any event, she raises an alarm, which awakens Harry from his hypnotic engagement with the veil:

> She sounded scared...yet Harry thought the archway had a kind of beauty about it, old though it was. The gently rippling veil intrigued him; he felt a very strong inclination to climb up on the dais and walk through it....He had just heard something. There were faint whispering, murmuring noises coming from the other side of the veil....
> "Can't anyone else hear it?" Harry demanded, for the whispering and murmuring was becoming louder; without really meaning to put it there, he found his foot was on the dais.
> "I can hear them too," breathed Luna, joining them around the side of the archway and gazing at the swaying veil. "There are people *in there*."
> "What do you mean, '*in there*'?" demanded Hermione, jumping down from the bottom step and sounding much angrier than the occasion warranted. "There isn't any '*in there*,' it's just an archway, there's no room for anybody to be there—Harry, stop it, come away—
> She grabbed his arm and pulled, but he resisted.
> "Harry, we are supposed to be here for Sirius!" she said in a high-pitched, strained voice. (p. 774)

At this, Harry relents, and returns to the search for Sirius; but he has seen, heard, and felt enough in this moment of *katabasis* to draw the necessary nourishment that will help carry him through the agonizing mourning that awaits him. For as he admiringly circumambulates this archway and veil, he unconsciously penetrates its appearance, and thus approaches the dawning realization of what Lao Tzu taught so long ago:

> Perhaps life and death
> Are not truly opposed.
>
> To conceive death as against Nature—
> As a cold termination of Life—
> Is the distorted perspective
> Of a violent inner tyranny.
> (*Tao Te Ching*, Chapter 42)

Later, Harry and his friends are driven back into the room containing the pit and the veil, chased by a group of Voldemort's Death Eaters, who are in pursuit of the prophecy that is believed to carry the secret of both Harry's and Voldemort's future. This time, Harry's descent is precipitous, violent, and painful:

> He was falling down steep stone step after steep stone step, bouncing on every tier until at last, with a crash that knocked all the breath out of his body, he landed flat on his back in the sunken pit where the stone archway stood on its dais. The whole room was ringing with the Death Eaters' laughter....He backed away, looking around, trying to keep all the Death Eaters within his sights. The back of his legs hit something solid; he had reached the dais where the archway stood. He climbed backward onto it. (p. 799).

Obviously, the adherents of the Voldemort-consciousness regarding death are frozen in fear by Harry's bold movement onto the dais supporting the death-veil; but Harry has already *felt the reality* that lies beneath this symbol's surface. Therefore, he connects fearlessly with this pedestal of Death, and is given just enough time and space for the help he needs to arrive.

Then the adult members of the Order of the Phoenix appear, and the ensuing battle scene in the death-room culminates in the death of Sirius, who is killed by a spell cast by his own cousin. As with his treatment of the house-elf, Kreacher, Sirius is undone by his haughty sense of contempt: he dies amid his own taunts against his cousin. Yet, as he falls through the veil and into the realm of the Formless, something else happens:

> And Harry saw the look of mingled fear and surprise on his godfather's wasted, once-handsome face as he fell through the ancient doorway and disappeared behind the veil, which fluttered for a moment as though in a high wind and then fell back into place. (p. 806).

Could this "look of surprise" be merely the shock of having been beaten in a duel, of having arrived so suddenly at the end of bodily life? Or might it represent something else: the sudden clearing of a lifetime's mistaken belief in death-as-termination? Perhaps that surprise is the same realization of which Chuang Tsu wrote so long ago:

> How can I tell if love of life is not a delusion? How can I tell whether a man who fears death is not like a man who has left home and dreads returning? How can I tell whether the dead are not amazed that they ever clung to life?[82]

The Unnamed Force in the Locked Room: The Unconscious Potential Buried by Ego

After the battle is over and won, the scene shifts to Dumbledore's office, where, in every one of the Potter books, Harry receives his most enduring lessons in the way of natural magic. In their final interview of Chapter 37, Dumbledore describes for Harry a force kept in a locked room at the Department of Mysteries; he tells him that this force

> "...is at once more wonderful and more terrible than death, than human intelligence, than forces of nature. It is also, perhaps, the most mysterious of the many subjects for study that reside there. It is the power held within that room that you possess in such quantities and which Voldemort has not at all. That power took you to save Sirius tonight. That power also saved you from possession by Voldemort, because he could not bear to reside in a body so full of the force he detests. In the end, it mattered not that you could not close your mind. It was your heart that saved you." (pp. 843-844).

Perhaps Dumbledore is ironically reminding Harry that magic is not truly about power or Mystery—but that the magical strength that preserves life and perpetuates Being is already within us all, cloaked beneath an obscure and institutional penumbra of Mystery. The key to the locked door behind which this "force" resides is perhaps the same as the one that opens the Room of Requirement or the Chamber of Secrets: it is the natural desire to connect with the Formless in furthering the benefit of All. This spontaneous movement of the heart, which surpasses time, thought, and even death, goes by many names, the most common of which is Love. Dumbledore, as the teaching presence within the Potter stories, embodies and expresses this feeling. Even amid the violent combat of their climactic confrontation, he addresses Lord Voldemort as "Tom"—his original first name. This implies a recognition of the fact that "Tom" still lives deeply buried beneath the ego-distortions that comprise Lord Voldemort; we are once again reminded of Lao Tzu's advice to kill the "criminal thought" and not the man. This is the active mode of *agape*—the abiding Love of the original, pre-institutional, Gnostic Christianity—which feels and acknowledges the presence of the Beloved, even in those who dwell in the realm of inner death. Perhaps *agape*, this simple and immanent Presence, is what lies beyond the locked door within the Department of Mysteries. In any event, Harry does not need to open this door: as Dumbledore points out to him, whatever resides symbolically in that room is already present within Harry, an active part of his true nature. In fact, Harry is a far purer and worthier vessel for this Presence than a room in a dark and dusty corner of an institutional palace.

This, indeed, is true of every one of us. The work of inner growth is to liberate and recover this Presence within ourselves, from the oppressive and secretive grip of the banal and corrupt institutional leadership of Ego. This Presence may be said to be the primordial light of which Lao Tzu sang some 2,600 years ago:

> There is something whole and formless,
> That existed before any universe was born.
> It makes no sound,
> Has no substance,
> Can't be fixed in time or space--
> It is inexhaustible, unchanging, perduring:
> It is the uterus of being,
> And I call it Tao,
> Just so it has a home in my mind.
>
> It may also be called the great,
> Since all beings arise from it,
> And it is the home to which they return.

> Humans: honor the earth,
> As the earth loves its sky,
> As the sky reflects its Tao,
> And as the Tao moves in harmony
> With its own eternal Presence.
> (*Tao Te Ching*, Chapter 25)

Penetrating the Mysteries of Time and Death: Reaching Past the Appearance

Harry's experience with time and death, though unique to his personality, is not uncommon in its overall character of a deep and painful ambivalence. Like many before him, he has had a personal communication with the consciousness of the dead loved ones in his life; but after the loss of his godfather he is gripped and frozen within by that bitter sense of irreparable, irretrievable loss. Perhaps Harry will eventually be brought to another moment of *katabasis*—a going-down and turning-within, which will lead him to a deeper understanding and acceptance. At the end of Book Five, there is an intimation of such a moment.

Throughout the stories, Harry and his friends communicate with the school ghosts, as well as a child-ghost that directs them to the Chamber of Secrets. Finally, near the end of *Order of the Phoenix*, as Harry is still inwardly paralyzed with grief for the loss of Sirius, he chases down the mascot-ghost of Gryffindor, Nearly Headless Nick, and demands that he reveal the secrets of the hidden world in which the dead reside:

> "What d'you mean, 'gone on'?" said Harry quickly. "Gone on where? Listen—what happens when you die, anyway? Where do you go? Why doesn't everyone come back? Why isn't this place full of ghosts? Why?"
> "I cannot answer," said Nick.
> "You're dead, aren't you?" said Harry exasperatedly. "Who can answer better than you?"
> "I was afraid of death," said Nick. "I chose to remain behind. I sometimes wonder whether I oughtn't to have....Well, that is neither here nor there....In fact, *I* am neither here nor there...." He gave a small sad chuckle. "I

know nothing about the secrets of death, Harry, for I chose my feeble imitation of life instead." (p. 861).

As Harry walks away from this conversation in frustration, "wondering whether he would ever feel cheerful again," he runs into Luna Lovegood, and in this encounter, a ray of illumination enters the desperate night of his mourning. Luna reminds him of the voices that they both heard from the veil, and concludes, "they were just lurking out of sight, that's all. You heard them." (p. 863).

Harry parts with Luna feeling freer and more hopeful. Why? Perhaps because she simply recalled to him something that he had already recognized on the inner plane, that, as Lao Tzu again shows us, in Chapter 16 of the *Tao Te Ching*:

> Life is never exhausted
> It is only delusion that dies.

Luna expresses a trusting confidence in the continuity of life after death that awakens a responsive trust within Harry—after all, they *did* have similar experiences in that vein (specifically, in their common ability to see the thestrals—the equine reptiles that are visible only to those who have witnessed death).

This encounter with Luna is also meaningful for its circumstances. Harry finds Luna as she is posting notices around the hallways, asking that her belongings be returned to her by those who had taken them. "People take them and hide them, you know," Luna tells him (p. 862). She explains that it happens every year, and her things do always come back in the end. Once again, Luna's innocent teaching quietly penetrates Harry's consciousness: there is nothing to seek or to strive after, for nothing, and no one, is ever truly lost. This is the way of Returning, described in our earlier quote from Chuang Tsu, and in Hexagram 24 of the *I Ching*:

> Returning. Growing.
> Issuing-forth, entering, without affliction.
> Partnering coming, without fault.
> Reversing Returning one's tao.

> The seventh day coming: Returning.
> Harvesting: possessing directed going.

This verse (from the Ritsema/Karcher translation) tells of return as the way of growth, maturation, and transformation back to the origin (Tao). The harvest of life is never depleted, but reanimates itself in the field of transformation between form and non-form, eternally returning, returning. It is a universal theme, better sung than declaimed. Rumi's lyric is in the same key as that of the *I Ching*:

> God said to the mind, "Return from where you came."
> He said to the hand of Death,
>   "Grab hold of worldly men."
> He said to the soul, "Fly to the Unseen.
>   Take all the treasure you can carry
>   And cry no more."
> ("The Return", tr. Jonathan Star)

Perhaps the voices that Harry and Luna (the moon-girl) hear beyond the veil are not individual voices murmuring, but the echo of that Cosmic song of *agape,* this time in the lyric of the personal love which always lives beyond the grave. Near the end of *Prisoner of Azkaban*, Professor Dumbledore had reminded Harry of this presence:

> "You think the dead we have loved ever truly leave us? You think that we don't recall them more clearly than ever in times of great trouble? Your father is alive in you, Harry, and shows himself most plainly when you have need of him. How else could you have produced that *particular* Patronus?....So you did see your father last night, Harry...you found him inside yourself." (*Prisoner of Azkaban*, pp. 427-428)

It is the same intimate yet universal note that Rilke's lover of "The Death of the Beloved" discovers:

> Then all at once he came to understand
> The dead through her, and joined them in their walk,
> Kin to them all; he let the others talk,
>
> And paid no heed to them, and called that land
> The fortunately-placed, the ever-sweet.—
> And groped out all its pathways for her feet.
> (tr. J.B. Leishman)

What Harry has begun to learn through these experiences is what Rilke's lover learned: that love, the pure and enduring energy of the Cosmic Whole, is never wasted or lost, no matter what appearances may seem to tell us. Its force is self-renewing; its feeling, poignant yet unsentimental; its voice, quiet and assured. Its presence is its purpose, for it knows that it alone is immortal.

In Chuang Tsu's *Inner Chapters*, the story is told of Chin Shih, who came to remember Lao Tzu at his funeral. Chin Shih's remarks are a guide to how we may face both time and death:

> "When I first arrived, I thought his spirit was really there. Now I know it wasn't. When I went in to mourn, the old people were wailing as though they had lost their son. The young ones were crying as though they had lost their mother. Since they were all together, they talked and wept without any control. This is avoiding heaven, indulging in sentiment, ignoring what is natural. In the old days, it was called the crime of violating the law of nature.
>
> "The Master came because it was time. He left because he followed the natural flow. Be content with the moment, and be willing to follow the flow....In the old days this was called freedom from bondage. The wood is consumed but the fire burns on, and we do not know when it will come to an end."[83]

The Use of Oracles: Drawing on Cosmic Resources

Isn't it extraordinary how, from childhood onward, our deepest and most purely felt experiences are repressed or rationalized, until we wind up behaving as if we couldn't feel anything? Thus, I am always amused to hear that the use of oracles is "mere superstition." Oracular traditions have developed in every known corner and culture of the earth: in the East, there are the *Nechung* of Tibet and the *Ling Qi Jing* and *I Ching* in China. In the West, we find astrology, runes, the Tarot, Kabbalah, and other practices still alive and well, while the ancients were known to have relied on guides such as the Delphic oracle in Greece and the Vestal Virgins of Rome. Throughout the world, shamanic traditions that incorporate oracular insight have thrived and continue to flourish. Oracles have been a part of human life and society for at least five thousand years, just as political organizations have been a part of human civilization throughout recorded history. Yet we do not commonly hear charges of superstition or fable-making leveled against the practice of politics, or against politicians (in spite of some very persuasive points that might be made to that effect).

It has been my experience, and that of many people I have known and worked with, that a practice of using an oracle to achieve personal insight into one's life is a beneficial and very practical way of broadening understanding and exercising the intuitive and feeling elements of the personality. Therefore, one of the best recommendations I can give to people who wish to discover a fresh and personal approach toward a deeper, more enduring understanding of life in time and amid death, is to work with an oracle. Once we clear ourselves of that Professor Trelawney nonsense about foretelling a predetermined future or the need for some special endowment to become "expert" in the use of oracles, there is a great deal of benefit to be had from working with the *I Ching*, the Tarot, Astrology, or nearly any other oracular guide.

We must first approach an oracle with the understanding that we are seeking insight into *an inner present* rather than some insider's lowdown on an external future. This is the first step in forming a connection between our inner truth and the

Cosmic teaching energy that speaks to us through the physical medium of the oracle. As with meditation, it is not only unnecessary but *unnatural* that we spend a great deal of time, effort, emotional energy, or money on developing a relationship with the Cosmic Teacher. Several of my counseling clients had never experienced an oracle before they began working with me; all of them were fully independent with the *I Ching* in just a few sessions. Many resources on oracles are freely or inexpensively available on the Internet or in bookstores. The list that follows is just an introduction, meant to help you begin your own exploration; further information may be found in the Recommended Reading section in the Appendix to this book.

Internet Directories: There are a number of online storehouses that include links to psycho-spiritual and oracular resources. You can explore a few of these sites and give yourself a sampling of what is available, always following your own personal feelings as to what resonates with your inner truth:
Spirit and Sky: http://www.spiritandsky.com/
Technoetic: http://technoetic.com/noosphere/Divination.html

I Ching Directories: Since I have had the most experience with the *I Ching*, I can confidently recommend the following:
Greg Whincup's Directory: http://pacificcoast.net/~wh/Index.html
Clarity I Ching: http://www.onlineclarity.co.uk/
The text of the *I Ching* is available at many of the pages in the above directories. The Wilhelm/Baynes translation is freely viewable in many places, including this site: http://akirarabelais.com/i/i.html#1 . If possible, however, it is best to purchase a copy of the complete book, which contains much supplementary material, including Jung's excellent Foreword.

The I Ching Institute: My most enthusiastic personal recommendation to anyone wishing to explore the use of the *I Ching* for drawing practical insight into all aspects of inner and outer life, would be to consider the various resources available through the I Ching Institute, where I have studied. Their website is http://www.ichingoracle.com/ and I would encourage anyone beginning a practice of the *I Ching* to consider the publications offered by the Institute, particularly Carol Anthony's *Guide to the I Ching* and *I Ching: The Oracle of the Cosmic Way* (which is quoted in several places in this book), by Carol Anthony and Hanna Moog. For anyone who is seeking help with romantic or interpersonal relationships, I recommend Carol Anthony's *Love: An Inner Connection*. These books are all available through the Institute's website.

I Ching Counseling: Finally, there is my own website, www.ichingcounseling.com which includes a presentation (compatible with MS Powerpoint) that introduces the simple methods involved in drawing on the teaching energy activated by the *I Ching*.

No matter what kind of oracle you choose, or how you use it, remember that there is nothing more crucial to the results you achieve than sincerity, openness, and a suspension of disbelief. An oracle can become a personal, organic guide to time, death, health, love, work, and relationships. It is meant to provide specific, practical, and nonsectarian insight into the problems and issues that *you* face in *your* life. An oracle can inspire a conversation between each individual and his unique connection with the teaching energy of the Cosmos. As such, an oracle cannot be a tool of belief, but rather a *living experience* that is re-created within the heart of every individual that uses it in a spirit of modesty and sincerity. As Carl Jung wrote in his Foreword to the Wilhelm translation of the *I Ching*, "The *I Ching* does not offer itself with proofs and results; it does not vaunt itself....Like a part of Nature, it waits until it is discovered."[84]

Chapter 11: Moaning Myrtle and Self-Distortions of the Human Psyche

> "We wanted to ask you if you've seen anything funny lately," said Hermione quickly. "Because a cat was attacked right outside your front door on Halloween."
> "I wasn't paying attention," said Myrtle dramatically. "Peeves upset me so much I came in here and tried to kill myself. Then, of course, I remembered that I'm—that I'm—"
> "Already dead," said Ron helpfully.
> Myrtle gave a tragic sob, rose up in the air, turned over, and dived headfirst into the toilet, splashing water all over them, and vanishing from sight, although from the direction of her muffled sobs, she had come to rest somewhere in the U-bend.
> Harry and Ron stood with their mouths open, but Hermione shrugged wearily and said, "Honestly, that was almost cheerful for Myrtle....Come on, let's go."
> (*Chamber of Secrets*, pp. 156-157)

One of the delights of art is its ability to surprise—to depart from convention and then to leave the audience with the feeling of a thoroughly natural experience. Ms. Rowling chooses to set certain crucial and transformative scenes of her Harry Potter novels amid the toilets, sinks, and mirrors of public bathrooms, yet I have never heard a reader of these books ask the question, "isn't a public toilet an odd stage for a magical drama?"

Perhaps the reason for this implicit acceptance is that the author is reflecting an unconscious (or pre-conscious) sense that naturally exists in all of us—the ability to work with the elements of daily experience on a metaphorical basis—in other words, *as living poetry*. When this inborn capacity is uncovered, every life becomes a poem, in which the most commonplace actions, functions and events acquire fresh depth, filled with message and meaning. Once awakened from the cultural trance of superficiality, this natural ability to see the poetic in the commonplace energizes the entire personality. It transcends the dull, predictable dyad of communication between outer sensation and intellectual rationalization that characterizes the torpid drill of conventional experience. This metaphorical encounter with the common objects and events of life is what happens in dreams, and a very common setting of dreams is the bathroom. In this context, using the bathroom as a background for metaphorical expression seems entirely natural, particularly for a bold and original artist such as Rowling, who is continually questioning the most ingrained elements of conventional wisdom and received belief.

The action of the stories first enters the lavatory in *Sorcerer's Stone*, at a moment in which the relationship uniting Harry, Ron, and Hermione takes a deeply maturational turn. Hermione is trapped in a girls' bathroom by a giant mountain troll; Ron and Harry help to rescue her, and Hermione takes the fall when the authority figures arrive to sort things out. The mutual loyalty, trust, and affection that arise from this encounter will sustain the three friends through many more trials.

In the following story, *Chamber of Secrets*, the essence of the narrative is set primarily in an abandoned girls' bathroom, within which demons are faced, ghosts encountered, and the alchemy of transformation effected. In *Goblet of Fire*, Harry returns to the bathroom, this time to discover the secret contained within a magical egg, which will provide him with essential information on navigating his course through the "triwizard tournament." In this beautifully colored, even sensual scene, the ghost of Moaning Myrtle returns, in an environment that reveals the flip side of the institutional ego's dualistic illusion. But before we enter the bathrooms of Hogwarts, it will help to first have some background on the private spaces of our inner lives, to which Rowling's metaphor is pointing us.

It is a place where the processes of elimination are carried out, where the body is cleansed in a variety of ways, and where a certain attention is given to our external appearance, before we take ourselves out into the world of social interaction. It is a place where the door is locked and the window made translucent—open to light but not to vision. It is as much (if not more) the domain of privacy as the bedroom, and it is typically this last attribute of the bathroom that becomes the focus of dream interpretation, whenever the unconscious takes us there. One question to be asked of this picture is, "must we accept this as the necessary metaphorical dynamic of the bathroom and the functions that are carried out there, or could we attempt a broader view of the poetry contained in our daily lives, and thereby gain a new perspective on ourselves and our bodies?"

Among the creations of Nature, it would seem that we humans are once again the oddballs in this respect, with our studiousness over privacy and rectitude in the matters of elimination, sex, and childbirth. It is indeed true that other creatures are careful and seemingly "private" about such matters, but for obviously different and more pressing reasons: the time and relative immobility that are required to complete an act of elimination or coitus involve exposure to predators and other dangers. But only humans, it seems, have constructed a complex fortress of ideological and moralistic walls over this ground of natural caution. This is why we may wish to look a little deeper than the privacy and exposure issues that are so commonly attached to the interpretation of dreams about the bathroom, or in understanding symptoms such as obsessive-compulsivity, which are typically framed in the anal contours of Freudian discourse.

The whole object of psycho-spiritual work, after all, is to uncover our true nature, the personality that we have been designed with, and which we are meant to reveal to the world. If that nature has been obscured, repressed, or encrusted with ideology (however well-intended or "therapeutic" it may be), then our inner work is not serving the true purpose of returning us to our natural, human self. The *I Ching* recurrently reminds us throughout its text of the importance of this purpose, and nowhere more pointedly than in Hexagram 24, "Return":

> Return.
> Returning will be blessed.
> He goes out and comes back in again without affliction.
> A friend comes and he suffers no harm.

> Forth and back on the road,
> In seven days he has returned.
> It is favorable to advance.
> (from the translation by Greg Whincup)

Return to one's true nature is blessed because it rejoins us to the creatures with whom we share our planet, as well as to ourselves. Return is accomplished through a process of separating ourselves from what is false, artificial, or projected onto our original self. In terms of interpersonal issues, this process focuses on the separation from a false sense of self, commonly found in the societal images of pride. This is a point made by Anthony and Moog in their commentary to this text:

> This hexagram chiefly concerns pride as the element that holds a person back from returning to humility. It also concerns indulging in hurt pride, which causes the heart to harden. The way of return is for the person to reopen his heart and apologize to the Cosmos for having allowed himself to indulge in hurt pride. (*I Ching: The Oracle of the Cosmic Way*, p. 292)

The problem with pride is that because it is so brittle, it is very easily injured. Once damaged or exposed, pride becomes a vortex of falsification, as when the patriot who is "proud of his country" is forced to manipulate history to disguise the depredations committed by his nation's leaders; or when the father who is proud of his son is pushed into denial when his child repudiates the pride through some culturally-defined act of misbehavior, or simply by a failure to live up to the rigid image in which his soul has been trapped. For not only does pride restrict the personality of the one projecting it, and expose him to a crushing disillusionment; it also imprisons the target of pride's myopic vision. In every case, without exception, pride opens the door to disgrace. The Bible's well-known verse (from *Proverbs*, 16:18) actually understates the effect of pride: it does not merely "goeth before the fall," but is *itself* the inner step off the edge of the precipice. From the standpoint of the true self, pride *is* the fall.

This brings us back to Moaning Myrtle. She is an injured, slighted, self-absorbed ghost of damaged pride; her death came amid a stereotypically petty moment of hurt pride:[85]

> "It happened right in here. I died in this very stall. I remember it so well. I'd hidden because Olive Hornby was teasing me about my glasses. The door was locked, and I was crying, and then I heard somebody come in. They said something funny. A different language, I think it must have been. Anyway, what really got me was that it was a boy speaking. So I unlocked the door, to tell him to go and use his own toilet, and then—" Myrtle swelled importantly, her face shining. "I died."
> "How?" said Harry.
> "No idea," said Myrtle in hushed tones. "I just remember seeing a pair of great, big, yellow eyes. My whole body sort of seized up, and then I was floating away...." She looked dreamily at Harry. "And then I came back again. I was determined to haunt Olive Hornby, you see. Oh, she was sorry she'd ever laughed at my glasses." (*Chamber of Secrets*, p. 299).

Pride externalizes everything: instead of looking within for the solutions to our interpersonal conflicts, pride drives us to seek revenge—even if that means condemning ourselves to an eternity of disgrace and empty longing.

When we scratch the media-surface of the pride-realm and its grasping images of aggrandizement, in which treachery is celebrated, greed rewarded, and ignorance reinforced, we find nothing but desolation. For what is commonly regarded as selfishness—being the last "survivor," winning the jackpot while others are left empty-handed, or climbing higher on the corporate ladder—is really the work of the same decadent Voldemort-consciousness as that which occupies and oppresses foreign nations in the name of a pious morality mouthed by a few wealthy corporate oil barons. It is, at its core, the black heart of a demon that smugly cries, "God is with us!" At Hogwarts, it becomes a bathroom filled with distorted images and inner decrepitude:

> It was the gloomiest, most depressing bathroom Harry had ever set foot in. Under a large, cracked, and spotted mirror were a row of chipped sinks. The floor was damp and reflected the dull light given off by the stubs of a few candles, burning low in their holders; the wooden doors to the stalls were flaking and scratched and one of them was dangling off its hinges. (*Chamber of Secrets*, p. 155).

The inner depravity of a group-consciousness that projects its manufactured delusion onto Nature ends in betraying Her. Rather than spreading reform or morality among people and nations, it actually obstructs the free flow of Nature's inherent ability to heal, its capacity for creative solutions, and its restorative energies. Lao Tzu recognized this, and wrote this warning to the adherents of the hungry-ghost ideology of the pride-realm:

> To those who would alter Nature,
> Or spread reform upon the earth,
> I say this: though your efforts be endless,
> You will not succeed.
>
> Alteration, control, improvement:
> They are repugnant to Nature,
> For its perfection requires no refinement.
>
> The impulse to control
> Only deforms what you wish to manage.
> Thus, it is lost to you.
>
> The Sage withdraws from excess,
> And retreats from display.
> Where arrogance boasts,
> Where pride struts,
> The Sage will never be found.
> (from *Tao Te Ching*, Chapter 29)

In preparing my own translation of Lao Tzu's poems, I discovered that when he spoke of "the Sage," he was not typically referring to a human sage, but rather to a teaching energy of Cosmic Consciousness. This is the harvest of that awareness of life-as-poetry. Just as there exists "magic" for washing dishes, sending mail, protecting oneself from harm, or lighting one's way through dark places, there is also a specific energy stream of the consciousness that pervades natural magic, which teaches us precisely what we need to learn to make progress in our individual lives and thus be of service to others as well.

Therefore, when Lao Tzu speaks of the pride-realm as a place where "the Sage will never be found," he means that no true learning or growth happens there. The way to an enduring experience of the practical wisdom that we call "natural magic" is to be found in the disburdenment of excess, display, arrogance, and pride, and the ideological foundation on which these rest. Lao Tzu's solution is a deeply individual, autonomous response that each person creates for himself and his path. It is true that most of us are affected by some of the same general manifestations of fixed belief, but each of us finds a unique personification or collection of such problems, along with responsive solutions, that can only be realized fully through independent experience. To enter the stream of that living experience is to live the way of natural magic, and thereby step out of the arenas of opposition and pride.

The Egg in the Bath: The Birth of Insight

The bathroom that Harry enters in *Goblet of Fire* is at the opposite extreme of appearances from what he had encountered in *Chamber of Secrets*. He goes at night, alone, carrying the heavy golden egg that he had taken from the dragon's nest in the first task of the triwizard tournament. This egg, when opened, is said to contain a clue or hint to what he will encounter in the next task of the tournament. However, whenever to this point he has opened the egg, only shrill, indecipherable noise has emerged from it; but his fellow competitor, Cedric Diggory, has confidentially assured him that if he will take it into the bathroom with him, he will be able to receive the egg's true message. Cedric has also recommended that, for the sake of privacy, he use the exclusive "prefects' bathroom," and has given him the password, as Cedric is a prefect himself.

So, even before he enters this space, Harry knows he is coming into an "upscale" version of the private realm. Sure enough, the first hint comes with the password itself: "Pine fresh". With these two well-chosen words, taken as if from the script of an advertisement for cleaning products, Rowling begins to create the reader's experience, along with Harry's: she is taking us into the gleaming world of vanity—the head of the dragon whose tail is pride.

> His immediate reaction was that it would be worth becoming a prefect just to be able to use this bathroom. It was softly lit by a splendid candle-filled chandelier, and everything was made of white marble, including what looked like an empty, rectangular swimming pool sunk into the middle of the floor. About a hundred golden taps stood all around the pool's edges, each with a differently colored jewel set into its handle. There was also a diving board. Long white linen curtains hung at the windows; a large pile of fluffy white towels sat in a corner, and there was a single golden-framed painting on the wall. It featured a blonde mermaid who was fast asleep on a rock, her long hair over her face. It fluttered every time she snored. (*Goblet of Fire*, p. 459).

Just as in his first visit to the Ministry of Magic offices, Harry is presented with the glitter of artifice: gold, marble, and gems—this time with the addition of an Olympic-sized Jacuzzi! Harry is at first suspicious—he wonders whether "Cedric might have been having him on"; but then he begins to play with those gemstone water taps, and is quickly drawn in. Once he has relented to the commercial allure of this luxury (the taps produce jets of colored bubble bath water that dance magically and with perfect, climate-controlled comfort into and around the pool), he indulges himself.

Then, as if to shock him into the realization that he has re-entered the same realm that had led him to the Chamber of Secrets two years earlier, Moaning Myrtle suddenly appears, as if from nowhere (as ghosts often do), to offer him some advice:

> "I'd try putting it in the water, if I were you."
> Harry had swallowed a considerable amount of

bubbles in shock. He stood up, sputtering, and saw the ghost of a very glum-looking girl sitting cross-legged on top of one of the taps. It was Moaning Myrtle, who was usually to be heard sobbing in the S-bend of a toilet three floors below.

"Myrtle!" Harry said in outrage, "I'm—I'm not wearing anything!"

The foam was so dense that this hardly mattered, but he had a nasty feeling that Myrtle had been spying on him from out of one of the taps ever since he had arrived. (*Goblet of Fire*, p. 461).

Harry's first reaction is the resentment of shame—another form of injured pride—that even the *ghost* of a girl has seen him naked. If the wailing noise of the egg had not completely broken the spell of his encounter with luxury, the smug pettiness of Moaning Myrtle's voice does the job. Of course, after another clumsy demonstration of self-consciousness, Harry follows Myrtle's advice, and submerges himself with the egg. Once again, as it was in Book Two, an enigma is solved, through a journey beneath the surface prompted by the ghostly, wormlike voice of ego. So the question arises: is ego really a friend—maybe, in fact, one of our "helpers"?

To borrow another underwater metaphor, we may think of the ego as the irritant, the grain of sand within the oyster of the self, around which the pearl of true nature seems to form. Granted, this is not quite exact, since the pearl is always there, waiting to be revealed, but the image of the irritating stimulus is apt to our purpose: the ego and its noisy, incomplete solutions to problems can be the occasion of the very dissatisfaction that causes us to turn within for the enduring solutions that our true self needs. I suspect that this is what Jung had in mind when he spoke of the appearance of neurosis as a kind of serendipity:

> I am not altogether pessimistic about neurosis. In many cases we have to say: "Thank heaven he could make up his mind to be neurotic." Neurosis is really an attempt at self-cure, just as any physical disease is in part an attempt at self-cure. [Neurosis] is an attempt of the self-regulating psychic system to restore the balance, in no way

different from the function of dreams—only rather more forceful and drastic. (from the Tavistock Lectures, CW 18, par. 389).

It is no different in the matter of psycho-spiritual practice. Returning to Sogyal Rinpoche, we hear indirectly the same message about the ego as the stimulating irritant that lights the lamp of awareness:

> Two people have been living in you all your life. One is the ego, garrulous, demanding, hysterical, calculating; the other is the hidden spiritual being, whose still voice of wisdom you have only rarely heard or attended to. As you listen more and more to the teachings, contemplate them, and integrate them into your life, your inner voice, your innate wisdom of discernment, is awakened and strengthened, and you start to distinguish between its guidance and the various clamorous and enthralling voices of ego. The memory of our real nature, with all its splendor and confidence, begins to return to you. (*The Tibetan Book of Living and Dying*, p. 120)

Clearly, there is the occasional frustration, and even a certain mortification that seems necessary to this process, as the ego's noise recurs and its re-installation programs of guilt, aggrandizement, arrogance, and pride are played out within us. Harry experiences this again and again throughout the stories, like so many of us who leap from one seeming solution to another, amid both the outer and inner planes of our lives, frequently switching from one to the other. This book has been designed to present some suggestions that are meant to help you toward your own discovery of a personal path to freedom from ego. There is no fixed or formulaic, one-size-fits-all solution; there are only certain practices and approaches that can serve as guides, which help us to remain open to each moment's fresh truth, each situation's solution. We will have a little more to say about this before we close, but first it will be helpful to review our understanding of what has been learned within the bathrooms of Hogwarts, for this may provide the clearest perception of the opening to our path.

In each of the bathrooms that we have visited at Hogwarts, we have found metaphors for excess (of negative emotion, pride, arrogance, or accumulation). In the toilet of Book One there sits a sulking, tearful girl who becomes trapped by a troll, after spending an entire afternoon wallowing over a perceived insult; in the stalls of Book Two lives the shadow of another girl, whining out a repetitive song of petty pride and vengeance; in the palatial luxury of Book Four's bathroom, that same voice mutters amid the scented musk of indulgence and manufactured bliss. Clearly, none of these places is the metaphorical realm of one's natural self or some archetypal center of the psyche; yet from each encounter within the bathroom, some growth occurs, or a solution to a problem arises, incomplete though it might be. We have found that the defiant but shadowy voice of a self-absorbed isolation can be heard at the inlets to the pipes that lead to the Voldemort-consciousness of institutional religion; we have also felt the seductive touch of "pine-fresh" vanity amid the voyeuristic presence of a false, commercial sensuality. What element is common to these seeming extremes? In both, the body is perceived as an enemy, a stranger, an object of shame or petty indulgence. This, of course, is the fundamental distortion common to every major institutionalized religion known to mankind.

The demonization of the body, either through self-abasement or the perversions of titillation and indulgence, is the hallmark of Voldemort-consciousness, which arises from a global demonization of Nature. Lord Voldemort lost his body, and never truly recovered it, because he had aligned himself with the obsessive goal of immortality-as-power; with the power to live forever in a perpetual dominion over, and separation from, Nature. Such a toxic belief diffuses into every corner of life, in the forced separation between one's private and public selves; in the divorcing of work and home, which leads in turn to the marital divorces that are so familiar to our culture; it recurs again in the opposition of the genders and their mutual suspicion born of fear; it is evidenced among both children and adults in the division of Authority and subject, or the powerful and the dependent; and throughout all levels of the psyche, it is heard as the voice of conformity (or its rebellious antagonist), where, with the sword of guilt held to our inner throats, we hear the threat posed to us by every form of the institutional ego—"are you with us, or against us?"

The answer, which we must form firmly within ourselves, is "Mu." In his groundbreaking book, *Zen and the Art of Motorcycle Maintenance*, Robert Pirsig explains:

> Because we're unaccustomed to it, we don't usually see that there's a third possible logical term equal to yes and no which is capable of expanding our understanding in an unrecognized direction. We don't even have a term for it, so I'll have to use the Japanese mu.
>
> Mu means "no thing." Like "Quality" it points outside the process of dualistic discrimination. Mu simply says, "No class; not one, not zero, not yes, not no." It states that the context of the question is such that a yes or no answer is in error and should not be given. "Unask the question" is what it says.[86]

This is the response that Harry and his young friends are led to, time and again, with the example of Professor Dumbledore to guide them. True, the representatives of the Voldemort ideologies of our culture will frequently interpret our inner departure from the arena of opposition as enmity: this is what Dumbledore means when he reminds the students, during his last speech in *Goblet of Fire*, that "the time should come when you have to make a choice between what is right and what is easy." In this message, he speaks to the heart of every individual in the Great Hall: what is right is that which accords with each person's inner truth, however much it may seem to separate him from the collective. What is easy is the cloying allegiance to a system of group belief that defines your identity, lives your life for you, and leads you inevitably into opposition.

Exercise: Transformation Through a Word

One of the principles of both the metaphorical magic of Hogwarts and the natural magic of inner discovery involves the use of words. Language has been the most commonly assigned defining attribute of humanity, yet we use it in a careless, slovenly, and even destructive fashion—and here I am speaking specifically of the habits of the leaders of our culture in the realms of government, law, science, academia, and religion. I would sooner learn principles of proper human conduct from a first-grader than from a papal bull.

At Hogwarts, the students learn that the words of a charm must be learned thoroughly and spoken clearly, in order for the magic to happen as desired. We must learn the same lesson in our practice of natural magic: the words we use make a difference—sometimes, they make *all* the difference. What follows is an example of this principle; it is meant to speak directly to the issue regarding pride that has been discussed earlier in this chapter. I encourage you to try it and let your feelings guide you from there.

We have seen how pride, whether of the healthy, "button-bursting" variety or the injured pride of a tarnished self-image, tends to obstruct growth and insight, leading us into a cesspool of bitterness that only poisons everything and everyone around it, if it is not deprived of the energy feeding its projections. What if we began the work of reclaiming and transforming that energy by "downsizing" pride, through a simple use of our most uniquely human gift, the blessing of language? It would cost us only a little effort, and hardly any time, so perhaps it's worth a try.

Start by writing down, or simply saying to yourself, some common pride-expressions that you have used in your life, and then go over the list of these phrases again, replacing the words "pride" or "proud" with the words "gratitude" or "grateful". Then, either in a brief daily meditation or simply with a conscious awareness of your inner and outer speech over the course of a few days, consistently apply this verbal correction, with a particular awareness of those instances in which you forget to make the replacement, either in thought or speech. The following is a sample list of expressions to help you begin.

Old Phrase	New Phrase
"I'm proud to be an American"	"I am grateful to live in this country."
"I take pride in my work."	"I feel gratitude for the work that is accomplished through me, and for the success that the helpers bring to it."
"I'm so proud of how my kids turned out"	"I'm grateful for my kids, and the help they've had in their growth."
"I'm proud of my staff for the long hours they put in to complete this project."	"I'm very grateful to the people I work with for their effort in helping to create this success."
"You must be so proud to have {aced the test, finished the painting, won the game, gotten the promotion}."	"That's wonderful news—this is obviously the stream in which your talent flows—you must be very grateful to have discovered it."

Work with your personal "pride phrases," and add variations of your own invention. See which phrases tend to stir up emotional tension or guilt—such emotions may point you toward the ideas that you need to discard from within, using the "inner No" technique discussed in previous chapters.

Dumbledore's Response: Returning to the Room of Requirement

In *Goblet of Fire*, there is a fascinating exchange between Karkaroff, the former Death Eater who now heads up the visiting Durmstrang school[87], and Professor Dumbledore. Karkaroff is an oily character with an unctuous air, who is described as having a "smile [that] did not extend to his eyes, which remained cold and shrewd." (p. 247). His self-righteousness and lingering attachment to the compulsive ideologies of power are revealed throughout the story, and are evident in this conversation, which occurs amid the feast at the "Yule Ball":

> Dumbledore smiled, his eyes twinkling. "Igor, all this secrecy...one would almost think you didn't want visitors."
> "Well, Dumbledore," said Karkaroff, displaying his yellowing teeth to their fullest extent, "we are all protective of our private domains, are we not? Do we not jealously guard the halls of learning that have been entrusted to us? Are we not right to be proud that we alone know our school's secrets, and right to protect them?"
> "Oh, I would never dream of assuming I know all Hogwarts' secrets, Igor," said Dumbledore amicably. "Only this morning, for instance, I took a wrong turning on my way to the bathroom and found myself in a beautifully proportioned room I have never seen before, containing a really rather magnificent collection of chamber pots. When I went back to investigate more closely, I discovered that the room had vanished. But I must keep an eye out for it. Possibly it is only accessible at five-thirty in the morning. Or it may only appear at the quarter moon—or when the seeker has an exceptionally full bladder." (pp. 417-418).

As Harry recognizes in the next book, after his own encounter with it, Dumbledore had chanced upon the "Room of Requirement," in his search for a place to "go". It seems entirely fitting that our discussion of bathrooms and the private domains of consciousness has brought us back to this magical room, the inner space in which each need is answered in exactly the right measure and at the perfect moment.

The psyche is not a fixed entity of drives, wishes, and repressive inner machinery; nor is it comprised solely of electrochemical impulses traveling among cells bundled together in our heads. As with religious and national orthodoxies, each scientific ideology ("theoretical paradigm") that becomes fixed within the lumbering juggernaut of received belief seems to find its place on a pole of opposition and extremism; the Freudian-influenced models of psychological development, pathology, and healing have found themselves cast into a darkness of disrepute by the equally shrill, fixed, and monumental notions of biological psychiatry, which seem to currently pervade our culture. The problem within this dynamic is revealed by the psychotherapist Robert Fancher, in his *Cultures of Healing* (1995):

> If schools of care had genuinely identified what it means to be psychologically healthy, we could use them to know what to aspire to—we would know that their visions of health are attainable and good for us. [Yet] cultures sometimes demand of persons what is not possible, what constricts their development, or what has less to do with current reality than with the needs or interests of some bygone time and its archaic purposes. We can be about as certain that what cultures of healing promise us is possible and beneficial as that America can be whatever the current political hero tells us it can—and that we would be as well off if it were. (p. 38).[88]

As Fancher suggests further in his book, the problem with competing schools of belief and practice—especially when it comes to the conception and treatment of the human psyche—is not a matter of deciding which school's paradigm is "true," but rather in the attempt of each to close its collective grip on The Truth. In this effort, the sciences fall prey to the very same delusion of Voldemort-consciousness that religion and government have succumbed to throughout history. Truth, as we have discovered over the course of this journey through the world of Hogwarts, is alive, organic, never ceasing in its transformative movement: the Room of Requirement that I enter today will be considerably different from the one I discovered yesterday, as much as it will differ from the same Room that you are entering now. Truth is a deeply personal matter, which defies the grip of group belief. What is universal about truth—that each person contains a unique potential for clarity—also makes it the organic and unfolding experience of intimacy with oneself and one's Cosmic Origin, as Hexagram 61 of the *I Ching*, "Inner Truth," lyrically describes:

> Inner Truth. Pigs and fishes.
> Good fortune.
> It furthers one to cross the great water.
> Perseverance furthers.
> (from the Richard Wilhelm translation)

The translation varies slightly among different versions: the expression "pigs and fishes" is often rendered (as in the John

Blofeld translation) as "dolphins" (or, as Ritsema and Karcher express it, "hog-fish", meaning aquatic animals of intelligence). Yet the metaphor points in the same direction as the Room of Requirement: there is a treasure-trove of inner truth within each being born out of the Tao that is unique, intimate, and inviolate; for through this treasure comes each being's individual connection with the Source, the All. To enter this room of inner truth, and to care for it through one's whole life, is to remain truly a part of Nature, within whose realm the creatures of land and sea are as diverse and abundant as moments within Eternity. To nurture one's personal truth is to enable the "crossing of the great water"—the fulfillment of one's unique destiny as a life-form in the great sphere of consciousness.

This is a universal attribute of inner truth, and to this uniqueness is joined the way of Equality: the truth of a human being is of no greater quality or dimension than that of a pig or a dolphin. In brief, the mere existence of each of us confirms our purpose. Equality also extends to the surpassing of comparison or competition: the room where Professor Dumbledore is able to enjoy the refreshing feeling of elimination is the same room where Harry feels the first kiss of ecstasy; thus is the polar insanity of opposition and competition transcended. Think about this whenever you hear that voice telling you that your job, your house, your possessions, your talents, your thoughts, or your very life, are insignificant in comparison to those of others. As Lao Tzu reminds us in Chapter 5 of the *Tao Te Ching*:

> Equality is the Cosmic Way:
> Good and evil are born of fantasy.
> The Sage is neither partisan nor punishing:
> No one is special, no one excluded.
>
> Consciousness breathes,
> Expands and contracts.
> It never varies, and each moment is unique.
>
> Work with this and understand;
> Talk about it, and you lose your center.

We will now take Lao Tzu's advice and cease the talk (of course, by "talk about it" he meant to pour the concrete of dogma into the water of insight). First, however, I offer one final reflection, which you may adapt to the purposes of your own brief daily meditation, to affirm your life, its uniqueness, and your connection with the ground of being.

Think of yourself again as energy: the ceaseless movement whose order and disposition define the seeming matter of your body, and indeed of all form. You breathe out your excess into the Whole from which you came and to which you will return; you gently inhale the nourishment of renewed life-force—what the Chinese refer to as "chi". You can feel waves of movement, as of water or wind, passing through you with each breath—gently dissolving what is manifest but only derivative, while the energetic core of your personal inner truth is gradually revealed and strengthened. You are not, after all, your race, your gender, your occupation, your material possessions, your marital or family status, your sexual orientation, your socio-economic class, your political, national, or religious affiliation; nor are you what the voice from a television says you are. All these ingrained self-images dissolve with every breath, as the life-force enters and moves through you—dispelling the false, peeling away the appearance, revealing the core and center of your being, whose inimitable perfection dances in joyful separation from the realms of pride, guilt, and opposition.

Appendix: References and Further Reading

The Harry Potter Stories of J.K. Rowling:

Harry Potter and the Sorcerer's Stone (New York: Scholastic, 1997)
Harry Potter and the Chamber of Secrets (New York: Scholastic, 1999)
Harry Potter and the Prisoner of Azkaban (New York: Scholastic, 1999)
Harry Potter and the Goblet of Fire (New York: Scholastic, 2000)
Harry Potter and the Order of the Phoenix (New York: Scholastic, 2003)
Harry Potter and the Half-Blood Prince (New York: Scholastic, 2005)
Harry Potter and the Deathly Hallows (New York: Scholastic, 2007

The Poetry Referenced in this Volume:

Lao Tzu's *Tao Te Ching*: the translations of Lao Tzu in this book are from my own work, *Poems of the Universe: Lao Tzu's Tao Te Ching, A New English Translation.* 2005 (available at http://www.lulu.com/content/208185).

I also recommend:

Tao Te Ching, tr. Stephen Mitchell. New York: Harper & Row, 1988.
Tao Te Ching: The Definitive Edition, tr. Jonathan Star. New York: Jeremy P. Tarcher/Putnam, 2001.

The I Ching:

I Ching: The Classic Chinese Oracle of Change, tr. Rudolf Ritsema and Stephen Karcher. New York: Barnes & Noble Books, 1995.
Rediscovering the I Ching, tr. Gregory Whincup. New York: St. Martin's Press, 1986.
The I Ching, or Book of Changes, tr. Richard Wilhelm and Cary F. Baynes. New York: The Bollingen Foundation, Inc. / Princeton University Press, 1950/1977.
I Ching, tr. Kerson and Rosemary Huang. New York: Workman Publishing, 1985.
The Classic of Changes: A New Translation of the I Ching, Wang Bi, tr. Richard John Lynn. New York: Columbia University Press, 1994.
Carol Anthony and Hanna Moog. *I Ching: The Oracle of the Cosmic Way*. Stow, MA: ichingbooks / Anthony Publishing Company, 2002.
Carol K. Anthony, *A Guide to the I Ching*. Stow, MA: Anthony Publishing Company, 1988.
Carol K. Anthony, *Love, an Inner Connection: Based on Principles Drawn from the I Ching*. Stow, MA: Anthony Publishing Company, 1993/2002.

The Ling Qi Jing:

Ivan Kashiwa, ed., *Spirit Tokens of the Ling Qi Jing*. New York: Weatherhill, 1997.

<u>*Recommended Reading for Other Poetry Quoted in this Book:*</u>

Robert Bly, *The Man in the Black Coat Turns*. New York: Doubleday & Company, 1981.
Robert Bly, *Sleepers Joining Hands*. New York: Harper Perennial, 1973.
Robert Bly, James Hillman, Michael Meade, ed., *The Rag and Bone Shop of the Heart*. New York: Harper Perennial, 1992.
Yoel Hoffmann, ed., *Japanese Death Poems: Written by Zen Monks and Haiku Poets on the Verge of Death*. Rutland, VT: Charles E. Tuttle Company, 1986.
Rumi, tr. Jonathan Star, *In the Arms of the Beloved*. New York: Jeremy P. Tarcher / Putnam, 1997.
Rainer Maria Rilke, tr. Stephen Mitchell, *Ahead of All Parting: The Selected Poetry and Prose of Rainer Maria Rilke*. New York: The Modern Library, 1995.
D.J. Enright, ed., *The Oxford Book of Death*. Oxford: The Oxford University Press, 1987.
Shakespeare, W., ed. A.L. Rowse. *The Annotated Shakespeare*. New York: Greenwich House, 1988.
The Norton Anthology of English Literature, Fourth Edition ed. Abrams, Donaldson, Smith, Adamson, Monk, Lipking, Ford, Daiches. New York: W.W. Norton & Company, 1962/1979.
T.S. Eliot. *The Complete Poems and Plays*. New York: Harcourt, Brace & World, Inc., 1930/1971.

References

Akong Tulku Rinpoche, Taming the Tiger. Rochester, VT: Inner Traditions, 1995.

Alan W. Watts, The Way of Zen. New York: Vintage Books, 1957.

Alice Miller, Banished Knowledge: Facing Childhood Injuries. New York: Anchor Books/Doubleday, 1990.

American Psychiatric Association, Diagnostic and Statistical Manual of Mental Disorders (DSM-IV), Washington, DC: The American Psychiatric Association, 1994.

Anthony Storr, Churchill's Black Dog, Kafka's Mice, and Other Phenomena of the Human Mind. New York: Ballantine Books, 1965.

Anthony Storr, Freud. Oxford: Oxford University Press, 1989.

Benjamin Hoff, The Te of Piglet. New York: Penguin/Dutton, 1992.

Brian Greene, The Fabric of the Cosmos: Space. Time. And the Texture of Reality. New York: Alfred A. Knopf, 2004.

C.G. Jung, ed. Anthony Storr, The Essential Jung. Princeton, NJ: Princeton University Press, 1983.

Carol Anthony and Hanna Moog, I Ching: The Oracle of the Cosmic Way. Stow, MA: ichingbooks, 2002.

Carol K. Anthony, The Other Way: A Book of Meditation Experiences Based on the I Ching. Stow, MA: Anthony Publishing Company, 1991.

Chuang Tsu, tr. Gia-Fu Feng and Jane English. Inner Chapters. San Francisco: Amber Lotus Publishing, 1974.

D.J. Enright, ed., The Oxford Book of Death. Oxford: The Oxford University Press, 1987.

Eric Hoffer, The True Believer: Thoughts on the Nature of Mass Movements. New York: HarperCollins Perennial Classics, 1951.

Fritjof Capra, The Hidden Connections: Integrating the Biological, Cognitive, and Social Dimensions of Life into a Science of Sustainability. New York: Doubleday, 2002.

Fyodor Dostoyevsky, The Brothers Karamazov. New York: Bantam Books, 1981.

G.S. Kirk, J.E. Raven, ed., The Presocratic Philosophers: A Critical History with a Selection of Texts. London: The Cambridge University Press, 1971.

Gary Zukav, The Seat of the Soul. New York: Fireside, 1989.

George Orwell, 1984. New York: Signet Classic/New American Library, 1950/1977.

Gilles Marin, Healing From Within with Chi Nei Tsang: Applied Chi Kung in Internal Organs Treatment. Berkeley, CA: North Atlantic Books, 1999.

Hannah Arendt, Eichmann in Jerusalem: A Report on the Banality of Evil. New York: Penguin Books, 1977/1994.

Harry Stack Sullivan, M.D., The Psychiatric Interview. New York: W.W. Norton and Company, 1954.

Henry David Thoreau, Walden (1854). Koln, Germany: Konemann, 1996.

I Ching: The Classic Chinese Oracle of Change, tr. Rudolf Ritsema and Stephen Karcher. New York: Barnes & Noble Books, 1995.

J. Krishnamurti, D. Rajagopal, ed., Think on These Things. New York: Harper & Row, 1964.

Jean Chevalier and Alain Gheerbrant, tr. John Buchannan-Brown, The Penguin Dictionary of Symbols. London: Penguin Books, 1996.

Joan Borysenko, Ph.D., Fire in the Soul: A New Psychology of Spiritual Optimism. New York: Warner Books, 1993.

John Blofeld, tr., I Ching: The Book of Change. New York: Penguin Arkana, 1965/1991.

John Herman Randall, Jr., Justus Buchler, Evelyn Shirk, ed., Readings in Philosophy. New York: Barnes & Noble Books, 1972.

John Welwood, Love and Awakening: Discovering the Sacred Path of Intimate Relationship. New York: Harper Perennial, 1997.

Joseph Campbell, Primitive Mythology: The Masks of God. New York: Penguin Books, 1959.

Joseph Campbell, The Hero With a Thousand Faces. Princeton, NJ: The Princeton University Press, 1949/1968.

Joseph Conrad, Heart of Darkness and Other Tales (Oxford World's Classics). Oxford: Oxford University Press, 1998.

Karen Horney, M.D. Neurosis and Human Growth. New York: W.W. Norton and Company, 1950.

Leston Havens, A Safe Place. New York: Ballantine Books, 1989.

Lindsey Fraser, Conversations with J.K. Rowling. New York: Scholastic, Inc., 2000.

Mantak Chia, Taoist Ways to Transform Stress into Vitality: The Inner Smile, Six Healing Sounds. Huntington, NY: Healing Tao Books, 1985.

Nicholas Black Elk and John G. Neihardt, Black Elk Speaks: Being the Life Story of a Holy Man of the Oglala Sioux. Lincoln, NE: University of Nebraska Press, 1932/2000.

Norman Cousins, Anatomy of an Illness as Perceived by the Patient: Reflections on Healing and Regeneration. New York: Bantam Books, 1991.

Rainer Maria Rilke, tr. Robert Bly, Selected Poems. New York: Harper and Row/Perennial Library, 1981.

Ralph Waldo Emerson, The Essential Writings of Ralph Waldo Emerson. New York: The Modern Library, 2000.

Rediscovering the I Ching, tr. Gregory Whincup. New York: St. Martin's Press, 1986.

Robert Bly, Iron John: A Book About Men. Reading, MA: Addison-Wesley Publishing Company, Inc., 1990.

Robert Bly, Sleepers Joining Hands. New York: Harper Perennial, 1973.

Robert Bly, The Man in the Black Coat Turns. New York: Doubleday & Company, 1981.

Robert T. Fancher, Cultures of Healing: Correcting the Image of American Mental Health Care. New York: W.H. Freeman and Company, 1995.

Roshi Philip Kapleau, Zen: Merging of East and West. New York: Doubleday, 1989.

Rumi, tr. Jonathan Star, In the Arms of the Beloved. New York: Jeremy P. Tarcher / Putnam, 1997.

Shakespeare, ed. A.L. Rowse. The Annotated Shakespeare. New York: Greenwich House, 1988.

Shunryu Suzuki, Zen Mind, Beginner's Mind. New York: Weatherhill, 1970/1996.

Sigmund Freud, tr. James Strachey, Introductory Lectures on Psycho-Analysis. New York: W.W. Norton & Company, 1966.

Sogyal Rinpoche, The Tibetan Book of Living and Dying. New York: HarperSanFrancisco, 1993.

Soren Kierkegaard, tr. Alastair Hannay, The Sickness Unto Death. London: Penguin Books, 1849/1989.

Stephen Hawking, A Brief History of Time: From the Big Bang to Black Holes. New York: Bantam Books, 1990.

T.S Eliot, The Complete Poems and Plays. New York: Harcourt, Brace & World, Inc., 1930/1971.

The I Ching, or Book of Changes, tr. Richard Wilhelm and Cary F. Baynes. New York: The Bollingen Foundation, Inc. / Princeton University Press, 1950/1977.

The Norton Anthology of English Literature, Fourth Edition ed. Abrams, Donaldson, Smith, Adamson, Monk, Lipking, Ford, Daiches. New York: W.W. Norton & Company, 1962/1979.

Willis Barnstone and Marvin Meyer, ed., The Gnostic Bible. Boston: Shambhala, 2003.

Notes:

[1] "Magic Words," from *Technicians of the Sacred*, edited by Jerome Rothenberg; quoted in *The Rag and Bone Shop of the Heart: A Poetry Anthology*, edited by Robert Bly, James Hillman, and Michael Meade (1992).

[2] Chuang Tsu, tr. Gia-Fu Feng and Jane English: Inner Chapters.

[3] Blake, from *The Marriage of Heaven and Hell*.

[4] The poet is P'ang-yun, from the Ch'uan Teng Lu, 8 (paraphrased from the verse as quoted in Alan Watts' *The Way of Zen*, p. 133).

[5] Walden, "Economy". Thoreau adds that "what is called resignation is confirmed desperation...a stereotyped but unconscious despair is concealed even under what are called the games and amusements of mankind."

[6] The translation is from a rendering of the I Ching made by a Yale professor Law named Jack Balkin, *The Laws of Change: I Ching and the Philosophy of Life* (New York: Schocken Books, 2002), p. 136.

[7] Lovers of Shakespeare will recall that the victim of Leontes' madness in *The Winter's Tale* is named Hermione. Metaphorically (as Rowling must have seen herself), the demonization of the feminine through the scheming insanity of intellect acting in isolation as the "royal power" of the personality, is exactly what drives Leontes into psychosis, or the separation from a healthy experience of reality. When Hermione is falsely accused and banished, eventually to die, what is first lost to inner death is Leontes' true nature—all through the obsession with thought and action.

[8] Thus, her surname, Granger, meaning, of the "grange"—the farm, the earth, and growth.

[9] Still, this is not an uncommon error, and one of the reasons that children are driven away from some wonderful literary experiences. This happens when adults, some of whom laughably refer to themselves as "teachers," dictate to children what a book, a play, or a poem, means, leaving the kids no inner room to experience it for themselves.

[10] The characters representing this state-manifestation of evil are Dolores Umbridge and Cornelius Fudge, who are government officials trapped in a web of deceit and manipulation by Voldemort, through his appointed "lobbyist," Lucius Malfoy.

[11] It has long been assumed that snakes (Lord Voldemort's animal symbol) cannot hear, since they lack external ears. This has only recently been questioned by scientists, who now believe that snakes can hear. But the symbolic association between the deafness of ego and Lord Voldemort's "snake-deafness" seems compelling in this context.

[12] From *Think on these Things*, pp. 43-44. This book is a sparkling

collection of lectures and talks by Krishnamurti on education and thought. Krishnamurti's entire discussion of religion from this book is worth study: this comes from Chapter 4 of that work, "Listening".

[13] This connection between Falstaff and Ron is reinforced through that between the rather airy and ambitious Hotspur of Shakespeare and Ron's brother, Percy, which is Hotspur's given name.

[14] These are Professor Dumbledore's words, from his closing speech in The Goblet of Fire, after he has announced to the school the news of the return of Lord Voldemort.

[15] Draco's name comes from the Latin draco, dragon, and the French mal foi, or "bad faith."

[16] Alice Miller, Banished Knowledge: Facing Childhood Injuries (1990). Miller's work deserves far better recognition than the marginalization to which it has been subjected by the adherents of so-called scientific psychology. Her insight is based on the synergy of a lifetime of experience with troubled children combined with a lively common sense and an active, natural compassion. I think it is not the least excessive to recommend her writing to every parent, teacher, or childcare provider; if she occasionally goes "over the top" in her strident position against psychoanalysis (and she is more often than not directly on target with her criticisms in that vein, anyway), she is nevertheless incisive, revealing, and always genuine in her unremitting commitment to the health and natural growth of children. For this alone, she is worth reading and remembering.

[17] This phrase is from Chapter 50 of Tao Te Ching.

[18] Banished Knowledge, p. 52.

[19] The quotes in this section from Black Elk are from one of the classic volumes of psycho-spiritual literature, *Black Elk Speaks*, which is a collection of autobiographical interviews from 1931 of the Lakota healer and philosopher Black Elk, as arranged and transcribed by John Neihardt. Incidentally, the term "Wasichu" is a term from the Oglala Sioux for "white man." The book remains in print (University of Nebraska Press).

[20] And as we will discuss in a later chapter, the encounter with Lord Voldemort in the graveyard scene of Book Four comes as the result of the pursuit of the glory associated with an athletic prize. Harry's good fortune is that each of these consequences of allowing ego and its monumental desires to lead his personality leads him into an experience that will further deepen his humility and his recognition of his true place, as a human, within the totality of the earth and the Cosmos.

[21] In the spirit realm, Black Elk encounters horses, geese, eagles, elk—"animals of every kind"—as well as human figures. For his part, Harry is helped throughout the stories by non-human creatures: elves, hippogriffs, centaurs, dogs, and the deer-like creature produced by his patronus charm, which dispels the dementors.

[22] Robert Bly, *Iron John: A Book about Men*, pp. 207-216.

[23] Joseph Campbell, *Primitive Mythology*, p. 273. In this same chapter, he re-tells some of the old trickster stories, including one of a creation god

who is shot through the world by explosive farts, scattering villages and spreading disorder, until he finally leaves the earth for good, leaving behind the massive imprint of his buttocks on the land.

[24] The Hidden Connections (2002). In this book, Capra describes a living systems approach from a biological perspective, and then draws on that understanding to explore its applicability to management and human organizational spheres.

[25] This is from Augustine's *Confessions*, a beautifully written piece of delusory dogma.

[26] From *Iron John: A Book About Men*.

[27] Herman Hesse, *Siddhartha* (tr. Hilda Rosner); 1922/1951, New Direction Publishing Co, New York, p. 50. *Siddhartha* is a classic because it is a universal story: it reflects the search of each one of us who encounters it, and thus it speaks to us in every stage of life. It is the kind of novel that is best read many times over the course of one's life: in many moments of growth and regression, prosperity and reversal, happiness and despair; for its teaching ability is never lost to us, no matter where we are in life.

[28] According to legend, the basilisk was "a cock with a dragon's tail or a snake with cock's wings;" it is metaphorically related to the gorgon as a symbol of death and terror. "It represented kingly power which annihilates all who do not show it due respect." (Chevalier and Gheerbrant, *The Penguin Dictionary of Symbols*, p. 69).

[29] For instance, many of us are taught, from childhood on, that our sense of smell is relatively unimportant or menial—a function of the "reptilian brain," which must be superseded by the monarchical intellect.

[30] For the marvelous insight on the "inner No," I am indebted to Carol Anthony and Hanna Moog, who present the practice in their *I Ching: The Oracle of the Cosmic Way*. For a complete description of the practice and benefits of the inner No, see the Appendix to that book.

[31] The Feng Shui practitioner mentioned is a consultant named Gregg Nodelman, whose work I highly recommend. More information about Gregg can be found at his website, http://www.ddfengshui.com/content/publish/home.shtml .

[32] We later find that Neville's parents have been tortured into terminal dementia by followers of Lord Voldemort.

[33] Clearly, Freud did not mean by "ego" the same sort of concept that we are discussing here. To Freud, ego was a necessary structural component of the psyche that acted as a kind of mediator between the unconscious, roiling "drives" of id and the conscious, socially-oriented rationalism of civilized life—as such, ego was functionally an agent of compromise, standing with one foot in the deeply unconscious realm of dark, instinctual urges and the other in the open air of society and its necessary limitations on the expression and gratification of the instinctual drives. For our purposes, ego may be considered as the abstract embodiment of error— mistaken beliefs, assumptions, and self-images that distort Nature, the

Cosmos, and our own human nature. In the way of inner growth, there is nothing "necessary" about ego.

[34] Norman Cousins, *Anatomy of an Illness as Perceived by the Patient*

[35] We are, of course, referring to the sincere and malice-free laughter of natural humor, the joy of the true self freed from the oppression of ego. Unfortunately, it is possible that ego can poison and distort humor, as it does with anger, love, and other natural human feelings. The humor that is from ego can be easily detected, however: it is usually dark, malevolent, aggressive—as if coming from a chip on the shoulder.

[36] Shunyru Suzuki, *Zen Mind, Beginner's Mind*, p. 32.

[37] Walden, "Solitude".

[38] This very brief illustrative discussion of the inner No is drawn from the work of Carol Anthony and Hanna Moog, the directors of the I Ching Institute and authors of *I Ching: The Oracle of the Cosmic Way*. The appendix to that book contains more detailed instruction on performing the inner No, and it is recommended to the reader who is interested in further exploring the transformative capacity of the inner No in furthering inner growth, healing illness, and managing relationships.

[39] Christmas is, of course, a late-phase development of the solstice observance, which appears to go back as far as 5,000 B.C.E. Among the ancient Egyptians, December 21 was the date upon which the entombment of Osiris was memorialized: this represented a time of simultaneous death and rebirth. For Harry, this first solstice in the magical world is a moment replete with the promise of transformation—from his dependent, static past (the word "solstice" means "sun standing still") toward the active insights of the ever-broadening understanding whose path is so soon to open to him.

[40] Those more familiar with the film version of this story may be confused at this, because in the movie Harry only sees his mother and father. But Rowling's original version of the scene suggests an important point: she wants us to understand that Harry is having an experience that goes beyond the sentimental pabulum of Hollywood or Disney—he is being presented with images that go into the mists of his generational past, as if rooted in a mythology of the ancients.

[41] "One does not drink the mud of the well. No animals come to an old well." (Wilhelm translation). In the present context, the "mud" is the ideological crust of fixed belief that forms around the true self and makes the water of autonomous growth either inaccessible or so poisoned with falsehood as to be "undrinkable."

[42] The *I Ching* reference I have in mind here is from Hexagram 38, "Opposition", the third line of which reads, "One see the wagon dragged back, the oxen halted, a man's hair and nose cut off. Not a good beginning, but a good end." This, by the way, is a marvelous lesson in the opportunity or transformative potential that misfortune and adversity can contain, if we will only pay attention.

[43] The schizoid personality, as delineated within the various editions of the

American Psychiatric Association's DSM, is to be clearly distinguished from the psychotic state known as schizophrenia. The schizoid profile of self-absorbed depression and haughty, omnidirectional anger or hatred, is most frequently the mark of one who has been programmed from an early age with self-images of unworthiness and personal insufficiency, who carries the "template" of rejection-expectation, resentment, and further rejection: indeed, one of Welwood's clients describes himself as Prometheus bound in torment, the vulture gnawing at his liver. For another description of the schizoid personality, this time from literary history, see Anthony Storr's *Churchill's Black Dog, Kafka's Mice*, Chapter 2, "Kafka's Sense of Identity".

[44] Joseph Campbell, *The Hero with a Thousand Faces*.

[45] Here, it is worth recalling Rowling's description of Harry's cloak: "like water woven into material."

[46] The Love Song of J. Alfred Prufrock (1917)

[47] in *Iron John* (1990). The subtitle to this book is "A Book About Men", but it is a gift to anyone of either gender, which can be recommended to women every bit as much as to men.

[48] Mrs. Rowling's intriguing use of her unique brand of euphonious (if ungrammatical) Latin is another instance of the positive influences for children that flow throughout her stories. The first novel has already been translated into Latin, with an ancient Greek version to follow soon. As for the phrase "Priori Incantatem", it means "previous enchantment" and refers to the effect of the appearance of Voldemort's murdered victims during this scene. In the actual novel, it is explained as "the reverse spell effect" in Chapter 36, yet I'd prefer that we focus here on the inner direction of the metaphor over any superficial interpretation of the Latin expression.

[49] Harry's red is probably an angry scarlet, while Voldemort's green is best imagined as a kind of pale, slime-green. As every painter knows, red and green pigments make a brownish color; but the same mixture with light yields a different result: yellow. The color that arises from the connection between Harry's and Voldemort's spells is a kind of composite gold—a bright, gleaming yellow that contains a hint of the earth's brown.

[50] Many of these ideas are summarized and cogently presented for the general reader in Fritjof Capra's works, most notably, *The Web of Life* (1996) and *The Hidden Connections* (2002).

[51] See *The Art of War*, Ch. 6, "Weak Points and Strong"

[52] The owl, in classical Greek and Hindu symbology, is said to represent intuition and feeling-wisdom, since it is a nocturnal animal that thrives in the realm of reflected light (the moon); it is also associated with the movement between form and non-form, life and death, especially among Native American cultures such as the Algonquin. (See Chevalier and Gheerbrant, *The Penguin Dictionary of Symbols*)

[53] As always with Mrs. Rowling, the brutality and tension are interrupted by humor: in this case, it is the Puck-like twins, Fred and George Weasley,

who provide the comic relief ("you don't want to bottle up your anger like that Harry, let it all out...there might be a couple of people fifty miles away who didn't hear you.").

54 Both of these explanations are, of course, incorrect—the obvious explosion of ego in the Grimmauld Place episode, and the confused, false modesty of the Hogwarts quote—but clearly, Harry is closer to his center in the latter. One suspects that over the course of the final two volumes of the Potter series, Harry will come to a more complete and balanced understanding of his past and his role in drawing upon the help that seems to come to him when he is in danger.

55 Horney (1950), *Neurosis and Human Growth*. "Neurotic claims," she adds, "are neurotic needs which individuals have unwittingly turned into claims."(p. 42)

56 This book was largely written before the release of *Harry Potter and the Half-Blood Prince* and *Harry Potter and the Deathly Hallows*, and I have only been able to add a few references to these last two parts of the Potter story while I was editing the final draft. Future editions will no doubt include more reflections on those last two stories; though some commentary on them can be found now at my blog, www.dailyrevolution.net.

57 So much so that Jung declared the process of healing to include the act of convincing the neurotic person "that he throws a very long shadow before he is willing to withdraw his emotionally-toned projections from their object." (*Aion*, CW 9, ii, par. 16)

58 This is from Kapleau's *Zen: Merging of East and West*, p. 199.

59 This is from *The Book of Loss*, a novel set in 10th century Japan, excerpts of which I have had the good fortune of previewing, as Ms. Jedamus had asked me to comment on the I Ching references made within the story before it went to press. It is a marvelous work, which I recommend to anyone who would enjoy a fine piece of fiction informed by a vibrant insight into medieval Japanese culture.

60 An entire book could be written simply on the subject of the abdomen and its place in psycho-spiritual teachings. The ancient Chinese medicinal practice of abdominal massage, known as "Chi Nei Tsang" is based on working blocked "chi" and the physical residue of negative emotion and false belief from the gastro-intestinal tract. In Japanese martial arts and in Zen meditation, the "hara"—a point said to lie just below and behind the navel—is considered to be the center into which breath and the life-force are to be taken, and from which all successful outer action arises. Even in certain Western practices, such as the popular exercise regimen invented by Joseph Pilates, the abdomen's role as a psycho-physical center of strength and personal presence, is readily acknowledged.

61 This phrase is from Arendt's 1963 report on the Eichmann trial, in which she formulated a new understanding of the motivating force of evil activity in its most hideous and genocidal form. I find it to be no accident that Mrs. Rowling's work so prominently features exploration of the genocidal and

racist expressions of evil: at the time she was writing, the genocidal slaughters of Rwanda and Serbia were being perpetrated before the world.

[62] Voldemort's name expresses the paradoxical effect of his obsession with immortality: it is a combination of the Latin words *volens*, willing, causing, or permitting, and *demorior*, to die (off or away). Thus, the mad pursuit of physical immortality (or, to note its concomitant in our own culture, eternal youth) is revealed in Voldemort's very name as an attitude that actually promotes the only death worth fearing—the death of the true self and its connection with the formless realm of Life-Beyond-Time.

[63] "Occlumency" and "Legilimency" are, of course, further examples of Mrs. Rowling's delightful ability to form compound Latin neologisms. Occulumency is formed of *occludo* (close or shut down, as in the English word occlusion, meaning a blockage) and *mens*, mind. Legilimency finds its active root in the word *lego*, meaning to read, and again, *mens*, mind.

[64] Here, I cannot resist the temptation to speculate: Snape's ability at Occlumency is probably sufficient to enable him to lie before Voldemort (or his other followers) without being detected. This is perhaps the function he performs for Dumbledore and the Order of the Phoenix, and it is a mission that is likely to lead him either to death or to duplicity. But that, again, is mere speculation.

[65] One big reason why "public demonstrations" of clairvoyance frequently fail, and scientific studies of similar abilities often seem to be either negative in their findings or else inconclusive, is that our natural intuitive abilities retreat in the face of any attempt at display, for this comes out of the realm of ego. To try to "make a show of" or "prove" psychic abilities is to neutralize the Cosmic energy that enables such gifts in the first place; thus, no "evidence" of these abilities will be found to scrutiny that comes from the desire for display or rationalization.

[66] Snape is one of those morally ambivalent characters of literature that are all the more vibrant for the conflicting traits and values they embody. In the world of children's literature, a parallel example of such a character is to be found in that of Templeton the Rat from E.B. White's classic, *Charlotte's Web*. Such characters, irascible and venomous as their behavior may appear, perform valuable functions that further the positive teaching purposes of the story as a whole.

[67] Hermione reveals a striking intuitive sense of the danger coming from the archway and veil during the climactic Department of Mysteries scene, at a time when even Harry is absorbed in admiration of its beauty and attraction toward its siren-esque form and sound. Luna shares Harry's ability to perceive the "thestrals" and the voices coming from the aforementioned veil, and is able to share her understanding of this during their conversation at the end of the book (see Chapter 10 for a further discussion of this). Professor Dumbledore's year-long withdrawal from personal contact with Harry is finally explained in the last interview between them, in which Dumbledore tells Harry of his own challenge in managing his gift of inner sight: he had been forced to walk a line between

supporting Harry through his own crises and protecting himself and the Order from the destructive influences of Voldemort's consciousness.

[68] Dumbledore is gone, having been removed as Headmaster by Umbridge, McGonagall is in the hospital after being attacked, again by Umbridge, and Harry—blinded by his hatred of him, fails to think of appealing to Snape for help. In his acute distress, Harry remains incapable of perceiving the disastrous consequences that his opposition toward Snape is creating for him. Had he thought of turning to Snape immediately after having the dream, the scene that ended in Sirius' death might well have been averted.

[69] For a further discussion of these encounters, see Chapter 10.

[70] The Healing Tao Center of New York has a website at which interested readers can obtain further information: http://www.taozenlife.com/about.htm

[71] In the second book, *Harry Potter and the Chamber of Secrets*, the Ministry, under the manipulation of the wealthy Lucius Malfoy (who later turns out to be an adherent of Lord Voldemort), places Harry's friend Hagrid in prison on a vague, baseless suspicion having to do with his possible connection to a beast that may exist at the school, attacking the children. Already in this story, the obsession with the apparitional, which characterizes all institutional ideologies, is evident: the Minister is "forced to act" purely from the belief that he's "got to be seen doing something."(p. 261). This, he explains, is "doing my duty" (thus revealing another unnatural compulsion of the collective ego—the performance of "duty").

[72] This quote is from Part I of that text; I would recommend that the interested reader experience the whole of Anthony and Moog's discussion of the collective ego in its full and original setting—see the Recommended Reading section at the back of this book.

[73] From "Economy" (pp. 53-54 of the Konemann edition of *Walden*).

[74] See, for example, Chapter 3.

[75] Ralph Waldo Emerson, *Spiritual Laws* (1841)

[76] Anthony and Moog write of the person who, under the influence of group ideologies, accepts and carries fixed beliefs "as if his mind is like a bank of full postal boxes that contain his final opinions on every subject." (p. 636).

[77] In Chapter 76 of the *Tao Te Ching*. It should be added, in the context of the discussion about age and decrepitude, that Lao Tzu's work, though very old indeed, is reconceived, re-experienced, and renewed with every generation. Thus, it is never old, but always appropriate to its time. Any creative work, no matter how ingenious, that is left trapped in its own time and geographical origin, is sure to be forgotten. It is part of the natural function of artists in every generation to reanimate the great works of those who came before them; to bring them alive into each moment of history. This is one way that the song of Life endures.

[78] Jon Kabat-Zinn, *Wherever You Go, There You Are: Mindfulness Meditation in Everyday Life* (Hyperion, 1994). The mythical beasts referred to in the quote, Scylla and Charybdis, are monsters which

Odysseus must avoid during his metaphorical sea-journey home from Ilium in Homer's *Odyssey*. Kabat-Zinn's point in using these metaphors, I think, is that we (like Odysseus) must rid ourselves of conditioned falsehoods about Time and the order of Life (ideas that are symbolized by the crew of Odysseus' ship, six of whom are lost to Charybdis), so that we may find these dangers transformed within the truth of lived experience *in this moment*.

[79] It is possible that Hawking's recent reversal on his position regarding the status of energy within black holes may lead him to also reconsider his view of the broad relationship between Time and Matter.

[80] Brian Greene, *The Fabric of the Cosmos: Space. Time. And the Texture of Reality* (Knopf, 2004). Also see Greene's *The Elegant Universe*—both the book and the Public Broadcasting program that grew from it. In the section being quoted, Greene adds the following emphasis in a footnote: "the big bang theory...leaves unanswered the question of what happened at the initial moment of the universe's creation—if there actually was such a moment." (p. 519).

[81] Fr. 210, in *The Presocratic Philosophers* (G.S. Kirk and J.E. Raven, editors).

[82] From "The Equality of All Things" in *Chuang Tsu: Inner Chapters*, translated by Gia-fu Feng and Jane English (p. 45).

[83] From "The Secret of Growth" in *Chaung Tsu: Inner Chapters*, translated by Gia-fu Feng and Jane English (p. 59).

[84] From Carl Jung's Foreword to the Wilhelm/Baynes translation of the *I Ching* (Princeton Univ. Press, 1950).

[85] We should also recall that the same force of injured pride drove Hermione into the bathroom of Book One, where she was eventually trapped by the troll, whose size, stench, stupidity, and violence together make a perfect metaphor on the warped character of ego.

[86] Robert Pirsig, *Zen and the Art of Motorcycle Maintenance* (HarperTorch, 1974/1999).

[87] As David Colbert has pointed out (in his *The Magical Worlds of Harry Potter*), the name Durmstrang is a play on the phrase "Sturm und Drang" ("Storm and Stress"), the name for the German literary movement of the late 18th century marked by the work of Goethe. Curiously (and perhaps this implies the object of Mrs. Rowling's irony here), the name was derived from the title of an obscure play by an author named von Klinger (*Wirrwarr, oder Sturm und Drang*); but the only "Wirrwarr" (confusion, mix-up, mess) relative to Goethe's work is that its clarity, beauty, and naturalness of expression could ever be tagged with such a label as "Storm and Stress." I would suggest that Rowling may be thus identifying Karkaroff (whose inner reform from his days of following Voldemort is revealed to be questionable at best) with the way institutional ideologies grab hold of and distort the purest and most deeply satisfying creations of human art. This seems to have happened in many cultures; another example of it can be found in the feudal beliefs that were overlaid, as

revision and interpretative commentary, upon the text of the I Ching by editors of the Confucian School in China.

[88] Cultures of Healing: Correcting the Image of American Mental Health Care. Fancher's book explores and exposes the history and intersection of politics, belief, and ideology in American clinical psychology.

Printed in Great Britain
by Amazon